About the Author

Clive Hart ... here he spends as much ti... horseback. He is a small ... dedicated to recreating m... it originally was.

The horses on ... are Icaro and Charlie of Historic Equitation, ridden by Dominic Sewell and the author.

For information on other books, please visit
www.clivehart.net

By Clive Hart:
The Rise and Fall of the Mounted Knight
The Legend of Richard Keynes series (six books):
Book One: Golden Spurs
Book Two: Brothers in Arms
Book Three: Dogs of War
Book Four: Knight Errant
Book Five: King Breaker
Book Six: Crusader

Copyright © 2024 Clive Hart

All rights reserved. All characters in this publication are fictitious and any resemblance to real persons, living or dead, is purely coincidental.

Contents

Homeward Bound
Wrong Place, Wrong Time
Arrows
Hearth and Home
Duty
Dogs and Gods
Death Squad
Children
Wounds
Knight of the Cart
Knight of Nothing
Extinguished
What Now?
Fundraising
Exodus

Historical Note

HOMEWARD BOUND

They rode towards the orange glow of the setting sun. The still air allowed the distant sound of a chirping bird to drift across the road. The repeating sound of the call filtered through the trees that lined the road, the road that ran west, that ran to home. Neufchatel was their destination, and it lay not far beyond the settlement they now passed. A small village sprawled out from the north side of the road, the sails of its squat windmill hanging idle, its arms creaking despite the lack of wind. A gang of villagers returned their only pair of draught animals to a hedge-lined paddock, their autumn ploughing completed for the year.

Richard watched them end their labours, one group took to drinking straight away. 'They don't know what's coming, do they?'

Bowman sniffed in the cooling air. 'No, but do we?'

Richard shook his head while his new warhorse, the magnificent blue roan he had acquired from the Marshal, shook its head along with him. A swarm of flies flew away from the black mane but buzzed straight back. Richard looked behind him to where his palomino horse limped, angrily snapping at flies who came anywhere near his mouth. The horse dragged himself along with the small party, but looked far from comfortable. He limped on one of his hind legs, the one with the spear wound.

'He just needs stabling for a while,' Bowman said, 'walking for the past two days doesn't seem to have done him any harm.'

Richard wasn't so sure. The yellow horse's cross-shaped wound had scabbed over, but the two-day journey from Corbie may have taken a toll on him.

Richard's wife glanced back at the lame stallion. 'I'll pray for him,' she said, 'as I pray for all of you.'

'Pray for Nicholas,' Richard said, 'he needs it the most.'

Bowman looked away.

'I have,' Sophie said, 'but the monks in Corbie can do more for his soul than I can.'

Richard made the sign of the cross and glanced at the darkening sky. He wondered if Nicholas had gone that way or sunk down into the tortures of Hell, although most likely he was spending the foreseeable future languishing in purgatory. Richard remembered his church in Yvetot, the village that lay still further to the west, and wondered if the Priest there would pray for his soul if he himself died there. He doubted it.

'Can we go quicker?' Bowman asked. 'It's getting dark.'

Richard snatched another look back at his hobbling horse. 'Don't worry, we'll make it before nightfall,' he said, 'I'm not risking speeding up unless I have to.'

'The lord was very welcoming when I came this way,' Sophie said, 'there will be room for us whenever we arrive.'

Richard remembered Neufchatel as a battleground. He had been knighted in its church and fought all around its walls. But that memory felt like a long time ago. The memory made him look over the fields beyond the village that was readying itself for rest. To the north, before the Battle of Neufchatel, Richard had first tasted warfare. The flames and the bodies in the destroyed village of Fallencourt hadn't troubled his dreams of late, in fact he'd felt so exhausted for so long he couldn't remember dreaming at all. Richard checked the rest of the party was still behind him. Judas the black dog marked a tree by the road with a leg cocked in the air, a pleased look on his panting face. Gerold, Brian, and Maynard rode together at the rear.

'I can't wait to sit by my own hearth,' Richard said, 'and not to sleep in a hall full of stinking and snoring men.'

'Who are you calling stinking?' Bowman asked with the faintest hint of a smile. The cuts across his nose and cheek he'd sustained at the Corbie tournament had scabbed over, but his shoulder still didn't quite work yet.

'You know who I mean,' Richard replied, just glad Bowman wasn't sulking and drowning himself in grief at his half-brother's death. They had slipped away from Corbie and the Young King the day after they'd left Nicholas in his water-filled grave. Richard hadn't asked the Young King for permission to leave, merely taken his pay from a clerk and left. He'd had enough of kings, either of them, and wanted to be as far away from crowns as he possibly could.

Sophie patted the black palfrey that had been her wedding gift. 'I miss the children.'

'I can't believe you named them while I was away,' Richard said.

'We didn't know if you were coming home,' she said, 'you left me for more than a year.'

'I know, and I've apologised,' Richard said.

Sophie smiled. 'And I accepted. The villagers didn't once try to burn us out of the castle once while you were gone, and both of the children are alive and well.'

'Alexander and Lora,' Richard stared off into the undergrowth. He repeated the names several times over and over.

'And they will be eager to see you,' Sophie said, 'they don't remember you.'

Richard frowned.

Bowman chuckled to himself. 'You missed the year where they cry at all hours,' he said, 'so maybe Ireland wasn't such a waste of time in the end.'

'I thought you didn't like Ireland,' Sophie said.

'Oh, I hate Ireland,' Bowman grinned. 'I just hate children more.'

'I'm sure they'll hate you,' Richard said.

'They'll love me, young lord,' Bowman nodded towards a small hill up ahead, 'but Neufchatel is just over that, and I'm not sure they'll like us as much.'

The hill descended into a wide valley, dark now in the evening's gloom, with the town on the east side of a river that twinkled silver in the faint glow of the emerging moon.

Sophie raised her eyes and observed the pale disc floating in the sky. 'I don't enjoy being out at night,' she said, 'it's when Sarjeant starts drinking.'

Richard scratched his ear, the ear that was half gone. 'How bad is it? Is he at least doing his job?'

Sophie looked him in the eyes. Then nodded. 'He started to slip when the villagers started to fight.'

Richard groaned. 'I'm not tolerating them anymore. They will learn to live peacefully.'

'Or what?' Sophie asked. 'You'll use violence to cow them into obedience?'

Richard shrugged. 'I tried to be fair.'

'You did,' Bowman said, 'and look where it got you.'

'Right here. But things will be different now.'

'No more kings,' Bowman said.

'No more kings,' Richard nodded to him. 'I don't want to fight or die for either of them.'

'Me neither, although I'd kill for a good wine,' Bowman said.

Richard was glad to hear it, because Bowman had spent the past few days in a grief-ridden sulk, and today had been the first time he'd sounded somewhat like his old self.

'They had some wine,' Sophie said, 'but there was space enough in his hall for you to sleep.'

'Where did you sleep?' Richard frowned.

His wife laughed at him. 'Lord Walter was surprised I travelled alone, too.'

'I'd rather you didn't travel without company,' Richard said, 'do you know how dangerous these roads are?'

Sophie pressed her legs onto her palfrey, and he lifted himself into a comfortable amble towards Neufchatel.

'Women,' Bowman said as she went off alone. Then he looked sad.

Richard couldn't help him, seeing as the woman his friend yearned for was in Ireland and married to yet another king. Richard let his wife go on ahead and waited for the other three members of his party to catch up.

'The town is just over that hill,' Richard said to Gerold, 'we won't leave too early in the morning if it gives you a chance to rest.'

Gerold nodded, his face pale and his cheeks more sunken than before he'd fallen ill. 'Thank you.'

'Brian can find someone to help you, I'm sure there will be monks or healers around somewhere.'

Brian nodded. The monk shifted himself around in his saddle and took a foot out of one stirrup to stretch it. 'I've never heard of Neufchatel,' he said, 'to be honest, I would have rather stayed at the scriptorium in Corbie for longer.'

'You should have,' Bowman said.

The Irish monk scrunched up his face, then cried out as his calf muscle cramped.

Bowman shook his head in disdain.

'Be nice to him,' Richard said.

'Don't take his side,' the blonde man replied.

They rode into the valley that held the town with its long, partially stone walls. The castle stood tall at the eastern end of the urban area, and it was towards its gate that they went.

Richard handed his horse to the last member of the group when they reached Neufchatel. Maynard the squire took their horses as the bored looking guards yawned and let them in.

Walter the Good was the castellan of Neufchatel. He'd held the same role in other fortifications before in Normandy, once even in Essex, but Neufchatel was his biggest job yet. He sat in his castle hall, slouched in a tall chair painted blue, rubbing his double chin. The topmost chin was smaller than the bottom, even though the castellan was not an overly fat man. He had been trying to grow a beard to cover both chins, but the attempt had met with only jokes and whispers behind his back. Walter knew it wasn't working, but why should he care what others thought? He was in command of one of the principal fortresses in Normandy. He was an important man.

His eyes lit up when Sophie swept into the hall. Although her blue dress was dustier than it had been a week ago, she brought some feminine nobility to a castle that was severely lacking it.

'Did you find your husband?' Walter asked. The hall was so large that he raised his voice to be heard, and some of the squires and sarjeants who passed their evenings there turned to see who he addressed.

Sophie smiled and nodded. 'I did, he's right behind me.'

Walter groaned and slumped further into his chair when Richard appeared and paused to take stock of the chamber.

A hearth smouldered in the centre of the space, smoke drifting carelessly up into the ceiling. Three of the walls were bare stone, although on the fourth workmen were halfway through installing some wooden panelling. Their hammering of nails was the only real noise in the otherwise quiet room.

Richard squinted through the smoke at the lord in his blue chair.

'This is my husband,' Sophie told Walter, 'Richard of Yvetot.'

'Welcome,' Walter flicked a dog hair from his tunic sleeve.

Richard thanked him for his hospitality, then waited to find out what that might include.

Walter waved his arm at the tables. 'Eat and drink what you like, although we are a military post and not what you are used to.'

Richard considered the castellan. 'We aren't used to anything, this is perfectly fine,' he said.

'But you are a tournament champion or a war hero, are you not?' Walter asked. 'I forget which.'

Richard glanced at Sophie. 'What did you tell him?'

'The truth,' she sat down near the castellan and waited for someone to bring her food.

'A roof and a hearth are luxuries,' Richard said.

Walter snorted. 'A man of the court, then. A silver tongue to worm your way into a man's confidence.'

Richard blinked at the unexpected assault of words as the rest of his group sat down and stretched their limbs out after their journey.

'Have I offended you?' Richard asked.

Walter tapped his foot on the rushes that covered the floor. The tapping made a muffled rustling sound. He coughed and wiped his face with his arm. 'No.'

Richard sat halfway down the table that the castellan slouched at the head of.

Walter waved at a servant and shouted for food and drink to be brought for Sophie.

Bowman nudged a squire at the table and asked what the local wine was like.

'Not so great this far down the table,' the sour-looking squire replied.

Bowman sighed and looked up at Walter.

'Keep quiet,' Richard whispered back to his friend, 'I don't think he likes us.'

The squire stifled a laugh.

The castellan stared at Sophie. 'How did you find the roads to Amiens? I hardly travel there, for those who dwell in that direction are the enemies I guard Normandy against.'

'The roads are adequate,' Sophie said, 'and they are safe. I saw no brigands, and these lands are supposedly at peace.'

'For how long, though?' Bowman said.

Richard elbowed him.

'What was that?' Walter squinted down at the table.

'War is coming,' Richard said.

'And how would you know? You're a decadent tournament knight.'

'Walter, please,' Sophie said.

The castellan let out a deep breath. 'Richard, was it?'

Richard nodded.

'What are you then?'

Bowman chuckled. 'Good question.'

Richard ran his fingers over a protruding and twisted knot in the oak table. The knot was coming loose. 'I'm just trying to get home and live quietly,' he said.

'So you're a coward?'

Bowman and Sophie both spun around, but Richard held a hand up to Bowman.

'He is no coward,' Sophie said, 'look closely at him and you'll see how readily he puts himself in harm's way.'

The scar on Richard's face itched.

Walter reached for a pewter cup and drank from it. He slammed it down onto the table and burped. 'It's knights like you who come raiding towns like mine. Men like you who burn them.'

'I defended this town a few years ago when the Flemings and Matthew of Boulogne attacked it,' Richard stared back at the castellan, 'but I don't remember seeing you here?'

'I was at another castle,' Walter replied, 'so I wouldn't know if you're making that up.'

Bowman jumped to his feet. 'Are you calling the young lord a liar?'

Walter laughed. 'I think you protest too much.'

Richard closed his eyes. 'I don't need you to believe me. I'll find somewhere else to spend the night if you don't want me here.'

Walter's bottom chin shook from side to side as he laughed. 'Those who charge around the countryside burning and stealing win all the glory, but it is those of us who guard the defenceless that are the better men.'

'I'm not arguing against that,' Richard said.

'Why do you do it?' the castellan asked.

'Do what?'

'Burn and rob.'

'I've never burned anything,' Richard said, 'and I don't think I've ever robbed anyone, either.'

Bowman nodded. 'He's right, he always refuses to,' he said loudly.

Sophie looked at Walter with the expression she'd used when Richard had tried to read Eric and Enid out to her. 'Please leave my husband alone, tell us about your lands instead. Everyone would like to hear you speak.'

'Nothing much happens here,' Walter raised his chins and eyebrows, 'the Count of Aumale might raid a village every now and again, but nothing has happened since the Young King's failed rebellion last year.'

Bowman cleared his throat, and Richard shook his head at him.

Walter didn't notice. 'Normandy as a whole however, is never quiet, there's always one lord or another trying to dispossess a neighbour or settle a dispute by violence. Lord Tancarville has been stirring up trouble again, that traitorous scoundrel will bring good King Henry down on his own head, mark my words.'

'You support King Henry, then?' Richard asked.

'Who else would I support?' Walter replied. 'He is our king. I am the keeper of Neufchatel because he can trust and rely on me. If his devious sons turn up here I'll bar the gates to them, any of them. His whole brood are but pale shadows of their noble father.'

Richard went to speak, then decided it might be best if he kept his more positive views on the Young King to himself.

'Lord Tancarville deserves everything he gets,' Bowman sat back down and searched the table for anything not yet drunk.

'You know him?' Walter narrowed his eyes.

'We hate him,' Bowman grinned, 'and I know his son hates us.'

'Ah, the Little Lord,' Walter sat up in his chair and life filled his face, 'the story is that he attacked a woman who fought back and sliced off his manhood.'

Richard struggled to keep his eyes away from Sophie. 'Did this woman slice the whole thing off?' he asked.

'Nobody knows,' the castellan roared with laughter, 'we've had three different tales about it come through this hall. What they all agree on is that he's vowed revenge on those who humiliated him, and that his father has turned his attention to another son. The Little Lord is treated like an inconvenient bastard.'

Richard decided he'd have to look at increasing the security of his castle at Yvetot, or maybe even move Sophie to England if he could recover Keynes. He needed to get her away from the Little Lord.

'The Chamberlain has turned his attention to one of his neighbours, and they are quarrelling over land,' Walter continued, 'but recently rumours have gathered about King Henry's sons.'

Richard absentmindedly scratched his partially severed ear and remembered that the last thing he'd done in Corbie was to accidentally let slip to Brother Geoffrey that the Young King was going to rebel, and that he was heading to Normandy. The monk had grabbed his leg as they'd been about to ride away, and after trying to kick him away, Richard had told Brother Geoffrey he needed to get back to Yvetot before the Young King invaded. He winced at his own lack of attention, but he'd been tired. So very tired.

'King Henry's son, Count Richard, is hated by all the lords in the south,' the castellan continued, 'and the other son Duke Geoffrey has mustered troops in Brittany. With the Young King nearby, Normandy feels far too exposed for my liking. All three brothers could rebel at any moment, if that is, they can cease their own squabbling long enough to cooperate.'

'Well, we wouldn't know anything about that,' Bowman gave up his search for a drink.

The castellan raised his eyebrows. 'Of course you wouldn't,' he said, 'but just in case you do, know that I punish treason swiftly here.'

Richard's eyes ached and he would rather just sleep. 'None of us have any intention of treason,' he said, 'all I want on this earth is to go home and see my children.'

'What about the third one?' Bowman asked. 'The Red Child.'

'Do not speak of that,' Sophie snapped, 'I need to speak to Richard about it.'

'He's a he,' Richard said, 'and we will discuss him in private.'

Sophie folded her arms as a servant finally appeared with pork and a dark-coloured pear drink for her. She started on the pork instead of finishing the conversation.

Walter watched her eat.

'Can you not look at my wife like that?' Richard asked. 'You're making my skin crawl.'

'This is my hall, I'll look at whatever I like,' Walter said, 'but what red-coloured child did the rude knight speak of?'

Sophie kept eating and didn't look up.

'We are in the care of a bastard of the King,' Richard couldn't be bothered to make up anything other than the truth. 'A child that we will look to foster now that I'm home. We have two children who I want to focus on until they are old enough to send away.'

Sophie looked up. 'I thought for Alexander, Sir Roger might be the best household to send him.'

Richard nodded, Sir Roger de Cailly was everything he wished himself to be, who better to be a role model for Alexander? The sons of knights grew up in households of relatives or close friends, they did not spend their formative years at home. It was a convention that worked, everyone knew children behave worse around their parents than other adults, and it invariably produced better manners. 'Sir Roger would be my first choice,' he said. 'When Alexander is old enough.'

Sophie nodded. 'I'll miss him when the time comes. He has your eyes, Richard.'

Walter burped. 'Children disgust me,' he said, 'their screams and endless weeping are enough to drive a man mad.'

'A real man would learn to endure such things,' Richard said.

Bowman snorted next to him. 'As if you know anything of children, young lord,' he mumbled.

'I know they need their father,' Richard said mostly to himself, 'which is why we're on our way back home, away from kings and struggles over power.'

The castellan tossed a bone over his shoulder and a dog caught it in midair with a loud snap of its jaws. Richard had left Judas in a stable with Solis, a good decision, for the black dog would not have let the bone go without a fight.

Brian made a bed for Gerold at the far end of the hall, and the monk helped the veteran knight into it. Even from a distance, Richard could tell he shivered.

'Your company is strange,' Walter said, 'only one squire and a monk who acts more like a servant. But three knights.'

Richard shrugged. 'We are who we are.'

'I still don't know who that is,' Walter looked at Richard.

'What do you want to know?'

The castellan tipped his head to the side as if sizing up a colt. 'Who was the last man you killed?'

Richard blinked and groaned inside. 'That is none of your concern.'

'It is while you share my hall,' Walter said, 'I wish to know if you will sneak into my chamber to kill me, or steal my wealth while my lazy guards sleep at their posts.'

Bowman coughed. 'What wealth do you have? There is nothing hanging from the walls, no one singing at your hearth, no food being offered to guests.'

'Don't be rude,' Richard hissed at him.

'Get out of my hall,' Walter shouted with bulging eyes, 'ungrateful, spoiled knight.'

Bowman sprung up and left the bench. 'There's no food here anyway,' he said, 'and for once we've got the money to actually buy some. I've been waiting years for that. And you never asked me who the last man I killed was.'

'Should I care?' the castellan looked like he didn't.

Bowman reached the doorway and turned around. 'Eustace Martel,' he said, 'I severed his jawbone and carried it as a trophy.' The blonde knight left as everyone in the hall turned to watch him go. Some of the squires and sarjeants whispered to each other.

'Eustace Martel?' Walter's voice quietened and his gaze moved to Richard when Bowman disappeared outside with a flourish of his cloak. 'It is said that Eustace Martel is protected by demons and no blade could kill him.'

'I suppose a horse killed him in the very end,' Richard said, 'but Bowman did rip his jaw off. Eustace was the worst sort of man.' His death had lifted a weight from Richard's shoulders, but the constant worry over Eustace had for years kept Richard in tension, and without it there to hold him together, he felt as if the threads of his mind were unravelling.

Walter clasped his fingers together and rested them on his belly. 'The Martel family is one of the great families of Christendom. They are loyal to the king and are one of the pillars of justice in England,' he swallowed, 'Eustace is known as a rough jewel in their crown, but the crown still glimmers.'

'Eustace *was* known,' Richard said, 'he's very dead now.' Richard made the sign of the cross. But he didn't make it for the sake of Eustace's soul, instead the gesture was to protect himself from Eustace's evil spirit.

Walter frowned. 'If you are in the business of killing Martels,' he said, 'then I wonder if you are as loyal to the King as you say you are.'

Not this again, Richard thought and put his head in his hands. He rubbed his eyes and peered back up at the castellan. 'We fought with

King Henry in Brittany, I lost a finger there, and got this scar for my efforts.'

Walter squinted to get a better look at the scar on his face. He glanced over at Sophie as if to confirm Richard's story.

Sophie nodded. 'You will have no trouble from my husband, nor from his men,' she said.

Walter let out a breath. 'Do not blame me for my caution,' he said, 'we live in dangerous times and on a frontier. I know the Young King is nearby, and I must be on the lookout for spies. It only takes one traitorous swine to open the gates at night and let the Young King and his foul host in.'

Maynard twitched next to Brian. 'I'm not a spy,' he whispered.

Brian smiled at him. 'We know. Don't be afraid of this man, he won't harm you.'

Walter didn't hear them, instead his eyes returned to Sophie. They rested on her far longer than Richard could endure. 'Sophie,' he said, 'we should go into the town, there is no food for us here.'

'Speak for yourself,' Sophie flashed a thin grin at him, eating knife in hand.

Richard wondered if she was tolerating the castellan's lechery just because of the incident with Alice in Amiens. His wife half arched an eyebrow at him, and he decided that she probably was. Richard shook his head, finding himself almost impressed, but also reminded that Alice of Lusignan had left an impression in his mind he couldn't clear.

'If you leave my hall,' Walter said, 'my men will escort you.'

'To keep an eye on us,' Richard said rather than asked.

Walter sneered at him. 'I don't trust you. I know you've come from the Young King, and I know he cannot be trusted. I need to be sure you are not the traitors who will open my gates and slit my throat.'

'I do not serve the Young King,' Richard said, 'and I would not risk my life, or that of my wife, by coming here on his bidding.'

'What would you risk your life for?' Walter asked. 'What would you die for?'

Richard paused. That was a good question. He'd almost died for kings, friends, and his horse, but he'd never done so consciously.

A servant poked the fire with a black iron rod and showers of orange sparks floated up into the air. Embers floated down and Richard had to brush one off his woollen cloak. Not that another hole in it would really matter.

'I'm not sure,' Richard replied. 'I'm more concerned with staying alive until my children are adults.'

Walter drummed his fingers on the table as if weighing up the answer.

'A spy would have concocted a better answer,' he said to himself, 'although that's what a spy would want me to think.'

'I don't have an answer because I've never thought about it,' Richard said, 'who would have a ready answer for you?'

Gerold cleared his throat from the far end of the hall, under a wall where shadows from the hearth flickered. 'My duty is to your family,' his voice crackled like the fire, 'a household knight willingly dies for his lord.'

'See,' the castellan said, 'even your old man has a better answer than you.'

'He's not mine,' Richard said.

'Then why is he willing to die for you?'

Richard knew the answer. Loyalty, duty, and selflessness. But Richard himself owed nobody those things enough to die for them, so he stayed silent.

Sophie peered at him. 'I'm waiting for you to answer,' she said.

'I don't have one.'

'Not even your wife and your children?' she asked.

Richard cursed himself. 'Of course,' he said, 'but I don't think that's the sort of thing the castellan is asking about.'

'Maybe your husband cares for you less than you think he does,' Walter said.

'Enough,' Richard said, 'I might well die for my family, but make no mistake, I would kill for it. I *have* killed for it.'

The castellan's eyes fell to his own fingers for just a moment, but that was long enough for Richard to learn that physical bravery wasn't one of Walter the Good's virtues.

Richard pushed himself away from the table. 'I'm leaving. There is little hospitality here. Sophie, you can do what you want, but I'm going to find Bowman.'

His wife shrugged. 'I would rather not risk myself amongst the drunks and beggars of the town,' she said.

'Suit yourself,' Richard walked towards the door.

'Ha,' Walter chuckled, 'a husband who cannot control his wife. What is the world coming to?'

Richard sucked in a breath but held his tongue. He slipped out of the door and nodded to Gerold, then promised to bring him back something to eat. The older man thanked him as Brian and Maynard hurried out on Richard's heels.

They descended the wooden staircase that led into the courtyard of the castle, the courtyard Richard remembered entering with news of the enemy's arrival all those years ago. Too much had changed since that day, and Richard felt weary as he trudged down the cobblestones into Neufchatel.

He'd made the same journey before, with de Cailly by his side, on his way to be knighted. Nostalgia filled Richard as he recognised some houses and noticed a cluster that had been rebuilt, most likely after a fire. Groups of men huddled together, obscured by the night, drinking away what little wealth they had.

Brian clung close to Richard. 'All towns are the same after dark,' he said, 'nests of sin.'

Richard shrugged him off. 'You don't need to fear them, you've stood in battle and killed more threatening men than these drunks with nothing but a banner pole.'

'That wasn't me,' Brian said, 'that was the Lord's will.'

Richard ignored the drunks and rounded a corner that brought the church spire into view over the thatched roofs of Neufchatel.

Bowman also came into view. He threw a punch at a man who wore no cloak, and knocked him to the cobbles. The fallen drunk's two companions pounced at the blonde man, and one went to howl the Hue and Cry. Bowman pushed him backwards into the wall of a house before he could raise his voice enough to draw attention.

Richard raced down the slope and pulled one man off Bowman. The townsman reeked of urine, and as Richard peeled him away from his friend, he recognised his face. It was the tanner who had chased him through Neufchatel on his previous visit, accusing him of being the devil.

The tanner looked up at Richard's aged and scared face with its savaged ear, and backed off. His face reflected fear rather than recognition, so Richard ignored him and grabbed Bowman instead. 'Why did you have to get into a fight here? Can't we just sit down somewhere and eat something in peace?'

Bowman lunged at the tanner and Richard had to brace with everything he had just to slow him down.

Maynard, although small, ran in and held the tanner's companion back.

'Enough,' Richard shouted. 'What is your problem?'

Bowman's eyes were red, and Richard could smell alcohol on his breath, which was rapid.

'They doubted I could afford their drink,' he snarled.

'Is that all?' Richard had a mind to leave him to it.

The tanner, with deeper lines on his face than Richard remembered, slid a knife out from its sheath. 'Foreigners should be careful here,' he said, 'especially you English, no one else mangles our words as crudely as you do.'

Richard held his hands up. 'We aren't looking for trouble, I'll take my friend and we'll go in peace.'

The tanner swished the knife through the air as a threat.

Bowman pushed Richard away and laughed at the blade. 'Do you know how to use that?'

The tanner's eyes flickered between his two companions, but one was still on the cobbles and the other hadn't moved from the wall.

'There's four of us,' Richard said, 'and your friend over there looks too frightened to come to your aid. One knife is hardly enough to cause us concern.' He held his hand out to ask for the weapon.

The tanner waved it at Bowman and then back to Richard. His eyes rested on Richard's open palm. The palm with the burn scars.

Richard realised his mistake as the tanner jumped backwards. 'You,' he cried, 'the English devil with the bandaged hands. Why has the devil sent you back here?'

'What's he talking about?' Brian asked. 'Why are you a devil?'

'I'm not a devil,' Richard snapped, more harshly than he'd intended, 'this tanner is prone to causing trouble. Which we will not give him.' He closed his hand and moved it to the Little Lord's sword instead. They were not wearing their mail, but Richard's battered sword still hung from his hip.

The tanner glanced at the sword, and then at Richard and Bowman's golden spurs.

'You should kill him for what he tried to do to us before,' Bowman said, 'although I'd be happy to do it for you.'

'How did you manage to drink so much already?' Richard asked. 'You left just before we did.'

The tanner edged sideways away from them.

'Where do you think you're going?' Bowman hissed.

'Let him go,' Richard put a hand on his shoulder. 'I'm hungry and this isn't helping my headache.'

The will to fight drained away from the tanner and he slipped away down the cobbled street. His conscious companion leapt after him, leaving the third man on the stones. A soft moan escaped his lips.

'At least he isn't dead,' Richard said.

Bowman shrugged. 'They started it.'

'Did they?' Richard asked, and then swiftly decided he didn't care. 'Come on, there must be someone willing to sell us some food in the town square.'

Bowman's shoulders slumped, and Richard wondered what his problem was.

16

'Go on ahead and find somewhere,' he said to Brian and Maynard.

Once the pair of them were a few steps down the dimly lit street, Richard turned back to the blonde man. 'What is wrong with you? Are you trying to get yourself killed?'

'I could have saved him,' Bowman looked down and put his hands on his hips, 'but what hurts the most is that there was no point to it. What was his death for?'

A sadness gnawed at Richard, too, but he was determined to live through it. 'He saved us from Eustace, you know that. He bought us enough time to escape from that melee. Eustace would have killed others if Nicholas hadn't fought him.'

'I fought him, too,' the blonde man said, 'why did Nicholas die when I survived?'

'Brian would tell you it was God's will,' Richard said, 'but I think we both know by now it's just luck. There's no reason for it. Good men can die just as easily as bad men in battle. His time came, yours didn't.'

'But he was my brother.'

'You avenged him,' Richard said, 'you said you felt better.'

Bowman ran his hand through his hair. 'I did feel better, but it was a drop of water in a lake. A desolate, dank, dark lake.'

'Come on,' Richard pushed him around so he faced down towards the centre of the town, 'we all need something to eat, and we all need a rest.'

'I need wine,' Bowman said, 'or at least cider. I miss the English ale.'

'I think you should spend some time in the church,' Richard said, 'spend some time in a holy place.'

Bowman pulled his arm away from Richard and made to walk down the cobbles. 'The last thing I need is a church.'

Richard's eyes lit up. 'I could knight you in the church. You know, for real.'

Bowman kept walking. 'I don't care if we do it for real or not,' he said, 'the spurs make the man, not some words and a slap around the face.'

Richard followed behind. 'It would do you some good, you won't find peace at the bottom of a cup.'

'How do you know?' the blonde man shouted back to him as some dogs barked across the town.

'It hasn't worked for Sarjeant, has it?' Richard had to walk briskly to keep up. 'Or the last time you tried it.'

Bowman reached the town square, where Brian considered the entrance to the church. He stood on the steps that led up to it. 'Can I go in?' he asked.

'You don't have to ask me,' Richard said, 'although if you could drag Bowman with you, I'd appreciate it.'

'He can try,' Bowman strode off towards some cheering and music that drifted over from the far side of the square.

'Can I visit Rouen?' Brian asked.

'I don't care,' Richard said, 'you're a free man.'

'I want to write a chronicle,' the monk said, 'men in Rouen will sell me what I need to write.'

'That sounds expensive,' Richard frowned.

Brian rubbed his hands together and looked up at Richard with big round eyes.

'Oh, I see,' Richard said, 'you're asking for money.'

The monk nodded and turned a shade of pink.

'If I have any left by the time we get home, then I'll pay for it,' Richard said.

Brian smiled, thanked Richard, and made for the church.

Maynard went to speak but gave up.

'What do you want?' Richard asked.

The squire was young, thin, and dark haired. He'd been trying to grow a moustache, but so far had only achieved a wispy covering of dark brown hair on his top lip. 'Can I be your squire?'

'I told you in Corbie,' Richard replied, 'we'll get to Yvetot and I'll think about it then. Your lord is Sir Roger since Adam died, so you should probably ask him.'

The squire shifted his feet. 'Are you really planning on staying at home?' he asked.

Richard exhaled. 'Yes, so I don't understand why you want to be my squire. My adventures are over.'

'But won't you join the Young King?' Maynard asked.

'I'm not joining anyone.'

'What about the Old King?'

Richard shook his head. 'I wasn't lying to the castellan, I want to live a boring life for a while. To go home, see my children and get bored sorting out disputes over which cow trampled whose crop, and who cheated with their payments to me.'

Maynard frowned. 'So we're really just going back to your home?'

Richard nodded. 'Yes, we are.'

Maynard looked confused, but Richard wasn't interested. He yearned to go home, away from the ghosts from his past that lurked in every corner of Neufchatel.

However, and to Richard's great dismay, what greeted them the following day was not the prospect of going home, but banners on the horizon.

WRONG PLACE, WRONG TIME

Richard rubbed the sleep from his eyes and then rubbed them again to clear them. He pulled his cloak around himself to ward against the sharp air, for even though the sun had risen, the day didn't promise to be warm. Sophie climbed the stone steps of the battlements with him and they both beat the castellan to the platform at the very top of the keep. The town's highest point offered a breathtaking view of the valley, yet no one looked that way.

Richard squinted in the other direction. 'They're right, banners along the road we came in on.'

Sophie put her hands on the stone wall, but the stone chilled her so she removed them. 'They look red. Are they royal banners?'

'Of course,' Richard said, 'but which king?'

'There are four red banners,' Maynard said, his younger eyes the sharpest of everyone.

The squires of the castle lined the walls below as Walter heaved himself up the steps to look at what was causing all the commotion. 'Who is it, then?' he asked no one in particular.

'Either King Henry or his son,' Richard said.

'Pray for the elder,' Walter said, 'although he'll eat me out of castle and town. But at least he won't burn it like the younger one will.'

'We could have been on the road already,' Richard said to his wife.

'Giving Gerold time to rest shouldn't be regretted,' she replied, 'we can still ride away. I will go and wake him.'

'Good,' Richard said, 'we don't want to get trapped in here. Not when we don't care which side triumphs.'

'That's treason,' Walter pointed at Richard.

Richard ignored him and tried to make out the other banners on the horizon. The road cut across the front of a shallow hill and straightened as it led to the castle, and the army that marched along it did so without urgency. Richard couldn't decide which king would be worse for him, the elder one who could strip him of his village, or the younger who he'd just abandoned.

'Yellow with a black lion,' he stood up and turned back to the castellan. 'Count Philip of Flanders.'

'The Count plays both sides,' Walter rested with one arm on the wall.

'But he was with the Young King at Corbie.'

'I knew you were one of his men,' the castellan said. 'I will have to lock you up until the enemy has gone away.'

'Lock me up?' Richard couldn't help a mild laugh. 'None of your rusty and creaking men could hold me.'

Walter pushed his ample frame from the wall. 'Seize him,' he waggled a finger at Richard.

'They won't,' Richard noticed a new banner on the road, a gold and green one that hadn't been at Lagny or Corbie. A banner he recognised appeared over the horizon, the blue and white lines of the Lusignans. Richard groaned. He left the wall, the eyes of four squires on him. 'They're more scared of me than they are of you,' Richard walked down the steps, 'but don't worry about it, we're going home.'

He found everyone else in the stables that opened out onto the castle's courtyard. Brian and Sophie helped Gerold up into his saddle, and Bowman waited by the gate asking why everyone else was taking so long.

'Why are you in such a rush?' Richard asked him as Maynard handed him the blue roan.

'The Young King might ask for our wages back,' Bowman grinned.

Servants ran out of the stables and a hurried rider left the castle and rode down into the town. Soon after, the church bells started to ring.

Richard pulled himself into the saddle and waited for Maynard to bring out Solis and free Judas from the stable.

Dogs barked at the ringing bells and Judas barked back.

'We need to hurry,' Bowman walked his horse so it stood in the gateway, 'before they stop people leaving the town.'

'You'd think they'd want all the non-fighting people outside if there was going to be a siege,' Richard said.

'Who said there's going to be a siege?' Sophie walked her palfrey on.

'No one,' Richard replied, 'but everyone here is preparing anyway. I don't think they're ringing the bells just for the sake of it.'

Brian and Gerold said they were ready, and the party left the castle. Maynard led Solis on a rope, but the horse kept stopping to investigate the houses they rode past, and every time he did, the squire was nearly jerked from his own horse.

Richard didn't mind, it might put Maynard off wanting a place in his household.

Townspeople went about their day almost as normal, if they were bothered by the bells that still chimed, they didn't show it.

'It's better inside than outside,' Bowman said when he noticed Richard watching two men playing a board game outside a freshly painted house.

'If it's a siege, the surrounding land will be pillaged,' Richard said, 'so we'd better move quicker than those pillagers.'

'It'll be hard with the old man,' Bowman nodded back to Gerold.

'Don't worry about him,' Richard turned his horse west and towards the gate that would lead them back to Yvetot.

The gate was barred. A line of carts queued up to leave it, their contents being inspected by guards wearing iron helmets and tunics of layered wool.

Bowman reached the gate and demanded it be opened.

'And who are you?' a guard with a short ginger beard asked. The guard had a sword at his waist, which marked him apart from the others.

'Who am?' Bowman asked. 'Who are you?'

'I'm the captain of the guard, and the gates aren't open yet.'

'I know, that's why I'm complaining. We're leaving, so open them up for us,' Bowman said.

The captain sighed and peeled himself away from the cart his men were checking over.

'Don't be offended by this knight,' Richard said, 'he's in a rush. Would you be able to open the gate for us, please?'

The captain thought about it. Then shook his head. 'You can wait like everyone else. You knights think you're better than us, but you have no authority here.'

'Open the damned gates,' Bowman cried and pushed his horse into the captain's face.

'Don't be a fool,' Richard said, 'he's never going to open them if you threaten him.'

The captain jumped out of Bowman's way and went to stand behind a cart stacked high with rolls of coloured linen.

Sophie rode over and asked the captain his name and if he had a family.

The captain nodded and told her about his two daughters.

'If you were being kept from going back to them by a closed gate,' Sophie said, 'would you want to break it down?'

The captain rubbed the pommel of his sword, looked into Sophie's eyes, and relented. 'It's about time to open the gates, anyway,' he said, 'the carts who've paid their toll can leave.'

Two of his men gradually unbarred the gate.

'Hurry up,' Bowman shouted at them.

'You're not making it happen any quicker,' Richard told him.

The gate swung open and Bowman shot out through it, stirring up a cloud of dust one of the guards coughed on.

'We need to get him a wife,' Sophie watched him go.

'He needs something, that's for sure,' Richard walked his warhorse through the gate and it sniffed the air as they left the town.

Except that Richard bumped straight into Bowman's black horse. The horse threw a back leg at Richard's, who squealed back. Richard pulled the blue roan's head away to avoid a fight, but the stallion tried to lash out with a front hoof regardless. 'What are you doing?' Richard shouted.

'Young lord,' Bowman looked away to the west, 'we have a problem.'

Richard knew they had a problem, fighting stallions was a big problem.

'Look,' Bowman didn't have to point, because crossing the river in the distance, a line of figures snaked their way towards the town. All on horseback, but so far away that to begin with, they all looked black. It wasn't long before the sun behind Richard reflected off metal here and there, which meant the column was another army. 'Can we go around them?' he asked.

Bowman groaned. 'They'll see us, and if they are minded to, they'll catch up with us if you insist on going slowly for the old man and your crippled horse.'

'Don't call him crippled,' Richard shuddered at the idea of his horse not recovering.

Sophie joined them. She stayed silent for a moment. 'We're not leaving, are we?'

'The last time we stood here, right here,' Richard said, 'and watched an army cross that bridge, it was Lord Tancarville coming to reinforce the town.'

Bowman spat onto the ground as the first cart leaving the town reached them and stopped.

'If it's him again, I don't know if he is coming to help the town, or take it,' the blonde man said.

'It could be someone else,' Richard said, 'it could be Sir Roger.'

'Aye, it could,' Bowman said, 'but we can't ride across fields and open ground to escape them. We can't risk it.'

'I don't want to stay here,' Richard said, 'I don't want the Young King to find us. What if this army is on our side?'

'Our side?' Bowman leant on the high pommel of his saddle. 'Which side is that?'

Richard grimaced. Then he shook his head. 'Our own,' he said, 'we're on our own side.'

'And it's better served behind these nice high walls than racing across bad ground,' Bowman said, 'where if one horse falls, we're all lost.'

'You're right,' Richard said, 'we'll have to take our chance in the town. We have to go back to the castle.'

Brian sighed behind them.

Richard shot him a withering look and the monk turned his face away. 'I know Neufchatel is boring,' Richard said, 'but we can't help it.'

'What if it's them?' Sophie asked in a soft voice.

'The Tancarvilles?' Richard asked.

She nodded. 'You know which one.'

Richard did. 'From what the castellan said, and Brother Geoffrey, too, Lord Tancarville is no supporter of the old king. If he's here, he could be part of the Young King's invasion.'

Bowman watched the approaching snake, its black metal scales shimmering occasionally in the sun as it slithered towards them. 'I'll see their banner soon,' he said, 'I can make out the shape of it.'

'Brian, get Gerold back inside the keep,' Richard said, 'there isn't a safer place for him.'

'What about the church?'

Richard shrugged. 'I don't think the Young King would burn a church,' he said, 'and the Little Lord was knighted in this one, so maybe the Tancarvilles would also respect it. Very well, put him there, and you can stay there yourself.'

Brian nodded back and retreated into the town with Gerold.

'We should all claim sanctuary in the church,' Richard said, 'this is another man's war.'

'I'm not going into the church,' Bowman said.

'Even if it keeps us away from any fighting?'

The blonde man nodded. 'You can do what you fancy, young lord, but I'll watch whatever happens from the walls.'

Richard groaned in frustration. 'I'm not leaving you alone to get yourself killed,' he said, 'so I'll stand beside you.'

'We should have stayed with the Young King,' Bowman said.

'Why?' Richard could make out individual riders now. And a bannerman.

'Because that banner is red,' Bowman said, 'with a silver shield.'

Richard's heart sank. 'And silver rowels?'

'Probably,' Bowman said, 'my eyes aren't as good as they used to be.'

'I want to go back now,' Sophie said, her words cold.

Richard agreed, and they wheeled around and reentered Neufchatel. The first cart which had left reached the same conclusion, spun around, and returned to the safety of the walls. The captain of the guard slammed the gates shut behind everyone once they were all back in.

Richard rode back up the cobblestones next to Sophie, his mind racing.

'We must return to Yvetot,' Sophie said, 'Sarjeant promised not to drink while I was away, but I don't know how long he'll last.'

'You shouldn't have left him, then,' Richard snapped.

Sophie's face recoiled with hurt.

'I'm sorry,' Richard said, 'I'm worried too, but we're stuck in here now.'

'Trapped, you mean,' she said.

'Yes,' Richard said, 'trapped.'

Four men approached the castle. The surcoats over their mail told Richard who they were even before he recognised their faces. The fact that they wore their armour at all told him what their purpose was. Guy of Lusignan in his blue and white, and Count Robert whose heraldry matched the Martel's, stood either side of two men with red surcoats.

The Young King walked on foot close enough to shout up at the walls on which Walter and Richard stood.

'The fool,' Walter sneered, 'he's within crossbow range.'

'I think he's making a point,' Richard said.

The castellan had donned a generously sized mail shirt, but didn't have a surcoat. Some crossbowmen peered down from the stone battlements, bolts bristling from bags around their waists. One crossbowman leant over too far and bolts spilled from his bag all over the parapet floor.

'I wouldn't shoot the Young King,' Richard said, 'his father would string you up, even if one of your men did it accidentally.'

'I'm not an idiot,' Walter replied, 'I know who the next king is. He's standing down there, and once King Henry is dancing with angels, I want to be reconfirmed in my post.'

Richard hoped Walter's men had the same level of self preservation. Down in the courtyard behind Richard, men stacked large stones in a net which would hoist them up to the walls. Men on the wall readied a wooden crane to do the lifting.

'Who commands here?' the Young King shouted up.

Richard half hid himself behind a crenellation. He wondered if Count Philip had avoided being in the parley so he could claim neutrality if things went wrong.

'I do, Sir Walter,' the castellan replied in his proudest voice.

'Why are your gates closed to me? Are you unaware of who I am?'

'I am very aware who you are,' Walter said, 'but my gates remain closed.'

'You bar your gates to your king?'

'There can only be one king, and you march to my town with an army on both sides of me. You intend to take my castle. I am no village fool.'

'We come in peace,' the Young King said, 'merely journeying from one tournament to another. We seek a day's rest in your town, then to move on.'

The castellan snorted quietly to himself and turned to Richard. 'Does he think I'm a child he can win over with honeyed lies?'

'He could be telling the truth,' Richard said.

'Your honeyed lies are even less convincing,' Walter snapped. He leant over the wall. 'If you're passing through, then go around. The ground is dry, so you don't need to pass through my town, and then you can leave us in peace. I won't interfere with your march.'

'You deny your lord his rightful hospitality?' the Young King asked, exasperation creeping into his voice.

'I deny an invader a chance to take my town with a crude ruse,' the castellan said.

Count Robert said something to the Young King, who shrugged back at him.

'Would you allow only the counts and greater knights to spend the day in your town?' the Young King asked. 'No more than ten of us.'

Walter laughed, and his second chin wobbled. 'You think me stupid? You think my mother dropped me on my head when I was a child? As soon as my guards turn their backs, you'll be burying knives in them. I am loyal to the crown, and once you wear it I will gladly throw open my gates for you. Until then, ride around.'

'The four of us then,' the Young King waved at his companions, 'just the four of us. We'll leave our swords behind.'

The castellan rubbed his chins.

Richard could see his mind churning, calculating the size of the ransoms of the four men who stood below him. 'If you take those men hostage,' Richard said, 'they'll pay their ransoms for sure. But then they'll come back and burn you out.'

'You would say that, you're their spy.'

Richard restrained his urge to grab his sword. 'The Marshal is petty and vindictive, but Guy of Lusignan is worse, he's mad. He pulls the fingers off his own guards when they fall asleep on watch, and he kills just to relieve his boredom. Those are not men to toy with. Certainly not men to allow into your castle and then betray.'

Walter sniffed. 'We have all heard about Guy and his brethren.' The castellan looked down at the supplicants beneath him. 'Go away,' he shouted.

Guy pointed up at Walter and said something to the Young King. The young Angevin laughed. That unsettled Richard. Nothing Guy said was ever a laughing matter. The Marshal regarded Guy with balled fists and whispered in the Young King's other ear.

'There is dissension between them already,' Walter said with a smugness that was unwarranted.

'Guy killed the Marshal's uncle and held him captive for months,' Richard said.

'Then their alliance will falter as soon as they face resistance,' Walter said, 'and here they will face plenty of that.'

The Young King turned away and the four men of the parley walked back to their army. Tents were half erected in the shelter of the small hill on the horizon, and parties of men already dug pits for various uses. Wagons rolled in every direction and horses were tied up to lines and given fodder.

'Are we under siege?' Richard asked.

Walter shrugged. 'I don't know,' he said.

It felt like a siege to Richard, so he left the walls to find his companions. He found Bowman and Maynard in the castle, Bowman trying to shoo the squire away.

'We need to get away from Neufchatel,' Richard said to them. They were outside the kitchen building in the courtyard, and the smell of baking bread made his mouth water.

'Obviously,' Bowman said, 'but how do you propose we do it?'

'Tonight,' Richard said, 'when it's dark. We'll ride out of the gate to the northwest that we sallied out of the first time we were here. The Young King is trying to pretend that he doesn't want to take the town, and posting guards by that gate, so far from his camp, would ruin his ploy.'

'So your plan is just to ride out of the town at night,' Bowman frowned. 'Is that it?'

'We can disguise as lepers or monks if you prefer something more elaborate,' Richard said, 'but you're the one who's always telling me we don't live in a romance.'

'What if the siege is real?' Bowman asked. 'What if we run straight into a party of crossbowmen with orders to shoot?'

'We'll just have to be quick or quiet, then,' Richard said, 'although probably just quick, as you're always loud when we're trying to be quiet.'

Bowman's face dropped. 'Not anymore, I've got no one to argue with now.'

'You're doing a fair job of it at the moment,' Richard said.

'It would be safer to stay,' the blonde man said, 'we risk too much riding around in the night. That's when people get lost and accidents happen.'

Richard shook his head. 'If there is a fight in this town, I don't want to be caught up in it. When most children have a grievance with their father, all they can do is shout or stomp off for a while. The Young King can raise an army instead, and that's all this is. Dying here for their arguments would have no meaning at all. After Nicholas, I can't let that happen to anyone else.'

Bowman's eyes softened as they met Richard's. He nodded.

Maynard sniffed the distracting scent of bread in the air. 'We could just open the gates for the Young King,' he said, 'then no one at all has to die.'

In a flash Bowman clipped him round the back of his head and the young man stumbled forwards. He regained his footing and rubbed the back of his head. 'What did you do that for?'

'Because we didn't ask your opinion,' Bowman said.

The squire gave the blonde man a dirty look but turned to Richard. 'The Young King promised all the Martel land to you, but you had to stay in service to him.'

Richard had half forgotten that. 'That is a lot of land,' he said.

'Too much for you,' Bowman grinned. 'Do you think the man who rules that much land ever has a moment's peace?'

Richard shook his head. 'But we'd never be short of money ever again,' he said.

Bowman licked his lips in the direction of the kitchen. 'Or have to steal bread,' he mumbled.

'I don't actually care if you steal from the castellan,' Richard said, 'but if you do, just bring enough for me.'

Bowman's grin widened.

Maynard scratched his head. 'Are you opening the gates or not, then?' he asked.

This time Richard clapped him around the ear himself.

The squire flinched partly out of the way and shook his head once he stood far enough away from both knights. 'My ear's ringing now,' he said.

'Good,' Richard said, 'then you'll remember not to speak of treason. Never betray anyone.'

Bowman stifled a cough. 'That's a bit rich from the man who tried to stay loyal to two kings and ended up betraying both of them.'

'That's unfair,' Richard said.

'What about the one you killed?' Maynard said.

Richard and Bowman glared at him and both stepped forwards to clout him again. The squire spun and ran across the courtyard.

'He has a point, young lord,' Bowman said once he'd stopped laughing, 'you are hardly one to preach on either loyalty or kings.'

'Be quiet,' Richard said, 'but he does have another point. If I ruled the Martel lands, that would mean something could happen to Geoffrey Martel.'

Bowman's lip twitched. 'Don't tempt me. If I see him again, I'll kill him.'

'If we sided with the Young King, maybe you could do it legally,' Richard said.

'Are you just saying this to annoy me?' Bowman asked. 'Because I know you, and you have no intention of opening the gates. The Young King is just another strutting peacock.'

A servant left the kitchen with two fresh loaves of dark bread, and Richard's gaze followed them as they swept across the courtyard and into the castle. 'No,' he said, 'temptation was just grabbing me. It's sheer, sinful, greed to even think about it.'

'Maybe we should, though,' Bowman said.

'What?'

'Open the gates.'

'So you've changed your mind?' Richard asked.

The blonde man shook his head. 'I'd never had a view on it, young lord, but killing the man who holds my mother prisoner and then lording it up over his lands sounds like exactly what I should be wanting.'

Richard rolled his eyes. 'Your mother is quite happy with Geoffrey,' he said, 'don't use that as an excuse. And it wasn't Geoffrey Martel who killed your half-brother.'

'Brother,' Bowman's eyes narrowed. 'But he is the last Martel left, and he must die.'

'Is that all you care about?' Richard asked.

'What else should I care about?'

'Staying alive long enough to see your child again.'

'Don't throw that at me,' Bowman said, 'you can't just mention Eva and Isabel every time I beat you in an argument.'

Richard sniffed. 'Well, I just did, and you know I'm right.'

Bowman pursed his lips.

'If you open those gates, those guards will run you through with a spear. I'm sure they are terrible shots, but one of them will hit you with a bolt, and then you'll be dead.'

'Sounds like the talk of a coward to me,' Bowman crossed his arms.

'You're calling me a coward, are you?' Richard said. 'Just because you know I'm right.'

'Fine,' Bowman said, 'but when you've spent your tournament money and moan about being poor again, I'll remind you of this moment.'

'You do that,' Richard said with a wry grin, 'just steal some bread for our journey and start getting ready. Tonight we're leaving.'

Darkness fell with no action from either the Young King or Tancarville. The castle however, had been a hive of activity; food had been stockpiled along with firewood and everything else the castellan could cram into his storerooms. Richard had checked on the Tancarville army, but they had pitched their camp exactly in the same place as they had done years before, and were busy digging anti-cavalry pits. That told Richard that Lord Tancarville himself was in command. Then Richard went to the northwestern gate that opened out to the suburbs and the second bridge across the river. Except the gate was shut, but from the wall above it he couldn't see any banners in the distance, nor movement in the suburbs or trees that grew around the edge of the town. The trees were further away than during his last visit, and the stumps from those that had been removed dotted the ground, perfectly placed to cause a horse to trip in the dark. But that was the only hazard Richard could see, so he rounded up his party and prepared to leave.

The castellan was a man who thought power was best wielded from afar, and he was not in the courtyard to prevent them leading their horses out of the stables at twilight. Braziers dotted the battlements, their light seeming to glow brighter as a great cloud shrouded the otherwise dazzling moon.

Two large bags of bread hung from Bowman's saddle as they mounted and rode down the cobbles towards the main square. The knights wore their armour, except for Gerold who was too weak to put his on. They had neither shields nor lances, and if challenged it would be speed that Richard planned to rely on.

The guards on the northwestern gate were unsure if they should let anyone out of the town.

'What are your orders?' Richard asked the nervous looking man.

'Don't let anyone in.'

'Well then,' Richard said, 'you aren't disobeying anyone by letting us out, are you?'

The young guard went to speak to a comrade, who answered by waving at the gate. The sturdy wooden bar that ran across it was lifted from its iron brackets and the gate opened.

Richard rode out into the dark streets of the suburbs.

'It's very quiet,' Bowman said as the town gate creaked shut behind them.

'Of course it is,' Richard said, 'if I lived here I would have fled already. Both sides are likely to burn it all down if real fighting starts.'

A fox ran across the road, paused to watch the horses approach it, then scurried off before Judas caught up with Richard.

'I hate foxes,' Bowman said.

'I know,' Richard said, 'bad luck.'

'What more bad luck could possibly afflict me?' the blonde man moaned.

'Don't say that,' Richard hissed, 'every time you say something like that, we get attacked.'

Both men checked their surroundings as they rode away from the walls. The hovels were quiet, no smoke rose from their thatch, and no animals barked or brayed.

Richard looked twice at a stone enclosure on the side of the street.

Bowman nodded. 'It is.'

'Castle Peacock?'

'He'd probably want a palace now,' Bowman mumbled to himself.

'Castle what?' Sophie asked from her palfrey just behind Richard.

Richard shook his head at the memory. 'Don't worry about it, I think you had to be there.' His left knee ached for a moment in phantom pain, a memory of the injury that plagued him throughout his stay at Neufchatel. He thought of the boar that had killed Simon Martel and caused his own leg injury, and then flexed his hands in remembrance of the burns he'd received as a result of the whole affair.

Castle Peacock vanished into the night behind them, and Richard reached the crossroads which marked the end of the suburbs he recognised. A short way down the next street and the urban area petered out. Richard halted the blue roan there and peered into the treeline.

'Mind the stumps,' he whispered and Bowman nodded.

'Judas,' Richard called softly and the black dog slunk up to their horses. He sniffed the air.

'What do you want him for?' Bowman asked. 'He'll just bark at a squirrel and alert anyone who is out there.'

'That's what Adam said,' Richard replied, 'just before he warned us of the enemy and saved our lives.'

The black dog silently walked forwards, cocked a leg on a tree stump, and then advanced some more.

A silvery light washed over the treeline as the moon came out, but it reflected on no helmets or lance heads. Another cloud rolled in front of the moon and the world blackened once more. The only light shone from the distant castle behind them on its hill, tiny yellow dots in the night.

Richard shivered. Being out in the dark was unwise, even if you knew the land you fumbled over. But he could see no reason not to continue, so turned to his companions. 'I think the woods are clear, we're looking for a bridge.'

'I think we first entered Neufchatel over a bridge this way,' Bowman said.

'I hardly remember,' Richard walked the blue roan on and it took him into the trees.

There was a track, two grooves worn into the earth by the passing of a thousand carts, and they rode between the ruts even though they could barely see the ground. As soon as the trees closed in on both sides, Richard felt unsafe. Sophie looked from left to right with fleeting glances, but Bowman's eyes were fixed ahead. The black dog took the lead, his job accepted, occasionally stopping to listen or sniff the air.

Water trickled somewhere, which meant they neared the river. The soft sound filtered through the trees to their left and the track bent towards it.

'Once we're over the bridge we'll be safe, won't we?' Maynard whispered as Judas halted and inspected their surroundings. The squire looked more afraid of the dog than the night.

Bowman grimaced and used the widening of his eyes to tell the squire to be quiet.

Judas lowered his head and his hackles raised.

'What's he doing?' Maynard asked.

'Quiet,' Richard replied.

'Is something wrong?'

'I don't know,' Richard said, 'dogs can't speak. Be quiet.'

Bowman stepped his horse sideways so he could whisper to Richard. 'I think we should go back.'

'Oh, you believe the dog now, do you?' Richard almost smiled.

'I'd put men on the bridge,' the blonde man said, 'everyone leaving the town would have to cross it.'

'It could just be a deer,' Richard said, 'the herds here are huge. This is the time of night they start to move around.'

'I'll go forward and check,' Bowman said.

Richard shrugged.

Bowman didn't go anywhere.

'I thought you were going ahead?' Richard asked.

'I don't think it's a deer,' the blonde man turned his horse around.

'Why not?'

'Because deer don't wear iron horseshoes.'

'What?' Richard asked. Then he heard iron on wood. The same sound horseshoes would make as they rushed over a wooden bridge. 'Go,' he shouted and turned his horse, 'go back.'

Judas barked and Maynard yelped in fright as all their horses spun around towards Neufchatel.

There was no question of fighting, not against what was likely a properly equipped enemy.

A cry cut through the sound of the bubbling river as Richard's horse grunted and surged into a canter.

Then Richard made out the cry.

'Dex Aie the Marshal.'

'God's teeth,' Bowman shouted, 'anyone but him.'

Richard spurred his horse. 'Come on Sophie,' he shouted, but there was no need, she wore spurs too, and her palfrey was neck and neck with Richard.

Richard glanced behind him, but Maynard still had a hold of Solis's rope, and the palomino was cantering, albeit uncomfortably.

But for how long?

The blue roan strayed onto the rutted groove of the track and stumbled, but stayed on his feet. Shouts and jeers followed them, and when Richard snatched another look at his pursuers, he saw armoured knights with lances charging after him. They were closing the gap.

The woodland opened up and the blue roan left the track and had to jump an old stump that had grown fresh shoots. Maynard and Solis lagged behind, the squire unable to drag the stallion along any quicker than he wanted to go.

Richard hit the suburbs and raced up the street. The town gates will be shut, he thought, and the nervous young guard wouldn't be opening them in a hurry. Which meant that the gate likely meant death or capture.

Running wasn't an option either, for they wouldn't reach the gate or anywhere else before the Marshal. Richard took a right turn, and although Sophie was on his heels, Gerold looked like he was about to sway from his horse. Maynard was almost an entire street behind.

Richard saw a familiar enclosure and slammed his horse to a stop. 'In there,' he pointed. The stone walls had been built up since their first occupation of it, so Castle Peacock was more formidable than before.

Bowman's horse hopped to a stop with its legs braced and skidded over the road. 'There?' he almost laughed as Sophie entered Castle Peacock with Gerold not far behind. Maynard turned into their haven, but Solis kept going down the road and the squire was pulled out of the side of his saddle. The palomino turned and snorted at Maynard as he tumbled on the road, but to his credit he kept a firm hold of the rope. Richard drew his sword and stood in the entrance to the enclosure to block it once his party was inside.

'We can't kill them all,' Bowman said, 'so I'm assuming you have a plan.'

'I'm going to talk to him,' Richard said.

'Talk? You can't negotiate with a man who cannot understand anyone else,' Bowman said.

Maynard's loose horse followed the others in to avoid being left alone on the road, even though the blue roan bit his rump on the way.

The street was empty only for a moment.

The Marshal led his company of a dozen knights up to the enclosure and they surrounded the entrance in a semicircle of horses and iron.

'We've got them now,' Henry the Northerner shouted with glee. Two of their horses pawed at the hard earth and snorted in the icy air.

The Marshal slipped the helmet with the metal face plate off his head and squinted into the darkness. Moisture swirled in the atmosphere as the moon came out again and cast a pale glow over the knights besieging Castle Peacock.

'Richard?' the Marshal stepped his horse forwards.

'We're on our way back to Yvetot.'

'This helmet is not great in the dark,' the Marshal held the helmet up and looked into its eye slits.

'If you stand aside we'll be on our way,' Richard said.

The Marshal lowered the helmet and glanced at his old friend. 'What are you doing here?'

'I told you,' Richard said, 'we're on our way home.'

'You left us,' the Marshal's voice strained almost with hurt, 'why would you leave us? The Young King would have given you everything. You could have been as highly regarded as me. Well, almost. Why would you abandon him? He is your rightful lord.'

Richard slid his sword silently back into its scabbard. 'I don't want to fight anymore, I'm done with it. I've suffered my fair share for lords and kings, the rest of the time God gives me is for my family.'

'They're there for the taking,' Henry's deep voice echoed off the walls of the enclosure. 'He stole your blue roan, we can take it back.'

The Marshal eyed the horse. 'I should have it back, but I'm not sure what I wish to do here.'

With a frown on his face, Bowman almost growled at the Marshal. Judas did.

'Call your dog off,' Henry said.

'Are you scared of a dog?' Bowman sneered.

'I'll call him off if you let us leave,' Richard said.

The Marshal laughed. 'I don't care about a dog, even that one,' he said, 'but I know you have no ransom potential.'

'Seems like a simple choice for you,' Sophie raised her voice, 'letting us go solves everything.'

'Not really,' the Marshal said, 'my orders are to block the bridge, to let no one over it. We can't let the word out.'

'What word?' Richard asked.

'That the invasion has begun.'

Richard groaned. 'I don't care, none of us care. We'll go back to Yvetot and not tell another living soul. I'll swear it on anything that makes you happy.'

'It wouldn't make me happy,' the Marshal said, 'because I'd have disobeyed my lord. That might not mean a lot to you, but to me it is everything.'

'Pretentious turd,' Bowman mumbled.

'Capture that one,' Henry pointed, 'I've never liked him. Both of those men have disrespected me from the time they arrived. Life was better before they ruined everything.'

'I didn't ask you to speak,' the Marshal snapped, 'and you're not helping.'

'Stand aside,' Richard said, 'we're worth nothing.'

'Speak for yourself,' Bowman said.

Richard kept his eyes on the Marshal. 'Let us ride down to the river, then follow us after to take up your position on the bridge. No one would ever know we'd passed through.'

'I'd know,' the Marshal said, 'my honour cannot accept that.'

Bowman laughed. 'You live in your own little world, don't you?'

'I'll pay you,' Richard said, 'our earnings from Lagny and Corbie. You can have it all.'

'Hold on,' Bowman said, 'what are you doing? I'm not agreeing to that.'

The Marshal rode forwards until his horse and the blue roan could almost strain to sniff each other. 'You offer me coin to compensate for shredding my honour? An amount of coin which would barely be noticed by Wigain when he counts up my other winnings. I'm not sacrificing my hard-earned loyalty for that.'

'I don't think he's even joking,' Bowman said to Sophie.

Her face unimpressed, she cleared her throat. 'William,' she said, 'my children are waiting for me at home and I need to return to them.'

'Your children?' Richard said. 'You mean *our* children?'

'I'm sorry, Lady Sophie,' the Marshal said, 'duty means I cannot let you pass.'

'I'll give you the blue roan back,' Richard's shoulders hunched, 'anything to let us through. We need to go back to Yvetot.'

The Marshal half smiled. 'If I take the horse you'd have to walk back home.'

'Don't give him the horse,' Bowman said, 'he doesn't deserve it. And if you do, I'm not sharing my horse with you.'

'I'll give you the horse if you swap it for another one,' Richard said, 'I don't care how bad it is as long as it's sound.'

The moon illuminated the enclosure in white light, and the Marshal grinned. 'Are you in my castle?'

Richard nodded. 'You remember it too, then,' he said.

The Marshal rotated his shoulder that had been torn almost in the exact spot he now stood. The tattered green knighting cloak still hung on its shoulders, although most of the tattering had happened since the skirmish around Castle Peacock. 'How could I forget?' he mumbled.

A silence filled the air and Richard and the Marshal looked at each other and remembered how close to disaster they'd come between these stone walls.

'At least let Gerold and I leave,' Sophie said, 'he is sick and I must reach the children. They will do no harm to your lord or your honour, indeed it might be boosted by an act of charity to the needy.'

Richard raised his eyebrows at his wife. 'You'd happily leave me here?'

Sophie's expression entertained no humour. 'You wouldn't understand.'

Eyes turned to the Marshal to await his decision. None came.

'After everything we've been through,' Richard said, 'both here and while Guy held you, would you really betray me?'

'I wouldn't call taking you back to the Young King a betrayal,' the Marshal said, 'it is where you belong.'

'Once I've seen to my children, I could return to him,' Richard said, 'at some point.'

'Really?' the Marshal scoffed. 'That's a weak promise.'

Henry shifted forwards. 'He cheated when he jousted me, this is our chance to even that score.'

'Silence,' the Marshal threw the face plate helmet at him, 'put this on so your unsought-for words are at least muffled.'

Having no free hands, Henry fumbled the helmet when it hit him, but caught it between his elbows and chest.

'Do you remember,' Richard said, 'when the firehook dragged you from your horse?'

The Marshal nodded.

'Do you remember who took you back inside the town? Who saved you from the mob of Flemings who didn't want to capture you, but to cut your throat?'

The Marshal did remember, but he fought to admit it. He sighed. 'I can't let you go,' he said, 'but I suppose I can let you stay. Then we're even for the Flemings. Which is ironic, because they're on our side now.'

'You always have to keep an account, don't you,' Bowman said, 'a good deed can only be considered if someone has done one for you first.'

'Stop it,' Richard said, 'before he changes his mind.'

'Go on,' the Marshal backed his horse up, 'before I decide I want my blue roan back more than I care about you. Look at his proud head, the nobility of it.'

Richard pushed his warhorse out of Castle Peacock and had to keep a grip of it as it tried to get close to the Marshal's horse to fight it.

Henry's horse flinched out of the way and Bowman laughed at him as he left the enclosure.

Richard led his party back up the street towards Neufchatel's walls and the Marshal turned his back and faded into the gloom.

'Well, that went well,' Bowman said.

'Don't,' Richard said

Bowman grinned. 'But at least I'm now certain you aren't planning on replacing me with the Irish monk.'

Richard shot him a puzzled look.

'You forgot to bring him with us,' Bowman said, 'he's still in that damned church.'

'Don't tell him we tried to leave,' Richard groaned, 'he'd be devastated.'

Bowman laughed. 'That sounds like your problem, not mine,' he said.

Richard sighed. He thought of his next problem instead, which was the prospect of arguing with the guards to get back into town. The thought made him feel very weary.

ARROWS

The next morning Richard found himself feeling that events were repeating themselves. Once again, Walter the Good looked down from his wall at the Young King as Richard watched from the most obscure part of the wall he could find.

The Young King repeated his request to be allowed into the castle, but now with just five companions by his side.

The castellan laughed. 'Even if you ask to enter alone, you will be denied.'

The Young King's mask, the one he had explained to Richard, cracked for a heartbeat and anger burst across his youthful face. 'You leave me with little choice,' he said, 'you have two days to throw the gates open, or I'll storm the castle.'

Walter almost jumped up with excitement. 'I knew it, I knew you were up to no good. Wait until your father hears about this.'

'Whatever happens here will be on your conscience,' the Young King said, 'I meant no harm.'

'Threatening to storm my castle sounds like harm,' Walter said.

'Your castle? The castle belongs to the crown.'

'Not your crown,' the castellan said, 'not yet.'

'You have two days,' the Young King shook his head.

The castellan left the wall before the Young King even walked away, an act of disrespect which the young Angevin's eyes flashed red at.

'The young fool,' Walter said to one of the guards next to him, 'that's two more days to strengthen the town wall, make more arrows, and gather more food into the castle.'

Richard left his place and walked along the parapet in order to reach the steps that led down to the courtyard.

'We'll hold them at the town walls as long as we can,' Walter raised his voice so more could hear, 'blunt their attack, then pull back to the castle where they will never dislodge us. We may have to sit here for a few weeks, but King Henry will reward everyone once he relieves us.'

Richard didn't like the idea of being cooped up with the castellan for weeks. And weeks could turn into months if the Young King was as stubborn as his father.

'You,' Walter pointed at Richard, 'do you know what the weakest part of a castle is?'

'I don't really care,' Richard walked towards the stone stairway.

'Most men say it is the gate,' Walter said, 'but it's really the men inside. The weak ones who cave in to their fear, and the conniving ones who deliberately enter a castle to betray it.'

Richard sighed. 'I'm stuck here with you, I don't want to open the gates.'

The castellan reached for his sword but didn't draw it. 'The first act of a siege is to flush out the traitors. I am told someone rode out of the castle last night, then came back. To me, that sounds like spies conspiring with the enemy. Would you know anything about it?'

Richard didn't have the energy to lie, he had the energy to sit on a bench by a hearth and drink something Bowman had stolen. 'I just wanted to go home. Quietly and with no fuss. But the Young King's men chased us back into Neufchatel. I don't want to fight anyone, or talk to anyone. I'm trapped here with you, and the best thing for me is for the Young King to leave without having taken this castle. Why would I want to let him in?'

'Your lies are not my concern,' Walter said, 'but I have a dark cellar with a heavy door that could save me from your trouble.'

Anger coursed through Richard's veins and he balled his hands into fists so hard his fingernails cut into his skin. 'Do you know who I am?' he asked in a forcibly calm voice. 'Do you know where I lost this finger? I stormed a castle and took it, with nothing but one man beside me. Do you know who I stormed the castle for? Your King, the old one.'

Walter lowered his hand, then raised it again. 'Take him into the cellar. Lock him away,' he cried.

Richard pointed up to the jagged and proud flesh that cut down his face over his eye. 'This scar, do you know how I got that? Saving your Queen.'

'She's a witch,' Walter said, 'she hides behind her sons and plots against her husband. She's unnatural, the devil's own work.'

Richard drew his dagger, his eyes unblinking and glued to the castellan. 'This dagger,' he said, 'it used to belong to Sir John de la Londe, have you heard about that? Everyone else seems to have. I can see on your men's faces that they have, they know who I am.'

Walter wavered. He could see his guards shrink from Richard.

'But you might not know about my sword,' Richard replaced the dagger and drew the Little Lord's battered blade. 'This belonged to Lord Tancarville's son. You've all heard the stories about him. Who sliced the manhood from him, that is the mystery, but I know who did it. And I have this sword as a trophy. Do you think that makes me a friend of the Tancarvilles?'

Walter rubbed his cheek.

'I'll fight at the western gate,' Richard said, 'and if any Tancarville climbs onto that wall, I'll kill him for you. What you aren't doing is throwing me into a cell, so get out of my way.'

Walter glanced at his guards, but none of them returned his gaze or lifted a finger to block Richard.

He pushed past the castellan so roughly that the portly man bounced off his battlements and bruised his thigh. Richard descended the steps into the courtyard, where the occupants tried their best not to look at him. They quickly scattered, all except Sophie who stood with her hands on her waist and a wry smile on her lips.

'I think you may have finally grown up,' she said, 'even if all that posturing was rather vulgar.'

Richard shrugged. 'I'm not spending the next few weeks locked in a cellar, and I'm not letting that happen to you, either.'

'I'm very glad of it,' she smiled softly, 'but I'm going to the church to pray for all the men here to come to their senses and end this nonsense.'

Richard nodded. 'I wouldn't bother, there's no reasoning with any of them, even with divine backing. I'll find Bowman and Maynard and go and man the western gate. We have to keep the Tancarvilles out.'

Sophie's face turned white and she nodded back. 'Keep them out.'

The two-day deadline arrived with a frost. Richard's fingers, especially the one that had been shortened at Corbie, ached even as he wrapped his hands up in his cloak. Bowman commandeered a brazier, but it was so cold that it didn't help. Maynard sat against the wall behind Richard, deep in silence. Their breath steamed from their mouths and nostrils in plumes as the grassy plains around the town shone a twinkling white. The sun rose behind them and the frost began to recede, but it would be a while before the air warmed enough to make their watch comfortable.

The ginger-bearded captain of the guard kept his eyes on the Tancarville camp. A red shield rested on the wooden wall next to his spear.

Bowman blew warm air into his hands and stood up. He gazed out of Neufchatel and into what was the enemy camp. 'They're stirring,' he said, 'like a nest of ants when you kick it.'

Richard took a deep breath and watched the brazier flicker from Bowman's movement. He pushed himself up and rubbed his thighs which had seized up. When he peered over the wall, he could see the encampment was indeed springing into life.

Maynard refused to get up and look for himself.

'Where did those ladders come from?' the captain asked.

'Lord Tancarville is clever enough to hide their construction from us,' Bowman said, 'I hope your men have enough arrows and bolts.'

The captain scraped his fingers along the rough wood of the battlements. He'd been doing the same thing for the past two days. 'Don't worry about my men,' he said, 'worry about pushing those ladders off the walls when they get here.'

Companies of enemy crossbowmen formed up in groups halfway to the town, half on either side of the road.

'They're going to try for the gate,' the captain said.

'Of course they are,' Bowman said, 'this isn't our first siege.' The blonde man's eyes were dark and he had a sunken look to his face. He hadn't slept well recently.

Richard laced on his helmet then picked up the spear the captain had grudgingly provided.

'Don't get in our way,' the captain said before ordering his crossbowmen and normal archers to prepare for battle. A guardsman propped a bundle of short javelins up against the wall and ran off for more.

The captain nodded down to the missiles. 'You can use those, I assume being highborn, you're no stranger to hunting with them.'

'You'd be right,' Bowman replied with his nose in the air, 'we are so highborn we hardly do anything other than hunt.'

Richard picked up two of the javelins to use before his spear. He felt the weight of the weapons and nodded. He held one out to Maynard, but the squire shook his head and cradled the spear he'd also been given.

Tancarville sarjeants mingled with their crossbowmen, their textile armour supplemented sometimes by leather and helmets, sometimes not. Behind them the glint of mail revealed the massing of Tancarville's knights.

'Can you count them?' Richard asked.

Bowman shook his head. 'What's the point? There's a lot of them.'

Richard counted twenty and hadn't got half way so gave up. 'I suppose they didn't use the two days to sit around drinking wine,' he said as more siege equipment appeared.

Screens made from lashed together trees were brought up and held up in front of the crossbowmen.

The palisade Richard stood on was only the height of two men, and the two ladders that approached looked exactly the right length.

Defending crossbowmen and archers lined the walls on either side of the gateway and an archer with a normal bow took a place next to Bowman.

The enemy drained from their camp and poured into the plain below.

'We can't stop them, can we?' Richard asked.

The captain and Bowman both looked at Richard. 'No,' they said in unison.

The captain glanced over the wooden parapet. 'Keep your heads down,' he said.

Tancarville crossbowmen advanced behind their shields, the red and white Tancarville banner with its silver spurs moving with it. Lord Tancarville was probably beside it, but it was the wave of dirty-white textile and brownish leather armour that drew Richard's focus. It was a swarm.

Men with shields and iron helmets moved in front of the two ladders.

'We only need to break their ladders,' the captain shouted. 'Aim at the men who wish to climb them. We'll make the ladders too dangerous to use.'

Bowman leant over to Richard. 'He shouts a lot, and even though his face looks like it's covered in rust, he seems to know what he's doing.'

Richard didn't have time to respond because the first of the crossbows outside the wall loosed their bolts. A handful sunk into the walls but many fell short.

'Hold your volley,' the captain ordered as fingers shivered on the trigger levers of crossbows along the parapet.

A bolt whistled overhead and Richard swallowed. He ducked down so only his eyes showed over the wooden barrier.

'Loose,' the captain ordered, and the twang of bowstrings shook the air. A few attackers outside the town fell, a few bolts buried themselves in the shields around the ladders, but they kept coming.

The archers loosed more arrows while the crossbowmen reloaded, and Richard went through in his mind the action of casting the javelin. He would look for mailed men to target, for they would be the first up the ladders.

More bolts thudded into the wooden palisade, and this time many more sailed overhead. What they hit in the town, Richard didn't know. The archer next to Bowman spun around as a bolt caught him in the cheek. His neck snapped back and he fell backwards off the wall.

Bowman caught the bow before he went and had an arrow nocked on its string before its previous owner had hit the ground. His first arrow flew from the wall and Bowman drew another from the dead archer's bag.

The company advancing around the ladders neared the wall. Men fell from their ranks, but others pushed forwards and held their shields aloft. Bowman aimed under them and one of his arrows hit an unmailed foot.

Wind caught the Tancarville banner and it flourished behind the ladders.

'There's the old man himself,' Bowman drew the bow and pointed the arrow at the banner. A bolt grazed the top of the wall and spiralled up into the sky behind them. Bowman released the arrow and its fletching spun and guided it towards Lord Tancarville. The iron arrowhead hit the lord in his barrel-like chest just as he bellowed an order. It stopped him in his tracks and cut through his surcoat and some of the armour beneath it. But not enough, and Tancarville pulled the unbloodied arrow out and threw it to the ground.

'Don't shoot him,' Richard said, 'if you hurt him his men will be out for blood. Our blood.'

'I think they'll be out for that already,' Bowman nocked another arrow. 'What about the boy next to him in the same surcoat? I don't think it's the Little Lord.'

'That's Raoul Tancarville,' the captain clutched a javelin and moved into a position above the gate. 'The new favourite son.'

'Don't kill him,' Richard said, 'unless you want to die slowly. If you see the Little Lord, though, don't miss.'

Bowman sent an arrow towards the ladders instead, but the men carrying them were close enough to the walls to raise them up, one on either side of the gateway.

Richard stood up and hurled a javelin. Out of the corner of his eye he saw two crossbowmen level their weapons at him, so he never saw how successful he'd been. He threw himself to the parapet's floor and felt the vibration of the bolts smacking into the outside of the wall.

Bowman shot from a different place with each arrow. A man nearby on the wall screamed as he was hit. The captain cast a javelin down as the first ladder crashed into the wall above Richard. He stood up and grabbed the top of it, but it wasn't wood.

'I can't push it off,' Richard said as the captain joined him. The ladders were fixed with large iron hooks that reached over the wall and locked them in place.

'We can pull it sideways with fire hooks,' the captain said, 'or smash it with axes.'

'Have you got any hooks or axes?' Richard picked up a javelin.

The captain frowned and didn't reply.

'Maybe he isn't as good as we thought,' Bowman shot his last arrow and dropped the bow.

Richard threw his javelin straight down the ladder at the first man who climbed it. His red shield was raised above him, but the force of the missile knocked it aside. The captain's javelin followed quickly and drove deep into the man's ribcage despite his mail. The knight dropped from the ladder.

Crossbow bolts hit the men on the ladder from the side, and bolts from the ground hit the defenders who shot them.

The next knight who edged up the ladder withstood Richard's javelin and batted the captain's aside as he reached the top.

Richard reached for his spear as the knight recognised him.

'You,' Sir John cried and cut his sword through the air.

Richard was too far away to need to parry it, so he clutched his spear and waved it at Sir John to keep him back.

Sir John advanced another rung so his head rose above the battlements. 'You've made me a laughing stock,' he cried, his missing front teeth proof of the encounter where Richard had bested him.

With two hands on his spear, Richard thrust it. 'It wasn't personal,' he jammed the point at Sir John's head. The point grazed the knight's cheek and ripped into his ear.

At that moment the captain drove his spear at Sir John's chest. Had he been on the ground, or lodged on a horse, the strike would have penetrated his mail, but on a ladder it served only to eject him from it.

Sir John flipped backwards over the man below him on his way down to earth.

The attacker next up the ladder had a face that looked too young for war, and it would never get any older because Bowman's javelin found the face with an unpleasant crunch.

Maynard's voice, the words unclear, cut through the air from the other side of the gateway.

Richard stepped back and saw the squire fought with a knight at the top of the second ladder. Maynard held his spear across his body, blocking the downward cuts of a sword with the spear shaft.

The sword belonged to the Little Lord.

'Bowman,' Richard shouted, 'the other ladder.'

A helmet appeared next to Richard, and the captain's spear rang it like a bell.

Bowman charged the Little Lord, but his attacks pushed Maynard back.

The squire glanced down at his back foot as it reached the edge of the parapet, but the glance meant he wasn't looking at the Little Lord, who simply pushed him backwards and off the wall. Another Tancarville knight joined the Little Lord on the wall.

'Hold this ladder,' the captain roared and rushed over with Bowman to plug the gap Maynard had left.

Richard wondered if he'd survived the fall, but before he could look, a hand reached up from the ladder nearest him and grabbed the wall. He brought his spear down and the side of the blade chopped down like an axe to send fingers flying across the parapet.

The owner of the hand cried out and withdrew it.

Bowman clattered into the Little Lord, but the young Tancarville was stronger than before and was able to stay upright.

The captain's spear found the throat of the other knight who'd reached the wall, and although it didn't pierce the mail, his throat collapsed and he dropped to his knees.

Now alone, the Little Lord's courage evaporated and he leapt back to the ladder. Bowman helped him on his way with a great push and the Little Lord tumbled down and smacked into the Tancarville squire who tried to climb up it.

'Bloody knights,' the captain mumbled.

'Tell me about it,' Bowman nodded back to him.

The captain frowned, but turned his attention back to the ladder. No one else came up.

A guard with an axe hacked away at the ladder to sever one of the iron hooks.

A bolt sunk into his shoulder and the captain took the axe from him to finish the job.

Another guard with a firehook leant over the wall and used it to grab the ladder Richard waited above.

Tancarville crossbowmen aimed at him, but with a grunt he dragged the ladder sideways. It snapped, left its iron hooks on the parapet, and crashed to the ground where the rest of its rungs broke. Richard popped his head up and saw the army pulling back.

'They've given up,' Richard said, 'already.'

The captain smashed the axe down and severed the second iron hook from his ladder. Bowman grabbed the broken ladder and dragged it upwards. 'They'll have to build another one,' he said as the captain helped him steal the ladder from the enemy.

Bolts still flew at the wall, but the Little Lord limped away from the town supported by two men, and Tancarville himself already walked away from the failed attack.

The men on the wall cheered their retreat.

'That was too easy,' Richard said.

Bowman ducked his head down from the wall and caught his breath. 'They didn't try very hard, young lord, I think they just wanted to see if we'd actually fight back.'

The captain watched the enemy shuffle out of missile range. 'They could have pressed us harder. They could have tried to batter the gate down,' he said.

'Aye,' Bowman nodded, 'they'll be back.'

Maynard had been fortunate enough to land on one of the carts that had been waiting to leave Neufchatel, and the bundles of wool on it had made his fall rather soft. Tancarville however, was not soft on his men after their failed assault, and groups trudged off towards the nearest woods, returning later with felled trees dragged behind oxen. They left drag marks across the countryside that looked like claw marks in the grassland.

The news from across the town was that the Young King had appeared inside the northwestern suburbs, and it looked like the two enemy armies would race to see who could breach the town walls first.

Richard allowed himself to drift off to sleep as dusk swept over the town, but just as he started to dream about throwing Yvetot's priest off his own castle walls, Bowman shook him awake.

'Young lord,' the blonde man whispered, 'something's happening.'

Richard groaned. 'Why are you whispering?'

'It seems like the thing to do,' Bowman stood up and looked over the wall.

In the centre of the town the church bells started to ring. They kept ringing.

The sleep-fog cleared from Richard and he joined Bowman gazing out of the town. Fires dotted the Tancarville camp in the fading light, but hundreds of handheld torches were on the move.

'That's a lot of torches,' Maynard said.

Bowman kicked the bottom of the palisade. 'You remember how I hate fire arrows, and how usually they're a stupid idea?'

Richard looked at him, then his heart sank.

'Exactly,' Bowman said, 'and we're standing on a wooden wall. This is when they aren't a stupid idea.'

'Surely they wouldn't want to fire their own town?' Maynard asked.

Richard laughed, but it was a laugh of tired despair. 'They'd rather rule a town of ashes than leave it for someone else.'

The captain spat over the wall and shouted at all the guards to find buckets and fill them with water. 'Soak the thatch of any building you can,' he cried.

'We don't have time to do that, do we?' Richard sighed.

Bowman shrugged. 'It's not my town.'

'It is while we're in it,' Richard took hold of his spear and waited for the fire to come.

Flames arced up into the air and over the wall. Each arrow's yellow path traced a line through the black cloudy sky, and together they looked like a swarm of comets. The arrows landed on roofs and in the streets, streets full of townspeople very alert to the danger of fire. Fire was the principal and ever present threat to any town, and the locals were aware of the threat. They ran back and forth from the nearest well to douse their houses in water, and as soon as the arrows fell, they ran to extinguish them. A second volley of fire added to their misery. Buckets were poured onto arrows, and one man was thrown back when a flaming arrow found his chest.

Plenty of arrows reached the town with their fire throttled by flight, but a third volley whistled over and not every arrow could be put out.

'We'll need to get back to the castle, young lord,' Bowman whispered to him, 'before that fat castellan locks the gates.'

Richard knew that was true, but they couldn't be seen to abandon the gate quite yet.

A series of thuds sounded from the outside of the town gate as the enemy archers turned their attention to it.

'That will take the whole night to burn through,' Bowman said, 'they're doing that just to scare us.'

'It's working,' Maynard huddled down on the floor of the parapet.

The church bells clanged still, their echo mixing with the desperate shouts of the townspeople as they tried to save their homes.

A fire caught in the thatch of a house over the street behind them. Two guards with firehooks rushed to drag the unlit thatch away from the blaze.

'Take the thatch off all the buildings,' the captain ordered.

'It's a bit late for that,' Bowman grumbled as a burning smell came from the outside of the wall.

'I suppose the wall will take a while to burn, too,' Richard said.

Bowman was about to answer, but a ladder banged into the wall above where they crouched. Richard looked at him for a heartbeat, then they both sprang for their spears.

Richard stuck his head up to look down the ladder. A knight hiding behind a shield was halfway up. A crossbow bolt drove into the battlement by his head, between two planks of wood, and split them apart. He ducked down. There were more ladders this time, but fewer men defending the walls because half the guards were fighting fires.

'They're not wasting any time,' Bowman stood up and thrust his spear down. It thudded into a shield. A bolt cut through his cloak and left a small hole in it. A ladder to their right, just beyond the gateway, produced a mailed-clad knight with a sword that reflected the fire inside the town.

Maynard struck at him and forced him back a step.

Richard waited for the climbing knight to reach the top of his ladder before jamming the spear at his face. The knight brought his shield up and the spear glanced away.

Bowman tried to do the same but the knight held firm.

A scream to their left came from a defender, but the captain had already rushed the other way to help Maynard.

A Tancarville squire climbed onto the wall to their left. He landed between Richard and the nearest flight of steps that led back to the town.

'We're going to get cut off,' Richard stabbed with his spear and the enemy knight climbed up another rung to bring his sword to bear.

'I'm not very attached to this wall,' Bowman said, 'I'll happily leave it.'

The captain drove a dagger into the knight Maynard grappled with, but another was already at the top of their ladder.

Beyond them, the single guard fending off yet another ladder clutched his stomach as a spear point ruptured it. A moment later the same spear caved in his face.

The captain looked around. The four of them were stuck on the wall between a growing number of attackers on either side.

'You're not going to stand and die at your post are you?' Richard asked the captain.

The man grinned, his ginger beard wet from both his breath and the blood of the knight he'd just killed. The captain jumped off the wall and onto the wool-laden cart that had previously broken Maynard's fall.

Richard looked at Bowman. 'Fine, now you can go.'

The blonde man didn't need to be told again and jumped after the captain.

'Hurry up and jump,' Richard waved at Maynard to follow Bowman.

The squire looked down at the ground. 'But it hurt last time.'

Sir John's mailed feet landed on the parapet behind him.

Richard lunged with his spear and Sir John deflected it with his sword.

Maynard turned to look at them, his mouth gaping and his eyes unsure where to focus. Richard was tempted to leave him for Sir John, but instead elbowed the squire so he plummeted from the wall. Then he scythed the spear through the air to make Sir John jump out of the way, and followed.

Richard bounced off a roll of green wool and hit Maynard before the ground.

Bowman held his spear ready, his eyes on the top of the wall. 'We need to be going back towards the square,' he said.

Richard stood up and held a hand down to Maynard. 'Come on, it isn't over yet.'

The squire took his hand and Richard heaved him up to his feet. He collected his spear from the cobbles as the captain shouted an order to fall back away from the gateway.

The blazing house across the street streamed black smoke up into the sky. Richard was close enough that its heat banished the cold from his bones, but that was of little comfort. Another house further along collapsed in on itself in a cloud of dust, sparks, and timber. Thatch, some aflame, exploded up into the air and floated back down to cover the street. The church bells stopped ringing.

Richard felt exposed without his shield, and ran up the incline towards the church.

The captain rallied whichever guards could get off the wall, and some threw down their water buckets and joined their comrades.

They all jogged to the square and Richard headed for the church where he'd been knighted. In the distance, towards the gate they'd unsuccessfully tried to escape from, more plumes of dark smoke rose and merged into a dark cloud above the town.

'They'll be breaking through there, too,' Bowman said, 'we need to get to the castle.'

Richard swore. 'Fight with the captain once he regroups here, I need to get Sophie and Gerold out of the church.'

'Don't take too long,' Bowman planted his spear on the ground and waited.

Richard burst into the church and was met by a wall of song. Dozens of townspeople had taken refuge in the holy building, and the clergy were singing to them. Incense wormed its way into his nose, and for a moment Richard forgot the carnage unfolding outside.

Then he spotted his wife and the stricken Gerold. The knight lay along a wall under a pile of blankets, a child peering down at him and poking him with a stick.

Sophie shooed the child away.

'We need to go back up to the castle,' Richard said, then lowered his voice to a whisper, 'the walls are lost and the town is burning.'

His wife looked up and she swallowed.

Richard nodded. 'You really can't stay here, if he finds you,' he left the thought hanging in the air with the incense and Latin chorus.

Sophie glanced at Gerold. 'But he can't move. Not quickly.'

'We don't have time to wait, I'll carry him if I have to,' Richard said, 'the Little Lord won't respect the sanctity of this place.'

Gerold's eyes were glassy but he was awake. 'Leave me here, my lord, I'll only slow you down. It isn't the French or Irish who are outside, they won't fire a church.'

'Fire the church?' a townsman in a cheap tunic asked. His face rippled with fear.

Richard didn't reply.

'Is someone burning the church?' a woman further along the crowd asked.

Richard swore and was hushed by everyone nearby. 'Sophie, we need to leave before these people stampede out of here. Gerold, I'm not leaving you at the mercy of a Tancarville, that family doesn't understand the meaning of the word,' Richard bent down and scooped up the knight. He was far heavier than Richard had expected and he grunted as he slung him over his shoulder.

'Where's Brian?' Richard asked.

Sophie picked up a linen bag and flung it over her shoulder. 'I don't know, I haven't seen him since last night.'

'Lord forgive me for leaving him,' Richard said and walked towards the door.

A man ran out of the church and past Richard, judging by his smell his job was to collect horse droppings.

'Save yourselves,' the head of a family of four followed him in a hurry. Then it became a rush.

Richard reached the church doors and squeezed through as the stream of people fleeing became a torrent of frightened townspeople.

Sophie gritted her teeth and slapped a man who almost collided with Richard, but soon he was clear and carrying Gerold towards the castle one slow step at a time.

Bowman groaned. 'How long do you think we have?'

In the distance dogs barked as more smoke darkened the sky above the beleaguered town.

The captain and his guards appeared from the street that led to the western gate. The company moved slowly, a dozen crossbowmen at their rear ran up the slope of the square so they could shoot over their ranks.

'You need to be quicker than them,' Bowman said.

Richard groaned under Gerold's weight and kept putting one foot in front of the other. 'I can't go any quicker.'

'Carry him between us,' Bowman took his spear in one hand and held out the other.

A wave of noise flooded out of the western street as Tancarville knights and squires charged the guards.

Those who fled out of the church screamed and ran towards the town's other gate. Some thought twice about their choices and ran back into the church.

'This is what the end of days will look like,' Maynard shivered as he gripped his spear tightly.

'It'll be the end of your days if you don't pull yourself together,' Richard dropped Gerold between himself and Bowman so they could carry him. They grabbed each other's hands under the sick man to make a seat, and Gerold put an arm around each of his helper's shoulders.

'Thank you,' he croaked.

A gentle breeze stirred and whipped up the smoke, making Richard gag on acrid air. He coughed as he and Bowman started to carry Gerold up the cobbles towards the castle.

A handful of townspeople joined the guards to defend their town, brandishing axes and firehooks, but although Richard admired their bravery, he didn't fancy their chances.

His hand under Gerold started to lose feeling.

The guards retreated slowly up the cobbles towards them, but too quickly for Richard to get Gerold to reach safety first.

Tancarville soldiers gushed into the square and the defending crossbowmen shot at them. That made them think twice, and they went back to pressing the captain and his dwindling company instead of trying to outflank them.

A whiff of urine took the smoke out of Richard's nose, and the tanner appeared with an axe in his hand.

'Get out of our way,' Bowman waved his spear at him.

The tanner grimaced and stepped aside before running down to join the company as it fell back.

That was when Richard's worn leather sole finally failed. It had taken him from Brittany after he'd been given new leg armour there, through Ireland and two tournaments, but now, when Richard needed his footing the most, the leather gave out. The waxed linen thread that attached the soles to the mail rings of his leg armour wore through, and one sole flapped between his feet and the cold cobbles. The sole was so worn it broke off under the ball of his foot, and then Richard had nothing but a layer of wool between his feet and the stones.

Maynard spun around as they reached the halfway point to the castle. 'You aren't going quick enough,' he said.

'Then hold them back,' Richard snarled, his patience with everyone and everything utterly drained.

Sophie ran ahead and through the crossbowmen who sent bolts down into the Tancarville ranks. The red and silver banner flew above the attackers now, men in glinting iron helmets leading the way, slowing reducing the size of the captain's company.

More of the town burned behind them, but apparently not enough, because some Tancarville squires hurled flaming torches up into the thatch of houses on the street. Richard thought of Brian in the church and felt a pang of guilt. But he had Gerold and had to at least make sure the old knight made it to safety.

A war-cry echoed off the narrowing street and a surge of Tancarville knights split the captain's company in half.

The retreating company swallowed Richard.

A bolt slammed past his ears and into a Tancarville knight who made for them.

Bowman checked behind him. 'We're out of time, young lord.'

The tanner ran back away from the fight.

'You,' Richard said, 'make amends and take this man into the castle.'

'Amends?' the tanner laughed. 'To the devil?' He ran straight into Sophie.

'If you don't help them,' she roared, eyes red, 'you'll be meeting the devil before the sun finishes rising.'

Bowman almost threw Gerold at the tanner, and their reluctant new assistant took the blonde man's place.

'Walk backwards,' Richard said, 'at least we can face them if we walk backwards.'

'But it's uphill,' the tanner complained.

Richard didn't care and spun around anyway. Walking backwards uphill was hard, but now he could point his spear at the enemy. Who were close.

Maynard speared a man who was fighting someone else.

Bowman jammed his spear over the captain's shoulder and into the neck of the squire he fought.

Sir John, vengeance on his mind, led the assault and cut down a guard as the two sides locked together.

Two squires pushed through the melee and rushed at Richard.

The tanner swung his axe, but he held it in his weaker left hand and the first squire pushed it aside.

Richard stabbed the second squire into his thigh next to where his teardrop shield narrowed. Then he threw the spear at the first squire just as he was about to strike the tanner down.

They backed up a few more steps and Richard drew the Little Lord's sword.

Sophie banged on the castle gate, which remained steadfastly shut.

Archers on the castle's stone wall rained arrows down into the attackers, but they responded by raising their shields above their heads and their progress was unimpeded.

A blow sent the captain reeling to the ground, but Maynard picked him up and helped him to his feet.

Richard felt his way by sliding his feet backwards up the hill one at a time. He could hear Sophie shouting behind him, which meant the gate was still closed.

Sir John reached Bowman, who barely parried his first attack. A Tancarville knight wearing a red surcoat cut down two guards, red hair under his red-painted nasal-helm. But it wasn't the Little Lord.

The captain attacked the knight, who was Raoul Tancarville, but Raoul smashed his shield into his nose and sent him flying backwards.

Richard's creeping foot slid backwards and hit something solid. He turned around and came face to face with the castle wall. Next to him Sophie thumped her fist on the gate, tears streaming down her face.

Maynard stabbed at Raoul, but the knight swept it aside and nearly cut the spearhead off.

Bowman lost his spear as Sir John twisted it from his grip, but the blonde man head-butted him and Sir John's nose exploded with a crunch. Bowman kicked him backwards and ran to the castle gate.

Which creaked. Then one of the two horse-sized doors opened just enough to let a man slip through.

Sophie was through it before Richard blinked, but then Raoul aimed a cut at Maynard and the squire fell over trying to evade it.

Richard pushed Gerold towards the gate. 'Drag him inside,' he said to the tanner. The man happily obliged.

Richard blocked a strike that would have decapitated Maynard, then with his free hand he grabbed Raoul's mail coif and pulled. The knight fell off balance for a moment, and the captain, lying on the cobbles, reached out and pulled an ankle out from under him. The Tancarville knight crashed down, spilling his sword, and Maynard took his chance to scramble into the castle.

A Tancarville squire stabbed the captain in the leg and he cried out. Most of his guards filed through the narrow gate, but some gathered up together to protect him.

Free of Gerold's weight, Richard went to help.

'We can't let him die,' Bowman said, 'all the good ones we come across like this die.'

Richard sheathed his sword and bent down to pick up one of the captain's arms. Bowman grabbed the other and they dragged the wounded man to the gate.

'I need to be the last man through,' the captain looked up at them from the cobbles.

'Shut up,' Richard heaved him over the threshold and into the courtyard. The noise of battle dimmed instantly and more guards poured through the gate behind them.

Several of Walter's men waited inside, jittery and restless, and they slammed the gate shut and barred it as soon as the last guard was safe.

Withering arrow fire from the wall soon forced the Tancarvilles back out of range.

Sophie leant on one of many barrels that littered the yard and wiped tears from her eyes.

Richard's own face was blackened from the fires, but he felt better than either Gerold or the captain looked. His wound looked survivable, a slice down the outside of his thigh, but men often died from less.

Walter stormed down from the battlements as fast as his rotund legs could carry him. He pointed at Richard. 'This is your fault, we lost the town far too easily.'

The captain pushed himself up to his feet, glanced at his wound and then his lord. 'These knights held the wall for longer than I did. And if it wasn't for them, I might be on the wrong side of this gate.'

The castellan sniffed and couldn't reply because he had to catch his breath.

Richard caught his own, tore off what remained of his flapping leather sole, and checked that Bowman and Gerold were alright. Then he embraced Sophie.

'How can you face a battle knowing this is what happens in them?' she asked.

Richard shook his head. 'What choice is there? If you don't pick up your lance to defend your home, someone else will take it from you.'

'But the blood,' Sophie whispered.

Richard shrugged. 'We all bleed.'

A watchman high on the keep's platform called down that the guards retreating from the northwestern gate were being cut down by the converging enemy armies. Silence descended in the castle as men thought of those who hadn't made it to the castle in time. The next message he relayed was that the townspeople caught in the same place suffered the same fate as their guards.

'What sort of men kill their own people?' Sophie asked.

'I don't know,' Richard said, 'this is another man's war and I don't want to be here.'

'Well, you're stuck here,' Walter said, 'so start drawing water from the well and clear this courtyard of anything that might burn.'

Richard ignored the order, there were squires to do that, and instead took Sophie and Gerold back into the hall, where at least they wouldn't be able to hear the screams of the people of Neufchatel as they were slaughtered.

Once Gerold and Sophie were installed in the castle's hall, Richard went up to the top of the keep to see if the church had been set alight. Thankfully no flames tore through its roof, but that didn't mean those inside it were safe. He couldn't see the square, it was obscured by houses, and half of the town was ablaze. Fires merged and grew in ferocity, so much so that he saw the Tancarville banner retreating out of the town. Before long, houses collapsed into the street and spilled their burning contents over the cobbles to block the roads. The smoke clogged the air and sometimes the mild breeze blew the stench of roasting bodies up to the castle. That brought back too many memories, and Richard nearly retched. There was nothing he could do for Brian now except pray, so he found the castle's chapel and did that.

The town took over a day to burn. Fires roared well into the night, but the next morning only ash and charred roof beams remained amidst a mountain of ruins. The church stood, blessed by low winds and having no adjoining buildings, but the air tasted bitter and the mood in the castle was bleak.

The Young King approached the castle for a third time, but this time Bowman was up on the wall with Richard as Walter received him. Count Robert stood next to the Marshal beside the Young King as he implored the castellan to surrender.

'Our realm has suffered enough for your obstinance,' the Young King said, 'swear fealty to me and nothing else has to burn.'

'What about the people?' Bowman scoffed.

Walter rubbed his chins. 'Nothing has changed,' he said to the Young King.

The Marshal stepped forwards. 'You're wasting our time,' he said, 'we'll take this castle in the end. This is pointless.'

'Who are you even to speak to me?' Walter asked. 'I don't care what you have to say.'

'I took the northwestern gate,' the Marshal looked pleased with himself, 'and killed your whole garrison.'

'Not quite all of them,' Bowman murmured.

'And your townspeople,' the Marshal said, 'they threw themselves at us. We had no choice but to cut them down.'

Bowman simmered.

'Ignore him,' Richard said, 'better still, get down from the wall. You'll just get more angry if you have to listen to him.'

'Prancing peacock,' Bowman mumbled.

'You murdered my people,' Walter replied to the Marshal, 'who is going to pay my taxes and tolls now?'

'That's not my problem,' the Marshal said, 'but your problem is what will happen if you decline my lord's generous offer. We'll kill all of you.'

Walter shrugged because those were the rules of war if a garrison declined a sensible surrender. He knew that a castellan prone to surrendering rarely found himself in command of newer and better castles, so he couldn't surrender for at least a few weeks.

'All of you,' the Marshal said, 'your women and children, everyone. And it will be your fault.'

Bowman's eyes were red, and Richard could smell pear cider on his breath.

'That peacock,' the blonde man muttered, 'I hate him.'

'You hate everyone,' Richard rubbed his own eyes, but that meant he missed what Bowman did before it was too late.

The angry knight swiped a loaded crossbow from the man next to him and levelled it down at the parlaying knights.

'Don't,' Richard threw a hand out to grab the weapon. But not in time. Bowman squeezed the trigger lever just as Richard's hand pushed the crossbow a fraction to the side.

Walter looked over with wide eyes as the crossbow twanged.

The guards on the wall gasped, then craned their necks to see where the bolt went. The missile spiralled through the air but missed its intended target.

The Marshal looked to his left as the iron-tipped bolt pierced Count Robert's mail and entered his shoulder. It threw him to the ground and everyone held their breath.

Count Robert gulped a breath as he lay on the grass and clutched the feathered bolt that was buried deep.

'I'll kill whoever shot that,' the Marshal shouted, then bent down and crouched over Count Robert.

The Young King walked towards the castle on his own. Which was brave.

Bowman handed the crossbow back to its owner. 'You should keep a tighter hold of your weapons,' he said, then walked off the wall, the garrison's shocked eyes on him the entire way.

Walter's lips flapped open.

'This changes nothing. That's what you said, isn't it?' the Young King cried. 'We will take the castle and everyone inside must die. That is the way. I won't forget how you've treated us.'

Richard shrugged at the castellan. 'I don't think this makes much difference, apparently they were going to kill us all already,' he followed Bowman, 'but at least I don't have to stand around to hear more of this pointless posturing.'

Count Robert was carried on a litter back into their camp underneath the small hill, and Richard prayed for his survival. Tempers would be cooler if he lived. All in the castle began to give Bowman a wide berth, and even the castellan avoided saying anything on the matter. When Bowman sat at the long table now, he was offered food and drink. Squires stepped out of his way on the staircases.

But nothing else changed for a day, until the Flemish banner stirred in the Young King's camp, and then rode back the way it had come. Count Philip's company left with it, and gossip and rumours flowed up and down the corridors of the castle. The next day another company with a banner from the Low Countries left. A rumour went around that Count Robert had died and others had lost their enthusiasm for the siege.

The next morning, a guard ventured out into the smouldering ruins of the town and brought back word that Tancarville's camp was deserted. Men, horses, and tents were all gone. The Young King remained, but the path was now clear to leave Neufchatel, so that is what Richard did.

HEARTH AND HOME

The iron stirrup sucked the warmth out of Richard's foot. Without the leather sole to rest on it, he could feel the coolness of the bar of metal under his foot as they rode.

He'd picked Brian up at the church, the Irish monk blissfully unaware of the danger he'd been in, and shocked when he left the surviving holy building and saw the smoking ruins of the town. Gerold had been propped up in his saddle, and Maynard had led Solis up and over the debris that covered the streets.

The castellan had tried to block their escape, but Bowman had squared up to him and the gates had opened. They left the Castle of Neufchatel in a wake of whispers, and with the rising sun at their backs.

The road west was churned up by the passage of the Tancarville army, and the never ending slippery mud slowed their progress. The journey back to Yvetot should have been possible with a full day of good riding, but with the mud and Solis constantly hanging off Maynard, they did not manage good riding.

Gerold slowed them down too, and Brian rode ahead of him with a grin because he wasn't last, at least until the lack of rest stops caused him to ache and his pride faded.

Sophie rode her palfrey next to Richard. 'Can you not make them go any faster?' she asked.

'Not really,' Richard replied, 'I don't want to rush Solis, or have Gerold fall out of his saddle.'

'We need to get home,' Sophie said, 'Yvetot is right on the road and the Tancarvilles will have ridden past it.'

Richard was aware of that but had been trying not to think about it.

Solis stopped to graze on the bushes that lined the road, his sudden halt jerked the rope from Maynard's grasp and the squire dropped it.

Richard called the horse to keep up, but then he caught him and slipped the rope halter off the stallion's head instead of giving the rope back to the squire.

'Why are you doing that?' Maynard asked.

'He'll follow us,' Richard said, 'we're his herd. And having you drag him around is just annoying the both of you.'

Maynard looked offended but was quite glad to be rid of the duty, so kept quiet.

Gerold's face was pale but beads of sweat ran down it, the old knight keeping his mouth shut and his eyes forward. Richard knew better than to ask him how he was, Gerold just needed to lie beside a fire. They all did.

The sun was warm while it was up, but it sank towards the horizon ahead of them before they reached Yvetot.

An owl hooted on their left and Richard swore under his breath instead of making the sign of the cross.

Bowman pointed to their right when the road opened out. 'I caught a great stag with Eva in there,' he said of the more distant woodland.

'What happened to the princess?' Sophie asked. 'While she stayed with us, she was the closest thing I've ever had to a companion.'

Bowman's proud grin faded.

'She's the Queen of Leinster now,' Richard said, 'they call her Red Eva.'

Sophie smiled faintly. 'If only I had a friend in the world, I could tell them how I knew a queen,' she said.

Richard ignored the sadness in her voice, he knew his wife's life was not the most happy one.

She sighed. 'I want my hearth and I want my home,' she said. 'With the children running around me, not giving me a moment of peace.'

Richard wondered if he and Bowman would have to spend a lot of time hunting to find the peace that might elude him at home. The thought made him smile.

Bats darted back and forth overhead as the sun dipped below the horizon. Orange rays lit up the few clouds that dotted the sky. Richard couldn't believe they'd made it out of Neufchatel unscathed, and allowed himself a moment of satisfaction. All he had to do was live in Yvetot for a year and both kings would forget he even existed. Then he could recover the silver hoard and prepare for the Holy Land.

He sniffed the air when an unusual scent caught in his nose. Richard ignored it, it was just a memory of the foul smells that clogged their senses as they'd ridden through Neufchatel's gutted town. He probably just needed his cloak washing.

Bowman yelped with joy when he spotted the Flying Monk. 'It's still standing,' he grinned, 'I thought Sarjeant would have drunk it into ruin.'

'No,' Sophie said, 'every traveller who comes by visits it. I dare say it has made ten times the coin you all have playing at war.'

'So we could have just stayed at home?' Richard asked.

'And more of our party would still be riding with us,' Bowman's face darkened as the orange in the sky retreated down to the horizon.

'Maybe the inn is my future. We had a good name for a new cider,' Richard said.

'If you name it after the King of Leinster,' Bowman said, 'I'll never drink in there.'

Richard smiled. 'That's the point.'

Bowman groaned, but Richard didn't hear it because in the sky beyond the Flying Monk he could see shapes circling in the sky. 'Crows,' he said.

'Can you smell that?' Bowman asked.

'Is this your village?' Brian forgot about his saddle sores and played with his reins.

'Yes,' Richard said, 'but there's no light coming from the Flying Monk.'

Sophie whispered something under her breath and kicked her palfrey on. She cantered down the road into the village, her horse slipped on the mud but kept going.

Richard followed without thought, worry convulsing his stomach. The blue roan surged up to the Flying Monk and Richard had to haul him down the turning into Yvetot because the warhorse thought he should continue down the main road.

The inn was large now, with tying rails for horses and barrels by the door, but the door was shut and no light shone around its frame. No smoke drifted out of its thatch, either, but Richard could smell smoke in the air.

Richard pushed his horse down the track through the orchard, the apple trees black twisted shadows in the night.

He emerged next to the church with its graveyard and the unstocked fishpond.

The blue roan almost crashed into the back of Sophie's stationary palfrey and immediately tried to mount it. Richard dragged him away and told him off, Judas appeared and barked at him for shouting.

But when his horse and dog stilled, everything else was silent.

Sophie stared out past the church and to the village. Or what was left of it.

'Not again,' Richard moaned, but this time the destruction looked total.

The church still stood, with the fallen chunk of masonry obscuring the doorway, but someone had patched up its roof. The old village was gone, only the outline of the houses remained, their wooden beams and thatch nothing but ash.

The new village, the one the outsiders had built, fared no better. Half of the large new barn still stood, but the other half had collapsed in on itself, black timbers snapped and scattered on the scorched earth.

The graveyard had a shovel stuck in a fresh mound of dirt, a line of bodies outside the fence ready to be interred. Richard squinted into the night and saw more lumps around the village that would be more corpses.

'My lady?' a voice rang out from the church.

Richard gripped his sword, but he recognised the voice before the Priest stepped out of his home. A black shadow at first, Judas growled and barked at him.

'Whose dog is that?' the Priest hesitated.

'Mine,' Richard said.

'Who is that?' the Priest asked.

'Your lord,' Sophie said, 'where are my children?'

The Priest slunk forwards carefully, his eyes failing to find the black dog in the gloom. 'A week ago, Lord Tancarville rode through. The younger Tancarville, the one who you,' his voice trailed off.

'I know who you mean,' Sophie said, 'hurry, tell me.'

'The Little Lord laid the village to waste,' the Priest waved his arm behind him, 'as you can see. It's worse in the daylight, although at night I fear treading outside for the spirits.'

'Spirits?' Bowman asked, as the rest of the group arrived.

'Until I can bury them all,' the Priest said, 'their spirits will haunt this place. I see movements in the shadows and the cries of children at night.'

'What about my children?' Sophie asked, more forcefully this time.

The Priest shrugged. 'I have seen no other living soul here,' he said, 'they struck as quick as lightning. Fire in hand, they charged through, burning and slashing. It lasted but a moment. The omens have all come true.'

'Don't try to blame me for this,' Richard said.

'Shouldn't I?' the Priest stepped forwards. 'Your first visit ended in death and your arrival as lord was heralded by more death. The birth of the Red Baby was preceded by storms and dragons in the sky.'

'I thought we agreed the dragon was merely a tale from your uncle,' Richard said.

'Who can say now? But your return caused the death here now.'

Sophie turned to Richard. 'Come with me to the castle. If we have to bury them, we do it tonight. We must allow their souls to rest.'

Richard nodded. His wife's voice wavered and he was afraid what his own would sound like. He swallowed hard. 'To the castle,' he said.

The Priest made to follow but the black dog lunged at him and sent him back into the church.

'I like that dog,' Bowman said, 'he reminds me of my brother.'

Richard led them towards the castle while Judas started digging at Sir Arthur's grave, but Richard had his children to find, so left him to it.

The last of the daylight dissolved into pitch black, the moon partial and only faintly able to light the ground as their horses rushed on.

The castle gate was open.

'There's no light from the windows,' Bowman said.

'Of course there isn't,' Richard said, 'everyone is dead.'

Sophie started to cry.

Richard didn't, and that worried him.

The inner bailey was occupied by only a cat that scampered away when Richard entered, it jumped up and over the wooden palisade to escape. The stables had been fired, but only one stall had collapsed and scorch marks blemished only a second.

'Stable the horses,' Richard said to Maynard and Brian, 'then wait here with Gerold while we go inside.'

'I don't know if I can go in,' Sophie said.

'You don't have to,' Richard swung his leg over his saddle and dismounted.

'I'll come with you, young lord,' Bowman joined him on the ground, his voice now serious.

Richard's legs were tight after the ride, but after a few steps across the bailey they loosened up. The inner gate was open too, and Richard heard Bowman draw a knife behind him.

'I don't think we'll need that.'

'It makes me feel better,' Bowman replied, 'so much is wrong here.'

The inner stone wall cast a dark shadow across the entrance to the keep, and Richard had to slow down to make his way up the steps. A rat, too large, scuttled across the doorway and fled outside.

'Your village has finally died,' Bowman tried to stomp on the rat but missed.

Richard put a hand on the stone wall, its coolness reminded him of Sir Rob's cooling corpse at Lagny. 'I don't feel anything,' he said, 'but when I find their bodies I'm going to go after the Little Lord.'

Bowman walked up the stairs. 'Seems fair,' he said, 'although I thought revenge didn't make you feel better.'

Richard frowned, but it was too dark for Bowman to notice. He walked up the stairs and followed the blonde man into his hall.

The hearth was grey, cold, and dead. The tables of uneven height had been knocked over and thrown onto the hearth, but they hadn't caught. A horn window had been shattered and a draught wafted through it.

Chairs lay scattered on the floor.

'It could be worse,' Bowman said.

Richard wanted to punch his friend. 'How? How could this be worse?'

'It could be rubble,' Bowman shrugged, 'I'll light the hearth and then the old man can sleep somewhere warm tonight.'

'I don't think I want to sleep here,' Richard said, 'and I don't think Sophie will be able to.'

'It's pitch black outside, young lord, like it or not, we are staying here tonight. We'll have to make our peace with whatever spirits the Priest has seen.'

That chilled Richard and he would sleep little that night, he knew that for sure.

He walked into the doorway and looked up the passage that led to his chamber. 'They're going to be up there, aren't they?' he asked himself.

'I can check if you want?' Bowman dragged the tables off the hearth and pushed the heap of ash to one side. Clouds of loose ash filled the air and the breeze from the window scattered it across the hall.

'No,' Richard turned to climb the stairs, 'whatever is up there is for me to see.'

Bowman grunted as he snapped the legs off a broken table to start building a fire.

Richard ascended the stairs. He would rather be going the other way, out of Yvetot, but he had to do this one thing. He couldn't live in the castle where his children had been murdered. But would he even know their bodies when he saw them? He entered his chamber. It was dark but the breeze blew a woollen window cover back and forth, bathing the chamber in dancing moonlight.

The bed blankets had been dragged off. A straw-filled pillow was up against a far wall, and the pole that held Sophie's clothes was on the floor with two of her dresses under it. But there were no children there, dead or alive. Under the bed he found the oxhide wrapped copy of Eric and Enid, and breathed a sigh of relief. He'd always wanted to keep it in a locked chest, but although he had the wood, he couldn't afford either the iron hinges or a lock. A bird, whether crow or raven, he couldn't tell, landed on the open window ledge and cawed at him. It fluttered off outside in a flurry of black wings, and Richard found himself with a feeling of profound loneliness. What had it all been for? All he'd accomplished in his life was to lose everything: family, village, children. Fingers.

Richard returned to the hall where Bowman had smoke streaming from a handful of linen char cloth that he always had with him.

'There's no one up there.'

'That's good,' Bowman said without looking up.

'It means we'll spend the night not knowing for sure,' Richard said, 'I think the waiting might kill Sophie.'

'This fire will help her,' Bowman gently slid the flaming tinder under a stack of snapped wood and sat back.

Richard picked up his own chair and righted it. He wobbled it but nothing seemed broken. He sat down in it for the first time in a very long time and ran his fingers along the armrest. 'I don't know what to do,' he said.

'Sit in the chair and watch the fire,' Bowman said, 'I'll fetch the others and bring them here. Today was the furthest I've ever ridden in one day, they will be feeling it more than us. In the morning I'll go out with you and search for the children.'

Richard nodded and couldn't find the words to say thank you. His eyelids grew heavy and as the hearth came back to life, he found himself wishing he was dead.

Bowman returned later after Richard had fed a chunk of his main table into the hearth.

'Your wife is insisting on searching for your children,' the blonde man said.

Brian and Maynard helped Gerold into the hall, who complained he was cold, and made him a bed near the fire. The knight shivered, and Richard suppressed the gnawing feeling that Gerold should have recovered by now.

Richard pushed himself out of his chair, but his body felt weighed down. 'I'll see if I can bring her in here,' he left the hall and looked for his wife.

He found Sophie sitting on her horse just outside the castle's main gate. She looked over the desolate village.

'Come inside,' Richard shouted as he walked over, his breath steaming in the night air.

'They're out there somewhere,' Sophie didn't turn her head, 'but I don't know where to look.'

'We'll all look when it's light,' Richard reached her, 'they might have fled.'

'How?' Sophie asked. 'I took our only horse, and they are too young to reach another village, or even the Templar farm, on foot.'

'Keep hope until we find them,' Richard said.

'Don't be childish,' Sophie said, 'the Little Lord did this and he wanted to hurt us. To hurt me. His target was our family, the best we can hope is that he has stolen them.'

'Then we'll get them back,' Richard said, although quite unsure how he'd do it.

'I can't live here anymore,' Sophie said. 'Everything here dies. Slowly like Sir Arthur, or quickly like our children, but in the end everything perishes. It is a bad place.'

A light gust of wind ruffled their cloaks and Sophie's hair.

Judas bounded over from the church with something in his mouth, followed closely by the Priest who ran after him. 'The dog is evil,' he cried.

'I know,' Richard said, 'but just leave him alone.'

Judas dropped his trophy at Richard's feet and looked up with proud eyes. It was an arm bone. A human arm bone.

'The dog must be tried for blasphemy,' the Priest arrived short of breath, 'he desecrated a churchyard.'

'That's the least of our problems,' Richard said, 'leave the dog alone.'

'Do you know whose bone that is?' the Priest asked.

Richard shrugged. 'What difference does it make if the soul has left?'

'It is Sir Arthur's,' the Priest pointed at it. 'I think all the stories about you are true, you are a thing of the Devil, evil follows in your wake.'

Richard ruffled the dog's head. 'Good boy,' he said.

'We can't stay here,' Sophie said, 'not now.'

'I don't know where we can go,' Richard said. 'I have the duty of administering this village, a duty given to me by the King.'

'What village?' Sophie asked. 'A castle will not survive without a village. Tomorrow we can scavenge food, but not the day after. And if we build another one, they will just burn it down again.'

Richard knew she was right, but his choices were limited. He could go back to either king and hope they would accept him, but he'd rather not risk it. One fact loomed clearly in his mind, Yvetot was no longer their home.

The black dog lowered his head and stalked up the track that led north and towards the mill. He sniffed the ground.

A high-pitched sound floated across the empty village and the Priest jumped in fright. 'That's the spirits,' he said, 'they're coming for us. The spirits of the slain.'

Judas bolted forwards and was lost in the night. A scream cut through the night, which was swiftly followed by the sound of crying.

'He's angered the spirits,' the Priest wailed.

Richard grabbed him as he tried to run back to the church. 'You're not going anywhere, I don't trust you out of my sight.'

The black dog emerged from the shadows with his pink tongue out and his tail wagging.

'Who is there?' Richard shouted.

'Richard?' a voice shouted back. A voice Richard knew.

Sophie knew it too and hurried towards it.

'Don't succumb to them,' the Priest shouted but his warning wasn't heeded.

Richard followed his wife.

He found Sophie off her horse and squatting on the ground, her blue dress on the earth beneath her and draped in mud. But in her arms were two children.

Sarjeant stood behind them, his broad frame slightly less wide than when Richard had left Yvetot, his face more weathered. 'My boy,' he said, 'thank God you've returned.'

'God had little to do with it,' Richard approached him and embraced him, 'but I've missed you.'

The older man had tears in his eyes. 'I saw light from the castle windows, so I hoped Lady Sophie had returned.'

'She has,' Richard said, 'how did you survive the attack?'

Sarjeant had his arm around the third child, the one with red hair, a year older than Richard's twins. 'I never let them out of my sight while Lady Sophie was away, and I needed to pay the Templars a visit, so I took them with me.'

'I hope you didn't fight with them in front of the children.'

Sarjeant shook his head. 'Words only were exchanged. Boundary fences again and some escaped cattle,' his eyes lacked shine, 'but I suppose that hardly matters now. The Lord has seen fit to destroy the fruit of our labours.'

'The Little Lord you mean,' Richard said. His old friend at least looked sober.

Sophie fussed the children and held them so tight they complained.

'The Little Lord?' Sarjeant recoiled. 'We saw the flames from the mill, so we simply stayed there. I avoided the village until either Sophie returned or our food ran out.'

'I'm sure the miller's house is very well stocked,' Richard said, 'although I suppose that doesn't matter now either.'

'What matters is that the children are safe.'

The Red Child looked up at Richard. 'Who are you?' he asked. His face resembled neither the Little Lord, who was his real father, nor King Henry, who had claimed him to spite the Tancarvilles. Richard supposed that was probably fortunate, but the red hair was prominent and now the boy was old enough to speak well.

Richard mulled over his answer. 'I am Sir Richard, your mother is my wife,' he said.

'But you are not my father?'

The boy wasn't a fool, then. 'No, I'm not.'

'Lady Sophie hasn't spoken to him,' Sarjeant said, 'not a word since you left.'

Richard crouched down so his eyes were level with the child's. 'Are you a good boy?' he asked.

The Red Child nodded. 'But Uncle John says I'm annoying.'

Richard smiled. He'd forgotten Sarjeant's name was John. 'If you're good to me, I'll be good to you, understand?' Richard asked.

The Red Child nodded.

Richard turned to his children, who squirmed to escape their mother. The boy wriggled free and stopped at Richard's feet.

'Alexander,' Richard said, marvelling that a boy so old could be his.

Alexander's eyes widened in fear and he backed away. 'Who are you?'

The words cut into Richard's heart.

'He's your father,' Sophie turned her head, 'greet him properly.'

Alexander blushed. He looked at Richard, who still crouched, and frowned. 'I have never seen you before,' he said.

'I've been away,' Richard said, 'for too long and I'm very sorry about that.'

Lora ducked out of Sophie's arm and jumped at Richard. She hugged him as she jumped and pushed him backwards to the ground. She giggled at him and Richard didn't care that wet mud soaked through all his clothing, instead he laughed with her.

'We should be inside,' Sophie said.

Richard held his daughter and she kissed him on the forehead. 'Yes,' Richard said, 'Bowman has lit a fire in the hall.'

'Who is Bowman?' Alexander edged towards Sarjeant.

'You'll either love him or hate him,' Richard grinned.

Sophie hugged Richard when he stood back up. Puffy eyed, she had no words to show her joy or her relief.

Richard carried Lora back into the castle while Alexander asked Sarjeant why their home had been ransacked. Sarjeant had no answer for him.

The hall was warm now, the old table burned brightly and Richard hung up his sodden cloak to dry next to it.

Sophie didn't seem to notice the state of her hall, she sat in her chair and watched her children, her eyes half closed.

Bowman dried Judas off with his cloak and then introduced him to Alexander, who seemed to relax when he could stroke the dog's black belly. His coat stank of wet mud, but that seemed trivial to everyone, and no one paid it any mind.

Brian sat next to the Priest at the back of the hall, the two refusing to speak to each other.

Bowman threw the last leg from the table into the hearth. 'What now though, young lord?'

Richard didn't want to answer that, not tonight. 'We can worry about tomorrow when the sun rises,' he said.

'This castle is sound,' the blonde man said, 'but I think it's plain to everyone that tomorrow we must leave it.'

'This is our home,' Richard said.

Sophie raised her eyebrows at him. 'So now you clearly cannot stay here, you don't want to leave? You've wanted to leave us every day you've spent here.'

Richard didn't want to argue in front of everyone. 'I really did want nothing more than to spend the next few years here,' he said, 'but now that the village is gone, what else can we do? I'm not a farmer, I can't plough the fields. I don't know when to plant the crops. The question isn't whether we stay here, it is where we go.'

'I never liked it here, anyway,' Bowman said. He prodded the hearth. 'It hasn't been the same since Eva left.'

'We left with her.'

'That's not the point,' Bowman said, 'but anywhere away from here is fine by me. The Young King did actually pay us, though. In case you'd forgotten.'

'I haven't,' Richard said, 'but have you forgotten that you just killed one of his closest companions?'

Bowman shrugged. 'He'll understand.'

'Will he? What about the Marshal? He knows you aimed that crossbow at him, and I'm sure you remember how badly he holds imaginary grudges. You've now given him a real one to brood over.'

'The Young King leads the company, not the peacock.'

'Are you willing to risk a treason charge just for a few shillings a day?' Richard asked.

'Give me a better plan,' Bowman crossed his arms.

Maynard waved at Richard to get his attention. 'The Young King is merciful,' he said, 'and you are still in his service, he never released you.'

'Who are you?' Sarjeant asked him.

'I'm Sir Richard's squire.'

Richard laughed. 'You aren't.'

'You said we could ride to Yvetot, then see,' Maynard said.

'I'm a knight without a castle,' Richard said, 'what need do I have for a squire? I can't even feed you.'

Maynard shrugged. 'I'm not fat.'

Bowman slapped his hands down on the only table that still stood.

'Ireland,' he said.

Richard coughed. 'You're joking.'

'Am I?' he asked. 'Everything I want is there. My daughter is there.'

'Your what?' Sophie frowned.

'Don't ask,' Richard told her, 'and you, you can't talk about that.'

Bowman's lips pressed together. 'Who cares what I want, anyway?'

Brian looked down at Gerold, who already slept. 'He'd want to return to England.'

'Who cares what he wants,' Bowman said, 'not if no one cares what I want.'

'Don't sulk,' Richard said, 'and there's nothing in England for any of us. The King may have installed a knight to Keynes by now, and I'm not fighting an innocent man over it. Besides, I hardly remember it anymore. My family is all gone from there and I don't long for it as I used to.'

'King Henry could still grant it to you,' Brian said, 'you served him well in Neufchatel, you know.'

'We were just trying to stay alive,' Richard glanced at Bowman, 'some more than others.'

The Irish monk peered out through the uncovered window. 'It matters little to me,' he said, 'I'll go where you go.'

'And who are you?' Sarjeant asked. 'Every time Richard goes away he comes back with more people.'

'I'm a monk.'

'I can see that,' Sarjeant said.

'You can trust him,' Richard said.

The Priest snorted and folded his arms.

'Which you can't say for everyone,' Richard said, 'you were only spared because you are related to Castle Tancarville's priest. And everything you hear will be told to him, I'm sure.'

'Am I not allowed to speak to my kin?'

Brian got up and walked away from him. 'Your tone is disrespectful, there is no religion in you.'

'Enough,' Richard said because the Priest uncrossed his arms and balled his hands into fists, 'there will be no fighting here.'

'Then decide where we're going,' Bowman said. 'Pick a king.'

'We can't exactly go back to Neufchatel and wait for old King Henry to swat his son away, can we?' Richard said. 'We'd starve in the woods beyond the town, and I'm not going back into the castle. Even if the Young King hasn't surrounded it by now. And speaking of the Young King, we can't rejoin him. You saw to that with your crossbow bolt.'

'I didn't shoot at *him*, did I?' Bowman said.

'Not really the point,' Richard said.

'He won't want you back,' Brian said, 'you foiled his invasion of Normandy.'

'We hardly foiled him,' Richard said, 'he might not even know we were there.'

'Everyone in that castle knows who shot the bolt,' the monk said, 'and they will talk. The Marshal knows too, I would rather we stayed away from them.'

'Would you?' Richard asked, then checked his annoyance because he felt the same way. Everyone watched him, except for Alexander who now had a dog. Richard rubbed his sole-less foot on the floorboards and felt blisters forming. 'I can only think of one person we can turn to,' he said. 'The only man who has helped us in Normandy and not spat at us for being too English. We'll spend the night in this haunted wasteland, and then when the sun rises, we'll ride to Cailly and find Sir Roger.'

DUTY

Richard's stomach gnawed at him by the time they spotted a small village nestled in a shallow valley far to the southeast of Yvetot. Trees lined the gentle slopes and washed it in green, but a river ran along its base and a castle perched on a raised mound next to the houses and wooden church. The village existed along a single road, but before the houses stood a line of tall haystacks. The villagers kept each stack under a thatch roof attached to a frame supported by four poles. Each pole had notches cut in so the height of the roof could be adjusted, and now the roofs were at their peak and bulging with hay. A barn on the other side of the road swelled with seasoned wood, and in the distance a cluster of beehives were attended by men with wicker discs in the openings of their hoods to protect their faces from bees.

'This is an organised village,' Richard said in awe.

'Not like yours,' Bowman grinned.

Richard fought the urge to reply. It had been a long ride and Solis lagged further and further behind, causing Richard even more worry about him. As they rode along the road and reached the barn, the group of villagers ahead on the road fled toward the castle.

Up on the grassy slopes above the houses, a herd of cattle was being driven along a pasture. Some had bells around their necks, and their clinking and clanking filled the valley and echoed from the slopes. Six enormous dogs mingled with the cattle, the thick collars around their necks sporting long iron spikes to defend against wolves. Judas knew they were there but decided not to antagonise them.

The village houses had sturdy walls lined with yet more firewood, and the street was clear of the detritus often found in such places.

'The church isn't made of stone,' Richard noticed the small wooden structure in the middle of the houses. He realised he'd been looking for flaws in the village and scolded himself for it before Brian said it out loud.

'But wild beasts have not disturbed its graveyard,' the Priest said. He walked on his own two feet, a punishment Richard had found himself taking too much enjoyment from.

'We should have buried all the villagers before we left,' the Priest added.

'You had only dug four graves in a week,' Richard said, 'we would be digging for another week even with all of us helping.'

'And we only had one shovel,' Bowman said.

'It is un-Christian.'

'So was killing them in the first place,' Richard said, 'the blame lies with those who swung the sword.'

'You'll burn for it,' the Priest slowed down and leant against a house wall.

'If I burn, it'll be for much worse than that,' Richard said, 'let the miller bury the dead, he was in league with the reeve, so was no saint himself.'

Maynard earlier gave Sarjeant his horse, and Sarjeant rode with Alexander clinging on behind him. 'My only regret will be that the Templars will inevitably take over the land,' Sarjeant said.

Richard was beyond caring.

Bowman chuckled. 'If Sir Roger tells you to go back and rebuild it, you will though, won't you?'

Richard sniffed. 'We'll worry about that if it happens. And he'd need to find me more farmers if he wanted that. But Yvetot isn't his land anymore, why should he care? Maybe we'll join his household, he once spoke of that idea.'

The castle was a stone tower ringed with two sets of wooden walls. The tower looked more or less identical to Yvetot's, but the walls were less impressive. A ditch too wide for a horse to jump surrounded the mound, and water from the river had been directed to fill it. The leaden sky seemed to colour it grey as they stopped by the wooden bridge that led into the open gateway. Men carrying firewood trudged over the bridge while others attached extra wood to the outside of the walls with hammers and nails. The striking of the nails mixed with the ringing sound of the cattle bells. A trio of women pushed past carrying baskets of food.

'Everywhere is preparing for trouble,' Bowman said.

'There is an invasion,' Richard said. He could feel Sophie's eyes on him, waiting to accuse him of being absent to command similar actions as those carried out by these villagers, but he didn't turn his head to her to find out.

A gust of wind funnelled down the valley from behind them and rippled the banner that hung on the keep. A diagonal blue line cut across the yellow backdrop.

'I'm sure I've seen that before,' Richard said.

'Probably,' Bowman looked up at it, 'but we've seen a hundred banners in the last fortnight alone.'

'Can we rest here for a while?' Maynard asked. His feet, unused to walking, had soon caused him to complain. The children had taken it in turns to walk with him, their bodies alternating between weariness from walking and soreness from riding. Richard felt almost sick at the fact that no one had taught them to ride, even a little, in his absence. They only had two years in which to start, after which they would be too old to ever master the art.

The Red Child's face made him even redder than the others, and Richard decided they may as well see if they could beg for some food here. The village looked as if it could spare a little bread.

'Dismount and I'll go in and see who the lord is,' he said.

Sophie dismounted first. 'We'll go in,' she said, 'no good knight will refuse a lady in need.'

Richard shrugged, handed his reins to Maynard, and walked over the bridge. He wore his mail, but the missing sole meant one foot could feel the lumps and bumps of the planks as he crossed.

Inside the outer bailey, thatched shelters were being expanded, similar to the adjustable haystacks, and packed with more provisions.

'They're expecting a siege,' Richard said.

'I can see that,' his wife strode next to him. 'If the lord is one of Sir Roger's knights, then you can hardly blame him for preparing. The Tancarvilles could come for him.'

'Walter told us he has been feuding with Sir Roger,' Richard said.

'Feuding means war, Richard.'

'I know,' Richard admired the stables which ranged along the inside of half of the wall. Several horses hung their heads over their stable doors to watch the activity in the bailey.

A crossbowman stood by the inner gate, a yellow and blue shield propped up against the wall behind him. A second guard spoke to him, and when he saw the newcomers, he jumped up and walked over.

'Who are you?' he asked in a gruff Norman accent.

'Richard, we have travelled far with our children and would like to rest on their behalf.'

The crossbowmen regarded Richard with suspicion. 'Who do you serve?'

'The king,' Richard replied.

'Which one?'

'Whichever one you like,' Richard said, 'my village has been destroyed and we are only passing through. We are no threat.'

'That's for me to decide,' the guard said.

'Would you fetch your lord, please,' Sophie said. 'I don't care how long you make us wait or how frightened you can make us by swinging your big crossbow around. Just tell him we're here.'

'He's very busy,' the guard frowned, then turned on his heels and went inside the inner bailey.

The lord who eventually emerged out of the inner gateway was an old one. Tall and slender, he was a man with a face set in a permanent frown. He wore a mail shirt with a hint of rust on the forearms and around his neck. That was a sign of actual use or continual wear.

The knight reached them and squinted at Sophie. 'I know you.'

That was when Richard's memory reached back into its more distant corners and remembered the face. 'Sir Thomas,' he said. 'Sir Thomas of Cleres.'

Sir Thomas cracked his frown to raise his eyebrows. 'Do I know you?'

Sophie let out a breath. 'Sir Thomas,' she said, 'it pleases me you still live. You buried my husband with dignity.'

Sir Thomas snorted and nodded in recognition. 'A lot of good that did me, those villagers of yours almost killed us all. Disloyal ingrates.'

Richard remembered Sir Thomas leading the Little Lord's company into Yvetot on his very first visit, how the Little Lord had killed Sophie's husband, and how Sir Thomas had brutally suppressed the resulting uprising.

But he was Tancarville's man, and that sent a tingle up Richard's spine.

'We have three children with us,' Richard said, 'would you have any bread you would donate to their comfort?'

'Who is their lord? Could he not provide for them himself?'

'Richard here is their lord,' Sophie said.

Richard wanted to nudge his wife into silence, but that was unlikely to work.

Sir Thomas peered at him again. The knight's years advanced him beyond Gerold's, and his eyes weren't as sharp as they once were. 'I have heard about you,' Sir Thomas said, 'the Lord of Yvetot. Merely a shadow of Sir Arthur, so they say.'

'Who says?' Richard asked.

Sir Thomas's weathered face hinted at a smile. 'Almost no one, but that is rather my point. Have I seen you before?'

Richard sighed. 'It doesn't matter. Will you allow my children to eat and rest?'

Sir Thomas nodded, turned around, and walked back towards his keep.

'I think that was a yes,' Sophie followed him.

Richard thought twice about it. Then his stomach rumbled, and he went back to bring his party inside the castle.

The hall inside the keep could have been his own, at least in size. In every other way, it was better. A single long table was neater than his own, the chairs actual chairs and not logs, and the walls painted in white. It felt airy because of the paint, even though the windows were covered with hanging cloth and the smoke from the hearth had few options to escape.

The barest scattering of reeds from the river covered the floorboards, and the cat and dog droppings it should have obscured were more visible than Sophie would have liked. She wrinkled her nose as she sat with her back to the hearth, but kept her opinions to herself.

'Your castle has excellent provisions,' Richard said, 'and your village is most orderly.'

'I do what I can with what I have,' Sir Thomas said, 'others with more do less. The youth of today are idle. Young men in my day worked hard.'

Richard sat down and dug a fingernail into his armrest to take his mind off the response he wanted to give.

His children entered the room behind Sarjeant with their eyes checking everything, and Richard wondered if they had ever left Yvetot before today. Maybe he had been wrong, selfish even, to leave for Ireland, for education had been neglected.

'I built the outer wall here with my own two hands,' their host told them.

Sophie looked at Richard and he raised his eyebrows back.

'It is a fine wall,' Richard said.

The red-faced Priest puffed as he entered the hall and threw himself onto a chair. He took his shoes off and rubbed his feet. 'The church is wood,' he said, 'even Yvetot had a stone church.'

Sir Thomas watched the Priest massage his feet with visible disgust. 'A stone church will not protect my people when others come to kill and rob them. That duty falls to me.'

'Perhaps if your villagers prayed harder, then evil men would be warded off.'

Richard spluttered a laugh. 'That's rich coming from you,' he said, 'the Priest of a village that was wiped off the earth only a week ago.'

The Priest blushed and looked down to his weary feet.

Sir Thomas blinked as he watched Richard. 'Perhaps you should have been a better lord. Sir Arthur wouldn't have allowed it.'

'Sir Arthur is gone,' Richard said, 'and we did our best.'

'I'm sure you did,' their host closed his eyes for a while. A servant brought in an austere serving of bread and heavily watered-down wine, but that was far better than nothing.

Sir Thomas opened his eyes as the last of the dark bread was eaten. 'Lady Sophie, I am glad that you survived. You were the light that shone in the blackness of that place.'

Richard watched her to see if she'd blush.

She didn't. 'Thank you,' Sophie said, 'and my husband is to thank for that.'

Richard almost choked on the last dry crumbs of bread.

'Remind me,' Sir Thomas looked at Richard, 'who are you?'

'I am Richard. Once of Yvetot.'

'Sir Roger's man, then?'

Richard shook his head. 'I hold. Well. I *held* Yvetot from old King Henry.'

'He's not old,' Sir Thomas coughed, then his face stilled. He nodded to a servant and beckoned him over. The tall, thin man bent over to hear a whisper, then left the hall.

'Some of you I have seen before,' Sir Thomas said, 'but I cannot place you.'

Sarjeant bounced Lora on his knee, only half listening. 'That would have been when we rode to Yvetot with you and the Little Lord,' he said.

The cracking and popping hearth covered Richard's gasp of dismay.

'I did not know,' Sir Thomas shifted his shoulders to redistribute his mail around them, 'but you look older than you did then, Richard of Yvetot. I was extremely disappointed to hear Sir Roger had chosen you to replace Sir Arthur. Yvetot could have flourished under better management.'

Richard pursed his lips and Sophie stared at him with a constant gaze that meant for him to restrain himself.

'So Yvetot is gone?' Sir Thomas asked.

Richard nodded.

A laugh escaped the elderly knight, a sound that had perhaps never been heard from him before. 'Perhaps there is a God dispensing justice onto the world. Those villagers deserved it, since their lord died, they have been the worst village in all of Normandy. A disgrace. Better to wipe the land clean and begin again.'

'You did your part to make them that way,' Richard said, 'you butchered them as if they were soldiers on a battlefield.'

Sir Thomas nodded. 'I did my duty, nothing more. They attacked us, which you would remember if you were there as you claim. My villagers accept protection from me in exchange for their labour and loyalty. I keep them safe, they feed me. In Yvetot, this bond was broken.'

'I'm not sure it ever existed under that old relic of a knight,' Bowman said.

'Sir Arthur was a better man than any here,' Sir Thomas said.

Sophie's face twitched.

'Who are you fortifying against?' Richard asked while looking at his wife. She didn't need to hear about her previous husband any longer.

'Did Lord Tancarville not call you to ride with him to Neufchatel?' Richard asked.

Their host nodded, and the rust on his mail shirt suddenly made sense. 'I did my duty to him and rode east, but when the Flemings deserted the siege, concern spread through everyone like a disease. Count Philip's departure doomed the siege the moment he rode away. Lord Tancarville foresaw it and made plans to leave.'

'To leave and burn my village,' Richard crossed his arms.

Sarjeant shook his head as Lora tugged on his hair. 'They came to us on their way east, not west. It was many, many days ago.'

'Indeed,' Sir Thomas said, 'when he left Neufchatel, Lord Tancarville decided to make use of his marshalled forces to inflict a mortal wound on Sir Roger.'

Richard's blood froze. 'The Tancarvilles could be at Cailly? We could be riding right into them.'

Sarjeant stopped playing, and Bowman stopped throwing Alexander up into the air and catching him.

'Why aren't you with them now?' Richard asked.

'I declined to join my lord,' Sir Thomas said.

'What about your duty?' Bowman sneered.

'How far is Cailly from here?' Richard asked.

'Not far, it is an easy morning's ride,' Sir Thomas said.

'We can't go there now,' Sarjeant said, 'the purpose of our journey is to elude them.'

Sir Thomas's eyes looked sad and glanced at the fire.

Maynard approached Richard. 'We can still ride away and find the Young King, it isn't too late for that.'

'Why do you love the Young King so much?' Bowman asked.

'He is a successful man,' the squire replied. 'I served in his company for over a year, and Sir Adam even paid me over and above my expenses. That doesn't happen to squires. The Young King is the future, he will look after you.'

'Fools,' Sir Thomas boomed. 'Young fools.'

Maynard turned his gaze away from the elder knight.

The Lord of Cleres scratched his lightly stubbled chin. 'My grandfather fought alongside Lord Tancarville's great, great grandfather at the Battle at Senlac Hill,' Sir Thomas looked up at the ceiling. 'Although it might have been his great grandfather. No matter, the king on the throne of England that day was another man, a man his followers expected to sit on that throne for many years to come. But matters took the crown in another direction. Do not assume the Young King will sit on the throne he covets. There is much life in the old king yet.'

No one thought to argue with a man a decade older than the Old King. The mention of Tancarville's ancestor and their long link to Cleres unsettled Richard, maybe they shouldn't have come into the castle.

'But the Young King has been crowned,' Richard said, 'he will follow his father.'

'If he lives long enough,' Sir Thomas looked to the doorway but no one was there. 'Until the right archbishop has thrown holy oil over a man, do not assume he will be king.'

'Perhaps,' Richard said, 'but then how do you know who to follow?'

Sir Thomas rubbed one of his eyes. 'I remain loyal to my lord, that is the end of the matter. You will hear nothing more complicated from me.'

The Priest edged forwards. 'My village has been consumed by flames and my flock culled, would you have a place for me here? You protected me from the rioting villagers when Sir Arthur died.'

'Those villagers were your flock,' Sir Thomas said. 'What use do I have for a priest who turns his own flock against him, then allows them to be massacred?'

The Priest swallowed and closed his eyes as if about to sob.

'But if my priest has a use for you, why should I care?' Sir Thomas said.

'Thank you,' the Priest jumped at the old knight and dropped to his knees. He bent down to kiss the lord's feet.

Sir Thomas kicked him in the teeth for his trouble, the Priest rolled to his side with red gums.

'Get out,' the knight said, 'priests are not welcome in my hall.'

The Priest scrambled to his feet, almost knocked the Red Child over, and fled to find himself a new home.

Richard was not sorry to see him go. 'If the Priest stays here, would you be able to stop him running straight back to Castle Tancarville?'

'Why should I care where he goes?' Sir Thomas asked.

'You don't,' Richard said, 'but I would rather he didn't run and tell the Little Lord where we are.'

'Why should I stop a man seeking an audience with my own lord?'

Richard frowned. 'I suppose you wouldn't mind holding him here for just two days instead?'

Sir Thomas raised his eyebrows and that answered Richard's question.

Bowman turned to the doorway as the sound of claws scrambling on stone burst through it.

Three of the intimidating dogs used to guard the cattle from wolves lunged into the hall, squires holding them back with long ropes. Their paws whirled at the stone to get to the visitors in the hall, all three children shot back behind Sarjeant.

The squires fought to restrain the hounds, but they pulled on their leashes and their paws scratched lines in the floorboards. One barked with the folds of its mouth flapping and foam flew across the hall.

'There's no need for whatever this is,' Richard said.

Bowman flicked his sword from his scabbard. 'If he makes me kill a dog, I'll kill him.'

They'd locked Judas in the stable with Solis, and Richard regretted it now. He readied himself to draw and looked at their host. 'Would you please remove those dogs? They are frightening my children.'

Sir Thomas remained motionless. All eyes turned to him and Sophie's breathing increased.

'Are we free to leave?' Richard asked.

The old knight exhaled. 'Why did you have to come here? My banner flies above my tower, you know who I serve.'

'We didn't recognise it,' Richard said, 'it's been years since we saw you.'

The knight shook his weathered head. 'Laziness. You young knights don't even try anymore, do you? You spend your time frivolously prancing about at tournaments like prize peacocks.'

'Who are you calling a peacock?' Bowman bristled.

The Lord of Cleres shook his head at the blonde man. 'My lord will not be pleased if I let you leave. He would hear of it. Nothing happens in secret, you see. It is easier for me to tell him you are here, and keep you here until he arrives. Then he shall not bother me. I am very sorry to do this to you, but perhaps it will teach you a lesson on knighthood and being a man.'

Richard slid the Little Lord's sword into the open air and laid it on the table before him. The iron hilt clunked as it settled onto the wood.

Sir Thomas eyed the bent blade with its dented edges. He knew it, for he'd seen it during the first visit to Yvetot. 'That is the blade that killed Sir Arthur.'

Richard folded his fingers together and rested them on the table next to the sword. The dogs barked behind him. He nodded. 'Then you know what the Tancarvilles will do to us if they capture us.'

The old knight nodded back. 'They will sing a story of the knight who forgot his heraldry. It will serve to warn the next generation that the failing state of knighthood is unacceptable.'

'You don't care if we die? Even the children and Sophie?'

Sir Thomas sighed when he looked at Sophie. 'There will be much to regret, but my duty is to my people, not yours.'

The three dogs all reacted to the tension in the air and barked louder. Sophie ignored them even as their howls were so forceful the rushing air from their barks moved her hair.

Richard had his back to the dogs but kept his gaze on his captor. 'You must do what your duty demands,' he said, 'and I must do the same for mine.'

'Of course,' Sir Thomas said. 'This is not personal.'

'It feels very personal,' Bowman said through gritted teeth.

Maynard crept around the table until he was next to Sarjeant. 'Perhaps if Lord Tancarville knew we served the Young King, he would release us all?'

'We don't serve the Young King,' Richard said.

'But if we did.'

'We don't,' Richard shouted.

The dogs howled, and one almost pulled a Cleres squire off his feet.

Richard locked eyes with Bowman but it was hardly necessary. He glanced at Sarjeant, and the man who had saved his children so recently had iron in his eyes. Maynard returned Richard's look with wide and uncertain eyes. His reaction to whatever happened next would tell Richard a lot.

Richard unlaced his fingers from themselves. 'It seems as if we have a conflict of duties,' he drew Sir John's dagger out, concealed under the table, and pushed it towards Sophie next to him. Her hand trembled as she grasped it, and her rapid, shallow breathing was visible through her dress.

'It seems so,' Sir Thomas's right hand rested on his sword pommel.

'I have failed in my duty too many times,' Richard said, 'it won't happen again.'

He looked up at Bowman and Sarjeant. 'Now.'

Sarjeant lunged one way round the table and Bowman jumped onto it with a clatter of plates and cups.

A squire released a dog and it sprung towards Sophie.

Richard picked up the Little Lord's sword and spun around, slashing through the air to meet the first dog before it reached his wife.

Sophie whirled around, dagger in her hand, and the fury of a threatened mother in her eyes.

Bowman leapt from the table, landed between them, and took care of the second hound. Sarjeant flew around the table at the final squire, who released his hound and fled out of the doorway. The hound pushed Sarjeant to the floor, drool fell on his face, but Sir John's dagger saved the man beneath the beast.

Richard left the others to confront the two remaining squires and instead thrust the point of his sword at Sir Thomas, halting a hair's-width from his eyes and showering him with blood that flicked from the blade.

The old knight didn't flinch.

Bowman killed a squire, and the other, faced with Sophie's uncertain charge, followed his companion out of the castle.

Sir Thomas glanced out of the side of his eye at the squire on the ground and sighed.

Richard's lungs heaved under his two layers of mail and the leather breastplate that covered them. 'It's nothing personal,' he said.

'Of course,' Sir Thomas moved his hand away from his sword. 'You may leave. At least Lord Tancarville has that body as evidence of my attempt.'

Richard wanted to sever his head for putting his family through that. Lora hid under the table, her eyes locked on the dead animals which littered the hall. Alexander craned his little neck at the fallen squire, tears in his eyes.

Sarjeant came back into the hall after having chased the squire away. 'They have four crossbowmen at the inner gateway. They are staying there.'

'Your men won't even come in to save you,' Richard said, 'maybe your duty means less to them than you think.'

'Do what you will,' Sir Thomas said.

'I'm not going to kill you,' Richard said, 'I know what it means to be trapped between bad choices and bad lords. You'll walk out in front of us and tell your men to stand aside. No more blood needs to run.'

Sophie kept the dagger but went to her children. The Red Child seemed unfazed, he crouched down by the dead squire who was still warm to the touch, and unlaced his sword belt.

Bowman looked up at Richard and shrugged.

The sword was almost as tall as the Red Child, but he tied it around himself all the same. The end of the scabbard dragged on the floor when he walked.

Richard looked for Maynard and found him rooted to the same spot he'd started on. That was unencouraging.

Sir Thomas went crossed-eyed looking at the tip of the blade that threatened him. 'Remove that and you have a deal.'

Richard lowered the blade and wiped it clean on his tattered old cloak, then put the weapon away. Sir Thomas got up of his own accord, stepped over the body of his squire, and led everyone out of the hall.

A crossbow bolt smacked into the doorframe as they left the keep, Sir Thomas's cheek was brushed by the fletchings as it spiralled past.

'Idiots,' he muttered.

His guards lowered their crossbows and shouted apologies as their lord waved them away. They let everyone pass by, but Richard walked behind Sir Thomas with a hand gripping his shoulder. No one interfered as Richard led his party out of the castle and Cleres as fast as he could.

He checked over his shoulder once they were beyond the last house in the village. No one followed. A wave of sweet relief washed over him and he glanced at Sarjeant who rode next to him. 'You've still got it.'

Sarjeant clutched Alexander to his chest as the boy sat in front of the saddle. The former steward of Yvetot smiled back. 'And I'm still sober.'

'Thank you,' Sophie said. Her face was pale and she gripped her saddle and daughter tightly.

'I liked Sir Thomas before,' Richard said. 'That was not the welcome I expected from him.'

'And they call me a rude knight,' Bowman grinned as they progressed along the valley.

Richard didn't look back again, because he was more concerned about what might lie ahead.

DOGS AND GODS

The next problem was the coming of night. They kept going along the shallow valley lined in dense undergrowth as the sun increasingly threatened to set behind them. Long shadows stretched out ahead as the road followed a small river. Biting insects came out at twilight to harass the horses, causing much swishing of tails and heads. The terrain flattened and opened out into a plain punctuated by large forests.

Bowman rode out front, but waited for Richard to catch him up as the road ahead disappeared into a treeline. 'I'm thinking we aren't going to reach Cailly before it's too dark to travel, young lord.'

Richard nodded. He cast his eyes around the landscape, but the light was dimming and there was no sign of shelter.

'We can find somewhere secluded in the forest,' Bowman said. 'It's a shame I have no bow or arrows.'

Richard's children look weary. 'They've never slept outside before. They will hardly get a moment of sleep, you know how loud the forest can be at night.'

'I don't know what we can do about that,' Bowman said, 'you can light a fire to keep wild animals away if you please, but you might attract people instead.'

'I'd rather not,' Richard said, 'for all we know, Tancarville scouts are camping in this very forest.'

'You should worry less,' Bowman said, 'at least about things that haven't happened yet.'

Richard coughed. 'How is that attitude working out for you?'

Bowman waved at his heels. 'I have golden spurs, don't I?'

They rode into the trees which seemed to wrap around them as if a blanket made from the deepest night. Once Richard's eyes adjusted to the gloom, he could make out individual trees and bushes. A coolness hung in the air, a freshness and stillness that surprisingly calmed Richard's nerves. He hated riding with his children through dangerous lands, worry clenched his stomach and wouldn't let go, but in the trees it loosened its grip a little. He let out a deep breath.

Bowman stopped by a tree and moved his head towards the branches and leaves which shrivelled around the edges. He reached out and held up a small wooden cross hanging from a branch. 'This tree is full of them,' he said.

The next tree was, too. Richard rode on and the air cooled even more. He stopped by a tree someone seemed to have blackened by burning. An array of small items hung from its lower limbs, including a comb, a wooden spoon, and a roll of parchment. That reminded Richard of the roll that still hung in Solis's mane, the one that asked after his father's fate.

'Why have they burned the tree?' Bowman asked as the party stopped alongside it.

Brian scoffed. 'Isn't that obvious?'

The blonde man looked at him. 'No, not really.'

'It symbolises the tree of knowledge in the Garden of Eden,' the monk said, 'that tree was black. It was a bad tree.'

'A bad tree?' Bowman laughed at him.

Richard frowned. 'How can knowledge be bad?'

'Has no one ever read the Holy Book to you?' Brian asked.

'Yes,' Richard said, 'but without knowledge, aren't we just animals?'

'Some people would burn you for saying that,' Brian said.

Bowman laughed again. 'Some have tried,' he grinned.

Brian dismissed the joke. 'Those are offerings or symbols of something given up. Places like this grow in lands where the church has less sway, people find their own way to honour the Lord.'

'Neither Sir Thomas nor Sir Roger are the church-going type,' Richard said, 'but we need to make a camp. Are we safe near this?'

Brian nodded. 'Well, unless you're of the devil.'

Bowman chuckled. 'Then we'll be riding on a while, will we, young lord?'

'That's not funny,' Richard pushed his horse beyond the black tree. 'And it was tested.'

Bowman rode on too. 'We should go off the road a short way,' he said, 'it's better to sleep out of sight of it.'

Richard agreed, but in the blackness ahead a shadow formed in their path. 'That looks like a building.'

'Out here?' Bowman snorted, but then squinted. 'But you might be right.'

The blur of the shadow solidified into the straight lines of an object until those lines became the outline of a stone building. The road split in two and curled around it, hugging the building closely as if containing it.

'A stone building?' Richard asked. 'Brian, what is it?'

The monk shrugged. 'How should I know?'

Richard dismounted next to the structure, an octagonal shaped tower of stone. He handed the blue roan to Maynard and went inside.

If it was dark in the forest, inside the tower it was even blacker. The building was a single chamber, twice the height of a man and with an octagonal hole in the floor. The hole was filled with water, although twigs and leaves had blown in and floated on the surface.

A Stone altar jutted out of the far wall but there was nothing on the ledge. Richard left. 'There's enough room for us to sleep inside, we just have to avoid rolling into the pool while we're asleep.'

'The pool?' Bowman asked and went in to look for himself.

Brian followed. He came out with a smile. 'It's a baptistry, Richard,' he said.

'Oh, I see,' Richard said. 'But don't we do baptisms in churches?'

'We do now,' the monk said, 'this is from longer ago.'

The horses were hobbled, and everyone crammed around the sides of the silent pool to make their beds. They carried Gerold in, his condition unchanged for over a week now. Weariness crept over everyone, and at least free from hunger for the night, they all fell asleep.

Richard awoke when a yellow glow washed the doorway of the baptistry. Lora was huddled next to him under his cloak but he didn't remember her getting there. He left his cloak on top of her and ventured outside. Birds sang in the treetops, a chorus of trill notes, and when he looked up, he could see huge nests swaying high in the tallest trees. The birds in them sounded like crows. The sun twinkled through the canopy and its light danced on the road. Richard stretched himself out and yawned. It felt fresh and early. He turned to look at the road ahead, but when he did he froze.

In the distance, unnatural shapes lurked between the tree trunks and low bushes. Shapes that looked like canvas shelters.

But more pressingly, in the middle of the road were a dozen men on foot, walking his way.

Richard's mouth gaped in horror. He reached for his sword and looked behind him for their horses, but they were scattered around the woods and far from being ready to escape on.

'Don't be worried,' the leader of the men said. He didn't quite shout, and stopped in front of Richard with his hands on his hips.

Richard readied his sword, but it would be harder to cut his way out of here than Sir Thomas's hall.

The leader of the men didn't look like a Tancarville scout. He wore full mail armour, right down to his toes, but his face was dark and his hair black. He wore his mail coif down behind him like an unused hood and carried no shield or spear. Various degrees of mail or textile armour protected his companions, but all had the same dark complexion.

'I had expected no one here,' the leader said, his accent harsh and words ill-formed.

'Where are you from?' Richard asked.

'Far away.'

'What do you want here?' Richard backed up a step and spoke loudly in the hope at least Bowman would hear.

'We came to see if this building holds anything we need,' the leader said, 'we not saw it in the night.'

Richard wondered if this was how he himself sounded to the native Normans. 'Who are you?'

'I am Sancho of Savannac,' the leader said, and it was then that Richard noticed the common colours between the men. Their tunics and the canvas sheets in the distance were all either gold or green. He'd seen those colours before, marching next to the Young King beyond Neufchatel's walls.

'Are you a mercenary?' Richard snatched a glance behind him and saw Brian's dark robes leave the baptistry.

'No,' Sancho said, 'dog of war.'

Richard didn't see the difference, but his heart sank.

'Does this monk live here?' Sancho asked.

Brian almost tripped when he saw the mercenaries.

'No,' Richard said, 'he's with me.'

'Does he have any gold crosses or silver cups?'

'No,' Richard decided to trust his memory. 'But we are with the Young King, who you also serve, yes?'

Sancho grinned, his white teeth gleaming. 'For today.'

'But I thought you said,' Brian began, but Richard whirled around and gave the monk such a glare he stopped talking.

'There's nothing of value inside,' Richard turned back to Sancho, 'just a pool of water they once used for baptising people.'

'Ah,' Sancho kept grinning, 'there is always an altar. We take what on that.'

'There's nothing,' Richard said, 'but you're welcome to look once my company has left.'

'Company?' Sancho laughed. He turned to his companions and said something in a foreign tongue. They laughed back.

The mercenary stepped forwards. 'I look inside. There always rich things in holy buildings.'

'Please,' Richard said, 'my family is inside and they are tired. We will leave, then you can do what you want. Do not storm in there, you will frighten my children.'

'How much are your children worth to you?' Sancho weighed up Richard. 'You can have them back for maybe ten silver coins.'

'Are you ransoming my children back to me?' Richard couldn't believe what he was hearing.

Sancho shrugged. 'When one man is frightened of another, the other get rich.'

'This is a holy palace,' Brian said, 'begone from it.'

'Monk is brave,' the mercenary said something else to his men, who found it amusing.

'This is a place of baptism,' Brian said, 'do you know what that is?'

Sancho held his hands up in mock offence. 'You think dogs from the south ungodly?'

'What?' Brian asked.

'No,' Richard said, 'he just means you have to respect this place.'

Brian understood. 'I see, but you cannot defile our Lord's ground with your filthy ways. You can't rob such sites.'

Richard raised his eyes to the monk. 'Remember Meath?'

Brian looked away. 'That was different.'

'I have been baptised,' Sancho said. 'But God no be angry at me for finding food for my dogs. My duty feed my dogs.'

'Not duty again,' Richard moaned. 'If you can wait here for a very short while, you can go inside.'

Sancho fingered the dagger at his waist. 'Me think we go in when we want. Fetch our ransom.'

'I have no silver in the world,' Richard said. He glanced at Brian to make sure he added nothing to that, but the monk's bravado had gone and he was white-faced and nervous.

'I have no wealth and no land,' Richard said, 'that is why I serve the Young King. If you take my children I cannot pay, so I have no choice but to stop you taking them.'

Sancho bent double with laughter. He told his men what Richard had said, and they joined in.

Richard heard footsteps behind him. Then a sigh.

'I told you we should have camped off the road,' Bowman said.

'You didn't force the matter once we found a nice, dry building to shelter it, did you?' Richard snapped back.

'You argue like women,' Sancho said.

Bowman stood next to Richard and looked down at the shorter

mercenary.

Sancho looked up at him with eyes that judged enemies by their skill and not their size.

Bowman looked at the tents. 'Who are this lot, then?'

'The Young King's mercenaries,' Richard said, 'which is lucky because we are on our way back to him.'

The blonde man nodded, for too long, then walked up to Sancho. He went to pat him on the shoulder and all the mercenaries behind him sprang into life and drew daggers or swords.

'Come, now,' Bowman didn't flinch and grabbed Sancho with a friendly squeeze. 'Have you got any food for us? I could eat a whole peacock.'

Sancho shrugged him off, his smile gone. 'Two knights,' he said, 'two pairs gold spurs feed my dogs for long time.'

Bowman drew his dagger in the blink of an eye and held it to Sancho's neck.

Richard kept himself still and let Bowman do whatever he planned.

The dogs of war raised their weapons but looked to their leader for instruction.

Bowman moved his head closer to Sancho, then pushed him away and laughed. He sheathed the dagger. 'I'm just playing with you,' he walked off through the dogs, pushing between them and strode off towards the camp in the distance.

Sancho scratched his neck then stroked the dark hair on his chin.

'I'm going to get my family,' Richard turned and returned to the baptistry's door. He looked back towards the mercenary's leader. 'The Young King is very fond of me, think about that,' he ducked back inside, leaving Brian quivering alone on the road.

Next to the leafy pool Sophie wrapped the children in their small cloaks with urgency.

'We need to go,' Richard said.

'I know,' Sophie hissed, 'get Gerold out. Sarjeant, bring us the nearest two horses for us and the children. It doesn't matter if they're the right ones.'

Richard went to speak, but everyone already jumped to obey his wife and he didn't need to add to her instructions.

Maynard alone looked at Richard for direction.

'You heard her,' Richard said, 'help me carry him out of here.'

Gerold wasn't as heavy as he had been in Neufchatel. He still had enough strength to make himself an easy weight to carry, and could lean on the cold and weathered baptistry walls while Sarjeant rounded up some horses. Richard went to check on Brian.

'You can leave now, Brian,' he found the monk where he'd left him.

Brian stood his ground, even though he shook so much his robe vibrated.

'Come on,' Richard walked to him.

'No.'

'No?' Richard asked. 'Why not?'

'They're going to desecrate it,' Brian said.

Richard sighed. 'There's nothing to desecrate. Unless the water is holy? Does holy water wear out after a while?'

Brian's hands clenched.

Richard watched Sancho as he spoke. 'Brian, this is not a monastery in Meath. You missed your chance to martyr yourself for a good cause. This baptistry isn't a good cause, it isn't even a cause at all. It's just some stone and some soiled water.'

'Monks like dying,' Sancho approached, the grin back on his face.

Bowman walked back from the tents towards the dogs of war. 'Look who I found,' he shouted.

Judas, pink tongue out, bounded towards the mercenaries. He stopped when one drew a dagger. The black dog retracted his tongue, lowered his head, and raised his hackles.

Sancho said something to his men, which shamed them into pretending to be unconcerned by the hound. And they should have been unconcerned, for well travelled mercenaries would have met real warhounds before, beats much larger than Judas.

Richard took Brian's wrist and pulled him away.

The monk snatched it back. 'Someone has to stand up for right. Better to do it late than not at all.'

'Look,' Richard said, 'your death will make no difference to anything.'

'It will to me.'

Bowman walked through the mercenaries and they parted to let him through. 'I think they are from Iberia,' he said. 'I've seen their kind before.'

'Navarre,' Sancho replied.

Bowman shrugged. 'Whatever. Come on, dog.'

Judas didn't walk through the Spanish mercenaries, instead he prowled around them, drawing their eyes.

Sancho faced Judas as he circled. 'They tell me about devil's-wolf at tournament,' he said, 'I wonder if he this dog.'

Richard kept his face impassive. 'Luckily there's no need for you to find out. We'll be on our way,' he said.

Bowman walked close to Richard on his way back towards their horses. 'Hurry up,' he hissed without turning his head.

'Come on, Brian,' Richard clutched the monk's arm and this time gave him no choice but to retreat.

'Are you trying to get yourself killed?' Richard asked him as they reached the baptistry.

Sarjeant held Sophie's palfrey as she mounted, then passed up Lora to her.

Brian remained tightlipped and looked at Richard.

'Just prepare to leave,' Richard told him and went to fetch the blue roan.

The stallion led their herd now, and the wounded Solis had gained a large red bite mark on his neck that saw to it, but the new warhorse still plodded over to Richard when called for.

'Should we go back?' Maynard asked when those with horses were all mounted.

Richard shook his head. 'There is nothing for us that way.'

'Can we at least go around those men?' Sarjeant asked. 'I don't like the way they're looking at us.'

'We go on,' Richard said, 'their bravado is for the benefit of each other. They are no different to the squires at Castle Tancarville, all trying to appear to be the strongest.'

Bowman donned his mail shirt in a heartbeat and tied up the lacing on the side of his leather breastplate. 'I'll ride at the front.'

Richard placed himself next to his wife and asked his son if he wanted to ride with him.

Alexander shook his head and raised his arms to Sarjeant instead.

Richard frowned but didn't have time to change his mind. They rode past the baptistry as Sancho entered it, his eyes searching for plunder.

'It's best if we are gone before they realise it's empty,' Bowman turned in his saddle to tell Richard.

They marched steadily towards the gold and green town of tents. Most of the shelters flanked the road, tied between trees, fires in the clear ground between them. Men glanced up from fires and piles of blankets to watch the unexpected visitors ride by. Richard and his party avoided eye contact.

Jeers and insults in a foreign tongue followed them, but they were preferable to swords or arrows.

Solis, roaming free, stopped at one shelter and thrust his nose down at the occupants. He nudged a cup with his lips and tipped the drink all over its owner. The Spaniard cried out and tried to grab the horse. Solis bit him and he recoiled with a flap of skin flayed from his forearm. His companions laughed at him and Solis squealed and jumped away.

'Idiot,' Richard muttered. He twisted his head around to look back at the baptistry, where he saw Sancho and his gang returning towards the camp empty-handed.

'Come on Solie,' he shouted and the palomino pricked its ears up and caught up with him at an awkward hobble. 'Squire,' Richard shouted at Maynard, 'put a rope on Solis and lead him.'

Maynard approached the stallion with the rope in his hand, but Solis saw it and walked away from him at a speed deliberately only slightly faster than the man.

'Do you know anything about horses?' Bowman asked.

'Hurry up,' Richard said, 'before he gets us into trouble.'

The man Solis had bitten stood up and followed them. He shouted at men in other shelters and a few joined him on the road.

Richard wondered how fast Maynard and the Red Child could run, but then the mercenaries had plenty of horses so running for it wasn't a viable option anyway. The Red Child's scabbard dragged along the road, the scraping noise of it cutting a line in the dirt grated at Richard.

Solis got them into trouble before Maynard could catch him. They reached the baggage train of the mercenary company and the horse stopped at a cart to which a small, shaggy horse had been tied. It was a mare, and Solis noticed with an enthusiastic sniff.

'Solie, no,' Richard shouted as the stallion completely ignored him.

A head popped out from underneath the cart's canvas cover. Richard recognised the head, which disappeared back under the cover, then reappeared with a wooden stave that jabbed at Solis.

The stallion fled as the stave poked his ribs, and the figure in the cart grinned under her long, grey hair.

'Nicola?' Richard asked. 'But that horse isn't Three-Legs?'

'No,' the woman replied, 'this is Two-Legs.'

Solis snorted toward the cart, but retreated to Richard instead of trying his luck again.

'What happened to Three-legs?' Richard asked as his little convoy halted.

'She was stolen,' Nicola said, 'so I had to name her replacement even less attractively.'

'I don't think the name change worked on my horse,' Richard grinned.

'Young lord,' Bowman said with a firm tone, 'we don't have time for this.'

The blonde man was right, Solis's bite victim approached with a dozen of his fellows, his face a picture of anger and pain. He brushed at the blood running down his arm and scowled.

'What are you doing here?' Richard asked.

'Me?' Nicola replied. 'You do not want to be amid these men.'

'But you're a woman,' Maynard said.

'Oh, am I?' Nicola sneered. 'I had best be away then. Thank you for pointing that out.'

'Are you spying for someone?' Richard asked.

'I'm not a spy,' she said, 'these men pay for everything when they have the money. And they usually have the money. Leave now, though, you don't belong here.'

Richard touched his legs to his horse.

'Although,' Nicola called after him, 'you should be rich or dead by now. And I'd wagered dead.'

'I've never been far from it,' Richard replied.

'Still waiting for the silver, then?' Nicola cracked a wry grin.

'Why does everyone keep talking about gold or silver around you?' Maynard asked.

'Shut up,' Bowman said. 'We need to go.'

'Forget about it,' Nicola said, 'it will kill you.'

'What, the silver?' Maynard asked.

'Too late,' Bowman groaned as the mercenaries arrived.

'Silver?' the man with a chunk out of his arm asked.

'If they don't kill you now,' Bowman said to the squire, 'I will.'

'God help me,' Richard raised his voice so half the camp could hear, 'we have no silver.'

The mercenary was thin, but strength lay in his wiry limbs, and his dark brow furrowed. 'You owe me. I will take silver,' his accent strong but his words more well formed than Sancho's.

Richard turned the blue roan to face the dog of war and rode so close that the horse's warm breath washed over the dark man's face.

'I'm not going to tell you again,' Richard said, 'there is no silver. Now if you don't want to die in this wood, turn around and leave us be.'

The mercenary laughed, which revealed a set of incomplete teeth. He strode up to the Red Child and put his hand on his head, almost as if holding him in place. 'What's this child worth to you?'

Sophie kicked her horse on and left.

'Leave the children alone,' Richard said. 'We ride for the Young King.'

'This is between us, it doesn't involve him,' the mercenary said as Sarjeant moved his horse and followed Sophie as she neared the boundary of the camp. Gerold's horse went with them of its own accord. Maynard finally caught Solis and slipped the rope halter over his head.

The Red Child tilted his head up and regarded the portly man who stood over him.

'Let him go,' Richard said.

Bowman groaned, then took his horse back to Richard. 'It's too early in the morning for this.'

The blue roan snorted and coated the mercenary in snot.

He wiped his face clean with the hand not on the Red Child, but only succeeded in wiping blood from his horse bite over his cheek.

'Do you know who this is?' Bowman asked.

'The man who will pay me,' the mercenary's companions lined up on either side of him. The black dog growled from next to Richard and some mercenaries reconsidered their bravado.

'This man,' Bowman said, 'saved the Young King's life not a week ago. The week before that, the Young King joined us to hunt down this man's captive horse. So if you take this boy, then the Young King will swoop down like a peregrine and massacre the lot of you.'

Richard drew his sword.

Bowman did the same. 'But more importantly, I lost a brother for the Young King last week,' for a moment his voice faltered, 'so I really, really, want to kill someone.'

The blue roan pawed the ground, throwing dust up behind him. His huge black head swished from side to side and one mercenary took a step back.

Their ringleader removed his hand from the Red Child's head and took half a step back himself.

Richard looked at the boy and saw no fear in his young eyes. Dark eyes. 'Come on,' Richard said, 'walk this way.'

The Red Child put one foot forward, but then used two hands to draw his new sword. The blade cleared its scabbard quickly enough, and the boy turned but the weight of the blade in his small hands unbalanced him. He caught himself before his momentum swung him off his feet, but the sword arced through the air. It nicked the mercenary's neck and the tip cut a gash in his windpipe.

The Red Child regained his balance and looked up at his victim who grabbed his throat as air wheezed from it. A small trickle of blood seeped through his fingers as his face paled.

'Come on,' Richard said again, but the Red Child gazed intently at the dying man.

'Henry,' Richard shouted.

The boy jumped on the spot, pulled his eyes from the blood as the mercenary fell to his knees, and ran.

'Like father, like son,' Bowman spun his horse around and didn't wait for Richard to follow him.

The blue roan tried to attack the nearest mercenary with his gnashing teeth, his aggression intimidating the crowd as they sprung back from him. Richard coaxed him away and pulled the Red Child up onto his horse. As he went he glimpsed Nicola's eyes under her canvas cover, watching everything, but the cover fell as the blue roan cantered down the road, leaving behind nothing but a cloud of dust and a dying mercenary.

Richard only caught up with everyone else after the camp was safely behind them. The sun peeked through the trees ahead, birds cawed, and the horses cleared their airways with loud snorts once they returned to a walk. Richard worried the mercenaries would chase them and kept checking over his shoulder.

Richard didn't tell anyone what had happened after they'd left, and Bowman for once kept quiet. The Red Child almost never spoke anyway, so they simply continued east in the direction of Cailly as the sun rose before them. Bowman rode ahead alone to check no Tancarville army sat outside Cailly, but he returned only a short time later to declare their path was clear. Richard didn't mind riding in silence, his eyes were heavy, and he was tired of eventful journeys.

Cailly looked much like any other Norman settlement. Three times as large as Yvetot had been, the village almost could be called a town. Fields stretched out for some distance on three sides, split by a modest but fresh river. A mound rose from the earth at the far end of the village, a square stone keep proudly perched at its summit, the highest point in the local landscape.

The horses clattered over the wooden bridge that crossed a wide ditch to enter the streets, a ditch that ringed the entire village. Behind the ditch a palisade lay under construction, piles of tree trunks cleared of their branches waited to be added to its length, and although early in the morning, a work party stood hammering fresh trunks into the defence. A makeshift wooden barrier made from the trunk of a huge old tree blocked the road, but was pulled out of the way when they neared. Richard noticed a bucket of twisted iron caltrops next to the road too, which sent a shiver up his spine.

The church and the castle nearby were made from flints set into mortar, the church a large one with an impressive rounded apse at the far end.

The castle had an equally impressive stone wall around the base of its mound, and another ditch with a wooden wall outside of that.

'I'd wager they're expecting the Tancarvilles,' Bowman watched some villagers stacking up more cut wood by the entrance to the castle.

Richard nodded. 'At least Sancho's mercenaries probably don't have the stomach to attack here if they didn't even want to fight the four of us.'

Bowman looked pleased with himself. 'They were bullies, you just have to know how to treat them.'

'You would know,' Richard grinned.

The blonde man glanced down at the Red Child who still rode on the rump of Richard's horse. 'I think he understands.'

Richard didn't doubt that, but he also didn't want Sophie to know what the child had done. 'We'll never speak of that again.' He turned back to Maynard, who now walked gingerly due to his lack of a horse. 'Which way is Yquebeuf from here?'

The squire scanned around the houses of Cailly. He inspected the keep that rose above them and pointed in a general easterly direction. 'Over there.'

Richard frowned. 'Do you even know where your home is from here?'

'I do,' Maynard kept pointing, 'it's over there.'

'He's useless,' Bowman said, 'I think Adam must have kept him as a fool for entertainment.'

'He's not very entertaining though,' Richard said.

'That's enough,' Sophie said, 'we've all been through a lot, there's no use in mocking the poor boy.'

Gerold's horse walked into the back of Sophie's and the old knight wobbled in the saddle.

Maynard dropped Solis's rope and dashed over just in time to catch the knight as he slipped unconsciously towards the ground. The squire saved Gerold's head from colliding with the earth and then tried to pick him up.

'You're not strong enough to lift him,' Richard swung himself off his horse. He left the Red Child onboard and handed him the reins. 'He stops if you whistle,' he said, before running over to help Maynard.

The two of them took Gerold between them and carried him to the gate in the castle's outer wall.

A pair of crossbowmen considered the party for a moment, but had seen Gerold's fall and opened the gate.

'They should at least ask who we are,' Bowman rode in behind Richard, towing Gerold's horse by its reins.

The outer bailey had little open space, crammed full as it was by store buildings and stables, but in that area Sir Roger de Cailly stood and instructed his freemen in the art of war.

A pair of straw butts stood at the far end and a cluster of crossbowmen took it in turns to shoot at them. De Cailly himself waved a short stick in the air and barked orders at two dozen men with shields and spears who stood in two lines facing each other. Most had leather caps on their heads and fabric tunics to protect them, but one or two had leather armour strapped over the top of those.

De Cailly turned around when he heard hooves from his gate, and he squinted for a moment at Richard before his eyes widened. 'My boy,' he shouted and left his men to train without him.

'What is wrong with him?' de Cailly considered Gerold's limp body.

'He's sick,' Richard said.

'He looks almost as bad as you,' de Cailly grinned, his modest hunchback ever so slightly more pronounced than the last time Richard had seen it. 'What happened to your ear?'

'Eustace Martel.'

De Cailly swept back his dark hair and nodded. 'I heard about that. Something about him being beaten to death with his own jawbone?'

'Not quite,' Richard tilted his head towards Gerold. 'Do you have someone who can look after him? He's been ill for weeks.'

The Lord of Cailly shouted some orders and two young men relieved Richard and Maynard of their charge. A pair of older boys took all their horses and stabled them, before coming back with a large pewter flagon containing some very welcome wine.

Richard let some of the wine bring him back to life before Bowman drained the rest.

De Cailly glanced from face to face. 'These are all your people, Richard, why are they all here? Who is looking after Yvetot?'

Richard's face darkened, and the freshness of the wine was forgotten. He told the man who had knighted him and granted him Yvetot to begin with of its fate. Richard told him everything else too, although he left out Ireland entirely, as well as the matter of Eustace's jawbone. He also didn't mention Bowman's ill-aimed crossbow bolt.

'You should tell that to a singer,' de Cailly shook his head slowly, 'it is quite a tale.'

Brian rubbed his inner thighs and stretched his back out. 'I've told him that,' the monk said, 'but I'd like to write it all down.'

'Writing a story down kills it,' de Cailly said, 'but it is better than losing it forever.'

His blue banner, the one with the green top and yellow line through the middle, fluttered briefly in the gentle breeze. The knight sighed. 'I cannot believe all those villagers I sent you are gone.'

Richard shrugged. 'I never got to know them. I'm more concerned that we have nowhere else to go now, that's why we're here.'

'It is foul news you bring,' de Cailly said.

A crossbow bolt whistled past the butt and struck a house beyond, causing a ripple of laughter and insults to echo around the bailey. De Cailly spun around. 'Do you think this is a laughing matter? If he misses a Tancarville knight riding towards you, are you going to laugh then?'

The practising men looked at their toes and shook their heads.

'Well, keep trying until you can't miss,' de Cailly roared, 'then run around the bailey between each shot.'

'Why?' Maynard asked.

The lord gave him a passing glance for a moment before moving on to Richard. 'Since when do you have a squire?'

'I don't,' Richard replied. 'But I have some bad news to tell you about Adam.'

'Adam?'

'From Yquebeuf,' Richard said, 'he died at Corbie, and Maynard here was his squire. He followed us home.'

'You make him sound like a dog,' de Cailly said.

'Do you know him?' Richard asked.

De Cailly shifted his eyes back to the spindly squire. Then he shrugged. 'No.'

'Really,' Richard mumbled. 'I was hoping you would have him back, I have no need of a squire. I can hardly afford one.'

'What happened to Adam?' de Cailly asked.

Richard told him, but he left out the shameful false accusation Adam had made of the Marshal.

De Cailly closed his eyes for a moment. 'A loss for us all,' he said, 'he was a reliable man.'

'Can Maynard serve the new lord of Yquebeuf?' Richard asked.

'I wish to serve you,' Maynard said.

'So you keep saying, but your place is here,' Richard said, 'or at least in Yquebeuf.'

'That may be a problem,' De Cailly frowned. 'That is where the Tancarvilles went after they left Neufchatel.'

Richard wasn't surprised, but he felt exposed knowing the Little Lord might lurk nearby. 'How far away is the village from here?'

'You can reach it in a gallop before your horse even warms up,' de Cailly said. 'That's why these men are so hard at work.'

'At Neufchatel we heard Lord Tancarville had a feud with you,' Richard said, 'I didn't expect it to turn this violent.'

'It turned violent long before that,' de Cailly beckoned everyone to follow him towards his keep and the mound it stood atop.

Richard followed him up the steep slope to where the breeze strengthened from the height and the air flowed more freshly. De Cailly stopped at the entrance to the stone keep and motioned everyone other than Richard inside.

'I have spoken to few people about it,' de Cailly said once they were alone, 'but I know you share my enmity of the Little Lord.'

'We have heard stories about him,' Richard said, 'has he done something to you?'

'I heard what he tried to do to your wife,' de Cailly said, 'how is she?'

'Better than him,' Richard half-drew the Little Lord's sword and held the hilt up. 'I took this from him on the day Sophie took something else.'

'Praise the Lord,' de Cailly's face remained set like stone. 'Rarely do evil men taste justice in this life, but a more fitting punishment couldn't be designed.'

'I remember when he stormed off across Castle Tancarville to assault your daughter.'

The old knight looked away and rubbed his cheek. He turned back to Richard and met his gaze. 'Your rude friend stopped him doing what he intended, and I will always be grateful for that. But it only gained her a year's respite from that monster.'

Richard felt a sinking feeling in his stomach. 'We heard a story about the Little Lord and a killing.'

De Cailly gulped, and his stony face cracked apart. 'It is true.'

The wind whistled through Richard's hair as they looked out over Cailly and its endless fields.

'She's gone,' De Cailly sniffed, but his eyes remained mostly dry. Richard wondered if the tears were long dried up.

'I'm sorry,' Richard searched for more words but only found a memory of Matilda, from long ago, back before he understood the world.

'I will kill him,' de Cailly said without emotion.

'Someone needs to,' Richard said, 'while he lives my wife is in danger. So are my children.'

'Matilda was my only child. Lord Tancarville should have taught his son better. Should have corrected him. Should have made him a man. Now it is too late.'

'I couldn't agree more,' Richard said, 'but what about his father? He has a hundred knights. You have some crossbowmen whose aim is worse than mine. If you kill his son, he'll kill you.'

'I'm old enough,' de Cailly contemplated his village from their high vantage point, 'and I can only die the once. Lord Tancarville will indeed kill me, but he is too angry a man to prolong the agony.'

'The Little Lord isn't worth dying for,' Richard said, 'it sounds like you need something worth living for.'

'You're supposed to be the young knight, and I the one giving advice.'

'You aren't even that old,' Richard grinned.

'I feel that old,' de Cailly let out a deep breath and thought for a moment. 'And my age has made me think of defending these walls rather than reclaiming Yquebeuf. It is my village and I should defend it, it is my duty.'

'How many knights do you have?' Richard asked. 'To fight Lord Tancarville's hundred.'

'He had fewer than that with him at Neufchatel,' de Cailly said, 'and they are not all here now.'

'Who leads them?'

'The Little Lord.'

Richard's pulse quickened. 'How many mounted men do you have?'

De Cailly shrugged. 'Maybe ten.'

'You have two more knights now,' he said, 'and my other two men.'

'You'd join us to break the siege?' de Cailly asked.

Richard nodded. 'If Lord Tancarville is not there, this could be my only chance to get rid of his son.'

'You seek death eagerly,' de Cailly frowned, 'you used to avoid it.'

'I avoid it when I can,' Richard remembered letting men go who he could have killed, 'but if the Little Lord was dead and his father appeased, I might return to Yvetot in safety.'

'You wish to appease Lord Tancarville? That man has never been appeased in his life,' de Cailly said.

'I heard he favours his next son, Raoul,' Richard said, 'I imagine he sees the Little Lord as nothing but an embarrassment. He might look the other way.'

'That would be a brave roll of the dice.'

'It's the only one I have left.'

'I could give you another option,' de Cailly almost smiled.

'You'd grant me another village after what happened to Yvetot?' Richard frowned.

'If you help me save Yquebeuf from being destroyed, you can have it.'

Richard closed his eyes for a moment in a slow, resigned blink. 'I really don't know if I'm cut out to rule land. Every single thing I did in Yvetot went wrong. You gave me a small village and I left it a smoking ruin with only a miller left alive.'

'That was not your doing,' de Cailly said, 'lords cannot always stay at home. Until my rift with Lord Tancarville, I almost never spent a night here.'

'I don't think I can accept the village, Sir Roger, but I will help you save it.'

'Give me an answer if we succeed,' de Cailly ran his fingers around the disc pommel of his sword. 'One last battle for me, then. If I die, you can have Cailly, too.'

'I don't want Cailly,' Richard said, 'and Cailly won't want me. Besides, who do you hold Cailly from?'

'Lord Tancarville,' the old knight grimaced, 'so my refusal to leave here or Yquebeuf at his command is unlawful.'

'But he fights under the Young King's banner,' Richard said, 'which is a banner of rebellion. King Henry would view your defiance as you being loyal to the rightful crown.'

'What does that matter to me? It changes nothing here.'

'It matters if the Young King fails.'

De Cailly turned to Richard. 'I thought he was your lord? After you lost a man defending him.'

Richard shook his head. 'I serve neither king.'

'That really is treason,' de Cailly grinned.

'I just need to find a way for my family to be safe. Perhaps I could live here if the Little Lord wasn't alive to menace us.'

'That's my boy,' de Cailly said, 'let us prepare a force. We can march to Yquebeuf tomorrow morning before dawn. Scout the Tancarville camp and their strength.'

'Leave a garrison here,' Richard said, 'we met some of the Young King's mercenaries on the road not far from here.'

'They rode by yesterday,' de Cailly said, 'they circled the village twice but didn't try to force the ditch. We faced them with shields, spears, and crossbows. Men who fight for coin are cowards.'

Richard scratched his chin. 'Usually,' he said. 'Their leader was a coward though, or at least a bully.'

'Probably both,' de Cailly nodded and put a hand on Richard's shoulder, 'but he will not return here tomorrow, so we will take almost everyone who can fight with us. If we strike quickly, we can catch the Little Lord unawares.'

'We still might not have the strength to defeat them,' Richard said.

'We don't need to defeat them,' a twinkle shone in de Cailly's eye, 'we just need to kill the Little Lord.'

DEATH SQUAD

Richard confiscated the Red Child's sword before they left. He also found a man in Cailly who could repair his perished sole while he had time. The man lived in the poorest corner of the village, for the trade of repairing shoes was considered a low one. The cobblers who moulded and formed new leather into shoes lived in a more well-to-do area, but Richard didn't want to spend any of his tournament pay on anything other than food unless he had no choice.

Sophie hugged him as he walked out of the castle and descended the mound in the cold dawn.

'Finish what I started,' she said and closed his hands around Sir John's dagger. Richard nodded and wondered how such a caring mother could turn to such thoughts. Then he remembered the sight of her back in Yvetot, after the Little Lord had tried to force himself on her. Such wounds do not heal.

Richard had expected Sarjeant to accompany them on their attack, but the twins clung onto his legs and Richard had given in and left him behind. He left Solis behind too, the stallion belted the stable door with his front legs as Richard mounted the blue roan. He gave Brian instructions to care for the horses, Gerold, and his family, then left Cailly along with its fighting men.

Just over the boundary ditch, the blue roan almost trod on a toad that crossed the road.

'That's good luck,' Bowman said, 'at least because you didn't kill it.'

'We need luck,' Richard shifted his new blue, green, and yellow shield around to his front and adjusted the grip on his fresh lance.

Maynard wore a new leather breastplate, commandeered from a very grumpy spearman, and rode behind Richard with a beaming smile. De Cailly rode ahead of his modest column of infantry, and it wasn't long before he stopped and studied the surrounding terrain. The road to Yquebeuf barely deserved the name. It was little more than a track worn into the earth by the wheels of carts. But not that many carts, and grass grew knee high between the ruts, while tall trees leant over the track as if trying to reclaim it. Richard only just fit under their thin limbs. The foliage around them was still dense despite the falling of leaves, and a light coating of them, yellow and crispy orange, covered the ground and obscured the ruts.

'This is the perfect place for the ambush,' de Cailly said, 'the crossbowmen can stand here in the road and shoot up to that next bend. The spearmen can hide in the trees by the bend, and when the enemy stops to consider their next move, they shall fall on them.'

Richard followed de Cailly as he left the infantry to take their positions and led the mounted men further along the track. Only a dozen strong, their company followed it until they reached a clearing. Stumps dotted the open space and a charcoal burner's house stood in the very centre, grey smoke billowing from a great mound of earth nearby.

De Cailly pointed to the far end of the clearing. 'This looks just like the place you became a man,' he winked at Richard.

Richard remembered the incident only shrouded by a fog in his mind. 'What are we doing?' he asked.

'We shall ride around the village so we can inspect the situation without being noticed. They may have lookouts watching the road, but they will expect no one riding in from any other direction.'

That sounded sensible enough, so Richard followed the old knight as he picked his way through the stumps and back into more woodland. Branches closed in, and with the lack of road stunting their progress, the sun had risen long before they saw daylight through the trunks ahead of them. Maynard's face sported a red cut along his cheek from an unnoticed branch, and the horses snorted with the exertion of actually having to look where they placed their hooves. The cracking of branches and the crinkling of fallen leaves heralded their arrival at the edge of the wood, but luckily there was no one there to hear it.

The siege they found was a loose affair. Yquebeuf had only a dozen wooden houses and a long wooden hall instead of a castle. A wooden fence ran from one house to another, including the hall, to create a boundary wall. The single gate was resolutely shut, and Bowman told everyone who couldn't see them, that two archers stood on top of the wall.

'It's not a true wall,' de Cailly said, 'it only has a few platforms for them to stand on dotted around it. There are only twenty men inside, but they all have spears or bows.'

Pasture held in common, enclosed by hedges and the occasional wooden fence, occupied most of the land outside the village. A herd of cattle lay resting in one corner, the bells on two of them ringing when they shook their heads to free themselves from flies.

Only a few long fingers of fields lay in view, but of most interest was the camp pitched in the very centre of the pasture. Two red painted tents marked out the middle of the Tancarville encampment, with a few dozen low-lying canvas shelters surrounding them. Many shelters were draped between dozens of carts, and the smoke from many fires curled up lazily through the morning air.

'There's not a lot of movement,' Bowman said.

'They've been here a few days now,' de Cailly said, 'the novelty of this siege has worn off.'

'And they came straight from another one,' Richard said, 'although that wasn't so boring.'

A hundred horses, hobbled with either leather or rope tying their front legs closely together, grazed loosely off to one side of the camp. They were spread out over a large area and in a few distinct groups.

'I can see the blue and yellow diagonal stripes of Sir John,' de Cailly said.

'There's only two or three other banners,' Bowman said, 'this might actually work.'

'Although there will be plenty of men under those shelters,' de Cailly said, 'and they'll have spears and crossbows.'

Richard counted horses. 'Everyone here has a horse, even the infantry must have ridden here.'

De Cailly nodded. 'As is known to be best.'

Maynard grunted in agreement, but at least he'd been lent a young horse for the attack so his sore feet could be rested.

'We can't assault the camp,' de Cailly said. 'There are too few of us. They only need to pick up a spear or slide a bolt into a grove in order to be ready for us, and we cannot cover this ground fast enough to surprise them.'

'Then we move them from their camp,' Richard said.

De Cailly raised his eyebrows. 'Has someone given you a copy of Vegetius? I remember you liked your books.'

'No,' Richard said, 'but we can make them leave their camp.'

'And how would we do that? They have everything they need there.'

A large tree had been dragged into the camp, and two men with large axes began their day's work of chopping the branches off it. They were making a battering ram.

'Not everything they need is inside,' Richard said, 'their horses aren't.'

'We can't steal their horses,' de Cailly said, 'with hobbles they won't outpace a walking man. Most of them, at least, we've all seen a horse in hobbles jump or canter despite them, but most won't.'

'We don't need to steal them, just scatter them,' Richard grinned. 'We have a dozen mounted men here, if we gallop into that pasture we'll send horses hobbling in all directions. The enemy can either send men out to recover them, or face the prospect of walking all the way back to Castle Tancarville.'

'They won't like that,' Maynard shook his head and his feet twitched.

'We can kill some of the men they send out to search,' Richard said, 'and make the rest so miserable that they leave.'

De Cailly nodded. 'That would drive them into our trap back on the road.'

Bowman coughed. 'You placed them there without knowing how we'd funnel them back?'

'You really are the rudest knight I've ever met,' de Cailly replied, 'and when exactly did you win your golden spurs?'

'So when these Tancarville men flee into your ambush,' Bowman said, 'we'll ride into the back of them?'

'Don't avoid my question,' de Cailly turned to Richard, 'but we should move quickly, the earlier we do this, the less awake they shall be.'

'The horses are in three herds, if we split ourselves into three we can scatter them all,' Richard said, 'push them into the treeline beyond, then they'll be impossible to recover quickly.'

'My boy,' de Cailly smiled and the sun caught his dark hair, 'you may become a leader of men on the battlefield, if nowhere else.'

'Don't be so sure,' Bowman said, 'he messed it up last time.'

'That's not fair,' Richard said, 'we did our bit outside Corbie on the Amiens Road. And we'll do it here.'

'Hopefully this goes better,' Bowman pressed his lips together.

'If they flee today,' de Cailly said, 'we charge into the back of them as they are ambushed by my infantry. We all make for the red Tancarville banner and cut down that little turd. If we kill him, I'll win enough arms and armour to defend Cailly against Tancarville himself.'

Bowman picked his lance up and rested it on his foot. 'So we're a death squad.'

De Cailly nodded. 'The story of King William's death squad at Senlac Hill is more famous than ours shall ever be, but pray we can match his success.'

Richard licked his cracked lips. He'd look for the red Tancarville banner with the silver shield once the grazing horses were scattered. Then he'd end the danger to his family once and for all.

They charged. The blue roan grunted with the effort of launching its barrel-like body into a canter, and when he lowered his big black head and accelerated into a gallop, the pasture flew by beneath him so fast the ground smudged into a green blur. His iron-shod hooves drove into the soft earth and trampled long grass. His stride was longer and slower than Solis, but he covered the ground far quicker.

Bowman and Maynard flanked him, but both were left behind by the charging Italian warhorse as he surged across the pasture and towards one of the loose herds of hobbled horses.

Shouts burst from the camp, but Richard kept his eyes on the ground, searching for holes or old fencing, anything he might need to avoid riding over. The crossbowmen in the camp fumbled for their weapons, but by the time they found positions to shoot, de Cailly's men were long gone, fanned out and nothing more than specks in the distance.

Richard aimed the blue roan at the centre of his target herd by pushing his hips in that direction. The warhorse shifted his course effortlessly and Richard thought the animal was enjoying himself.

The horses grazing ahead thrust their heads up into the air and searched for the source of the sound that thundered towards them. Some had learnt to move quickly with both front legs acting as one, and they made for the trees behind them quicker than Richard expected. The rest had to shuffle as fast as their restraints allowed, and Richard had to pull his warhorse away from one startled horse before the blue roan flattened it. He gathered the stallion up and halted him. Horses spread out from him like the ripples from a stone thrown into a lake, and just as he'd planned, most headed for the trees.

Bowman's black horse puffed as it reached the blue roan, who arched his neck and bellowed a great snort to welcome it. 'So far so good, young lord,' Bowman grinned.

Richard swallowed a breath. 'I enjoyed that, we haven't been able to flat out race for months.'

'Years,' Bowman said.

Maynard arrived on his borrowed horse, then left again as he failed to stop it.

'He'll never be a knight,' Bowman said.

'I know, but I don't know how to tell him,' Richard turned to look back towards the camp.

De Cailly and five of his knights scattered the second herd into the trees, and a short time later the last division of the small company dispersed the final collection of horses in the pasture.

'There's movement in the camp,' Bowman squinted at it, 'but I can't see what they're doing.'

'We should push the rest of these horses into the woods, then hide inside it,' Richard said.

'The squire is already there,' Bowman nodded towards the wood, through which the sound of snapping branches echoed out of a horse-shaped gap in the foliage.

'Maybe he'll go back to walking after this,' Richard grinned and rode with Bowman to the treeline.

The less startled hobbled horses took to eating the bushes and trees as soon as they reached them, while some of the more inquisitive pushed their way deeper into the dense woodland and disappeared from view. Richard rode in where Maynard had gone and called his name. There was no reply.

'He'll come back eventually,' Bowman said, 'and if he doesn't, I won't mourn him.'

They waited at the edge of the trees, trying to make out the movement from the camp ahead, which was so far away it appeared only as a thick black line on the horizon.

Bowman yawned after a while of uneventful waiting.

'Don't fall asleep,' Richard said, 'we'll see men soon.'

'How are you so sure they'll just run after their horses without thinking of themselves?' Bowman asked. 'They saw us riding, they know we're here, and they'll also know we are a threat.'

'They only know we rode this way,' Richard said, 'they'll think we stole their horses and are long gone. The Tancarvilles are sure to come and try to recover the horses we haven't rustled.'

'Then why didn't we just steal the horses for real?' Bowman asked. 'Just twenty of these would be worth a fortune.'

'That's not what we're here for,' Richard said.

'When we go looking for money, we find fighting,' Bowman said, 'and now you go looking for a fight, we find money and have to give it up. How is that fair?'

'Don't sulk,' Richard said, 'nothing's fair. If things were fair, Yvetot would still stand and I wouldn't be hunting the Little Lord.'

'How sure are you that you're the hunter?'

'We are in a death squad,' Richard said, 'I think that makes us the hunters.'

'No,' Bowman nodded towards the camp, 'I think they're the hunters.'

Richard fought to focus his eyes across the pasture, but at first saw nothing new. Then the black line grew thick and wobbled. Soon it drew into view as a line of men marching in close order.

'There goes your plan, young lord,' Bowman said, 'what now?'

'We didn't expect this,' Richard looked far to his right where de Cailly was also hidden in the woods. But he couldn't see him and had no way of knowing what the Lord of Cailly would do.

'They'll have to split up to reclaim their horses,' Richard said, 'and they can't move through the trees in that formation.'

'We can't charge them either,' Bowman said, 'and the trees are so close together we can't go faster than a walk if we decide to retreat.'

Maynard appeared on foot back through the gap his horse had made in the vegetation. The squire dragged the horse behind him and had to pick his way over a squashed bush and a young tree the horse had snapped in half.

'Took for your time,' the blonde man said without turning to look.

Maynard brushed off twigs and leaves that stuck on his clothing. 'It's a very bad horse.'

'It's never the horse,' Richard said.

'If our plan is to flee through where he's just been,' Bowman said, 'we need to start now.'

Richard swore. 'I can't leave here without at least trying to get to the Little Lord. And we came here to break a siege, not scare off some horses and then run away.'

'You want to charge them?' Bowman asked. 'What if the others don't charge with us? What if the crossbowmen in the Tancarville ranks are better shots than Sir Roger's? They only need three good shots and we're done.'

'I lost my lance,' Maynard tried to remount his horse but it jumped when he put his foot in the stirrup and lurched away from him.

Bowman snorted and shook his head.

The blue roan pawed at the ground but hit a small tree instead. The thin trunk flew away from the hoof that struck it, then sprung back and smacked the horse straight on his nose. He shook his head then kicked out again. Richard had to haul him away. The horse certainly wanted to attack something.

'I'm not here to fight the foliage or run away,' Richard said.

'You've got very little time to come up with a bright idea,' Bowman said, 'their crossbows will reach us before this squire manages to remount.'

Maynard threw himself into the saddle, nearly toppled off, but grabbed the high wooden cantle and dragged himself into position on his unsettled mount.

Richard watched the infantry advance, still surrounded by a sea of grass. 'Can't we just ride around them?'

Bowman thought for a moment. Then he laughed. 'I was just waiting for you to say that,' he said, 'come on.'

The blue roan followed Bowman's horse without being asked.

Bowman aimed to canter around the Tancarville formation, sticking close to the trees to stay out of missile range.

Richard glanced back to ensure the squire was behind them, then followed at a full gallop. The power of the blue roan beneath him astonished Richard, no wonder the Marshal had been loathed to give him up. He snatched a glance over the pasture to where de Cailly had been, and sure enough, he and his horsemen also raced along the edge of the woods trying to skirt the other way around the infantry.

Some crossbowmen took shots at either party, but the bolts flew through the air with little chance of hitting anything.

Richard overtook Bowman, and the camp loomed into view ahead. The enemy infantry were increasingly far behind them, so they had to decide what to do next.

'We can burn the camp,' Bowman shouted over the rushing sound of the air.

'Not if it's defended,' Richard shouted back.

'Let's find out,' the blonde man urged his black horse over the now trampled grassland. If the camp burned to ash, that might throw the enemy back along the track in just as demoralised a state as the loss of their horses would.

Richard eased the pace before they got too close. There was movement within the camp, but no missiles came hurtling through the air towards them.

'They've got spears,' Bowman arrived next to Richard and his horse snorted.

'We've got lances,' Richard shrugged. He checked on the Tancarville infantry behind, but they were now very far away, still much nearer the woods than their camp.

'We don't have long, though,' Bowman said.

Richard took them closer to the camp, close enough that he could see the faces of the spearmen who clustered near the tents at its heart. Both the Tancarville and de la Londe banners swayed in the air above them.

'We can break in there,' Richard gripped his lance and rested it on his thigh.

'Careful now, young lord,' Bowman said, 'let's not rush in, Sir Roger is on his way.'

De Cailly and the rest of his company all joined back together where Richard waited for them. 'Are there any crossbowmen inside?' de Cailly asked, his cheeks red.

Maynard's horse cantered up to the group and he pulled on the reins to stop it. The horse jerked the reins out of his hands and ploughed on towards the camp.

'We're about to find out,' Bowman said, 'at least that squire will be of some use, after all.'

'It's not funny this time,' Richard said, 'we're beyond the time for jokes.' He rode after the squire to rescue him.

Maynard's horse cut left and right between two fires and slammed to a halt when it reached two carts which he declined to jump. Maynard wasn't ready for the sudden halt and fell headfirst down the shoulder of the horse.

Richard stopped in front of the horse just as it thought about running away, but instead it dropped its head and grazed on the flattened grass beneath it.

'Get back on,' Richard looked up and saw the heads of spears bobbing around in the camp, and they were coming his way.

The first enemy to appear didn't wield a spear.

Sir John de la Londe strode around the two carts and pointed his sword at Richard. Maynard jumped to his feet and remounted his horse that was too preoccupied with grazing to protest.

'I have been waiting to meet you again,' Sir John said, 'you have something of mine and I want it back.'

Richard lowered his lance as a deterrent. 'You've only got a sword, and you've got no crossbowmen in this camp. You don't frighten me.'

Sir John stayed where he was. 'I told that young fool not to send them all out after the horses, but he never listens.'

'Why do you serve him?' Richard asked. 'He isn't worth dying for.'

Sir John shook his head. 'But who is worth dying for?'

'Not his father, either,' Richard glared at Maynard to tell him to ride away, but the squire stared dumbfounded at the old knight who faced them.

'His father is a great man, history will at least remember him. And a knight must die for someone,' Sir John took a single step forward.

Maynard snapped out of his fright, turned his horse, and fled away from the advancing knight.

'He disgusts you, doesn't he,' Richard said, 'and you're missing your front teeth because of him.'

'You knocked them out.'

'We only fought because of him,' Richard said. 'I have no quarrel with you.'

'I have my duty,' Sir John batted the end of Richard's lowered lance aside so Richard backed his horse up to maintain the distance.

'Stand aside,' Richard said, 'my argument is with the Little Lord, it is him I seek.'

'And you've found me,' a shrill voice cut through the air above the carts.

Richard spun his horse around and moved it away from Sir John so he could see the Little Lord as he walked through the camp with his red and silver shield covering his body. Richard recognised his short red hair, round face, and broad shoulders, but he now looked closer to Bowman's age than Richard's.

Bowman himself entered the camp and shouted at Richard. 'Get out of there, the spearmen are coming for you.'

He was right, they were just behind the Little Lord. 'How is your little village?' the young Tancarville asked.

'How are things between your legs?' Richard asked back.

Sir John frowned, and Richard knew both he and the Little Lord were being childish.

'My wife survived your attack,' Richard edged his horse sideways away from the spearmen who arrived and flanked their lord. They lowered their weapons but hesitated.

'Your village burned easily,' the Little Lord said, 'as if it beckoned its own destruction.'

Bowman rode closer, between the fires. 'Leave them, young lord,' he shouted.

Richard pointed his lance at the Little Lord. If God favoured his charge, the point of the lance could be the last thing the Little Lord ever saw.

'You won't manage it,' Bowman closed in.

'I'm stronger than I was before,' the Little Lord stepped at Richard.

'Even with parts of you missing?' Bowman couldn't help himself.

The young Tancarville lunged forwards, knocked the lance aside and swung his sword at the blue roan. The horse coiled backwards to avoid it lashed out with his teeth, which made the Little Lord break off his attack. 'You'll die here, Richard,' he snarled, 'then I'll find your family and kill them. They are a stain on Normandy.'

'You're a stain on Normandy,' Richard nodded, 'but I'll fight you. A duel. To the death.'

'Don't agree,' Sir John said to his lord, 'allow me to fight for you.'

'That didn't work before, did it?' the Little Lord sneered at his knight. 'I'll have to do it myself this time. You and me Richard, on foot, now.'

Richard raised his lance.

'Don't even think about it, young lord,' Bowman reached him. 'He's bigger than you, and your anger won't cut through his mail, will it?'

'Let me duel,' Sir John said, 'I'd rather die than continue to live in the shadow of my previous defeat. Men mock me, I know they do. Every time I open my mouth they see my missing teeth and know how it happened. I'll soon be too old to fight anyway, let me reclaim my dagger and my honour.'

The Little Lord stepped back and shot his knight a condescending look. 'This is not about you, old man. Content yourself with serving me. This is about what Richard did to me, he stole my child and my village.'

'Will you kill the child too if you can't have him?' Richard asked.

'He will return to his true father with a glad heart,' the young Tancarville said. 'I will save him from you, you are of the devil.'

'You know that is nonsense as well as I do,' Richard said, 'you were in that chapel too, remember?'

'I was, and I know Sir Roger cooled the iron bar for you.'

'That's blasphemy,' Bowman said, 'can we stop talking now? Young lord, we need to get away from these spears.'

Richard backed his horse away, the blue roan stepped on a fire and swished his tail at its heat. 'Sir Roger did nothing, Our Lord declared my innocence. Do you want me to mention the pottage?'

The Little Lord charged.

'Stop,' Sir John cried, 'Don't be foolish.'

With his horse not moving, his lance would not be of any use against the attacking knight. Richard heaved the animal round on its hind legs and it jumped away from the Little Lord with a single leap, although it stood in the fire in the process.

The young Tancarville realised he couldn't catch a mounted foe and stopped by the fire. 'Charge him,' he ordered the spearmen.

They looked to Sir John, whose shoulders sunk. 'Very well, he is the lord.'

Spearmen poured around the two carts at Richard. Sir John stayed where he was, turned around and trudged back towards the two tents.

'Young lord,' Bowman shouted as he rode out of the camp, 'we aren't going to be alone for long.'

Richard jumped the blue roan over another fire and looked over the pasture to see the main infantry force closing in. 'Where's Sir Roger?'

Bowman pointed his lance back into the camp, where one of the tents collapsed in a creak of timber posts and the flap of falling canvas.

'When did he do that?' Richard asked.

'While you were bickering like a married couple,' Bowman said, 'they're torching the supplies on the carts.'

Richard took a moment to be impressed by de Cailly's initiative. His few knights rode back and forth through the empty part of the camp, with flames taken from the abandoned campfires, and set them onto the canvas covers and carts. Flames grew taller and grey smoke was joined by black plumes from the burning canvas.

The Little Lord ordered his spearmen to protect the camp instead of attacking Richard, so they peeled away and spread out through the encampment. De Cailly's men ranged to and fro, but now played a game of cat and mouse with the spearmen.

'Should we join them?' Bowman asked.

'We're here to do one thing,' Richard said, 'so we should do that.'

'He's still got spearmen around him, you'll get close enough, but you won't get out alive.'

Richard searched for his target through the smoke that grew like a morning mist over the camp. Then he spurred the blue roan towards the Little Lord.

'Don't be foolish,' the blonde man shouted after him, but Richard wasn't listening. He was intent on reaching the Little Lord and striking him down. The fear that dogged his family could end now. The warhorse dashed into the acrid smoke as Richard steeled himself for a final encounter.

Except, after standing on one, the blue roan was now afraid of fire. The horse was startled when the first campfire appeared before him in the smoke and he stopped dead. Richard overbalanced over the front of his saddle and dropped his lance so he could use the hand to hang on. The horse reversed and Richard had to push himself back down into place. Smoke obscured the tents and half the encampment already, and the blue roan snorted at the smoke as it wafted towards him, before he veered away and took Richard from it.

The warhorse stopped by Bowman. 'I see the horse has better sense than you,' the blonde man said.

Richard gulped down some air to catch his breath, but what got his attention was the returning infantry that fanned out across the pasture. 'Are they trying to encircle us?' he asked.

Bowman growled. 'Looks like it. I don't know if they'll manage, but Sir Roger and his men won't know they're about to be caught in the trap.'

'We can escape,' Maynard said.

Richard had forgotten he was there. 'We can't leave Sir Roger, we have to warn him. Although I don't know if my horse will go back into the smoke and flames now.'

'You shouldn't have let him back onto that fire,' Bowman said, 'you've ruined him now.'

'We can argue about that later,' Richard knew his friend was right, 'ride around the camp and find Sir Roger. Bowman, you ride first and maybe mine will follow you.'

The blonde knight's horse obeyed his rapid order to canter around the outside of the camp, through the smoke that drifted out across the pasture, and round to the side closest to the village of Yquebeuf.

De Cailly's few men had been very effective. A dozen blazing carts roared as their wooden frames were eaten by flames, and the provisions inside burned fiercely, each cartload that went up was another few days the besieging force would now be unable to eat.

Bowman threaded his horse past a fire, and the blue roan stayed close behind, although he bent his body away from the heat. The blonde knight led him past a flaming cart and the blue roan refused, spun on the spot, and reared up. Richard lent forwards to avoid pulling him over backwards. 'Go on without me,' he shouted, 'warn Sir Roger.'

Maynard's horse followed Bowman's black one, which left Richard feeling quite alone. He patted his horse and spoke to it softly, but the animal was skittish now, his bravado burned away by his new fear.

Two spearmen appeared and threw buckets of water at the cart, but the water had no effect. One looked over and noticed Richard. He threw the bucket at the blue roan, but it missed and the horse ignored it.

'I won't hurt you,' Richard said, 'just go. Let the cart burn.'

The spearmen exchanged glances and ran off, disappearing into the smoke.

Richard coughed as some of the bitter grey smog wafted over him. His horse twitched under him and Richard decided he needed to get the animal away from the fiery atmosphere.

He rode out of the camp, saw the enemy encircling them were more or less in crossbow range, and cantered toward the village.

De Cailly's men flew out of the devastation they'd caused one at a time. They regrouped in front of the gateway, so Richard made his way to meet them.

Bowman emerged from the chaos with de Cailly.

'We're two men short,' Richard counted.

De Cailly's face was blackened from the polluted air. He glanced back towards the wrecked camp. 'I'm not leaving anyone behind. I know all their families.'

'Look,' Bowman pointed to the billowing wall of smoke that rolled over the green pasture, 'we're about to get shot at.'

Men emerged from the grey wall, and a few raised crossbows and took aim.

De Cailly turned his horse away from them, and towards his intended escape route.

But Tancarville men were marching there as well.

'I'm feeling a little trapped,' Bowman said.

'We can punch through anywhere,' Richard said, 'it's better than standing here and being picked off.'

De Cailly shook his head. 'We'll lose men and horses in a charge, and I don't have any to spare.'

'We can't stay here,' Bowman said.

'No,' de Cailly said, 'we'll go into the village. We've torched all their carts, they will leave today or tomorrow.'

'But we'll be trapped in there,' Bowman said, 'more trapped than we are now.'

De Cailly walked his horse towards Yquebeuf. 'You're welcome to attempt to break out if you wish, but my men are going inside to fight another day.'

'I don't think we have much choice,' Maynard said.

'There's always a choice,' Bowman sighed.

Richard watched de Cailly's men file through the gateway and into temporary safety. 'Follow them,' he said, 'the horses are blown anyway. They need water and a rest.'

Bowman sniffed and coughed as the smoke cloud changed direction and blew over them.

Richard rode through the gate and into the small village. Nervous archers stood on platforms inside the wall, and one ducked when a crossbow bolt smacked into the wooden fence below him.

Richard dismounted and led the blue roan to a trough to stand in a queue beyond the other horses.

The gate was barred behind them, and without thinking too much about it, Richard was again under siege.

De Cailly climbed an archer's platform to look for his missing knights, but none arrived and the gate remained closed.

Richard took the saddle off his horse to give it a rest and waited for something to happen.

The squire in charge of the village spoke to de Cailly, but there was nothing to do until the intention of the Tancarville company outside became clear.

Smoke drifted over the fence and blocked the sun out, which made the air cool so much that Richard shivered.

The new wind direction acted to mask any activity within the encampment. Richard climbed up the wooden ladder onto a platform himself, but all he could see was grey smoke floating over the pasture and into his eyes. It stung. He could hear voices beyond, as well as the crackle of fire, but little else.

Midday came and went before the wind changed and blew the smoke to one side. An archer shouted down that the acrid cloud had cleared, and de Cailly raced up the ladder as if ten years younger to take a look.

'Prepare to leave,' he shouted back into the village.

Richard saddled the blue roan, who had fallen asleep where he stood, and checked Maynard's horse for him.

'Are we leaving?' the squire asked.

Richard nodded.

'What's happening outside?'

'I don't know,' Richard let him be as de Cailly mounted his own horse.

'They have left the camp,' de Cailly said so all could hear, 'we ride to reinforce our ambush.'

Bowman grumbled. 'Let's hope they walked slowly.'

Richard got up into his saddle and followed de Cailly out of the village.

The charred skeletons of carts were still alight, but their contents were ash. All the canvas had been consumed by now too, including both of the two tents. The campfires had largely burned themselves out, but the air was still thick with acrid smoke and the taste of destruction. It reminded Richard of Fallencourt.

De Cailly found one of his missing men dead, his legs charred, his body face down. The lord shook his head and pressed on.

The blue roan spooked at every fire that still flourished, but he walked behind Bowman's horse and soon they crossed through the camp.

'At least we raised the siege,' Maynard said once their hooves were back on unburnt grass.

'We?' Bowman scoffed.

Richard could see horses dotted around the pasture where they'd scattered them earlier. 'We should come back for those,' Richard said. 'They're worth a fortune.'

De Cailly led his company in silence to the track which led to their prepared ambush. The lord broke into a canter, aware that the ambush could already have been sprung, and the company hastened behind him.

It was darker on the track, trees above blocked out the sun and as they raced by, Richard couldn't see far into the undergrowth. Their hooves echoed on the ruts as the horses tried to canter on the best footing, and they rounded bend after bend.

The last bend came and de Cailly darted around it.

He slammed to a halt.

Richard stopped next to him and Maynard once again shot off on his own, his horse dropping its head and racing.

The ambush had already been sprung.

And it had already been broken.

A cluster of bodies covered the track where de Cailly's spearmen had charged the Tancarville force from both sides.

Richard looked down at dozens of fallen Tancarville men, but all of de Cailly's.

'No,' the old knight whispered, 'no.'

'They took many with them,' Bowman said, 'more than they lost.'

Further up the track lay a pile of Tancarville spearmen bristling with bolts, the fletchings protruding from their chests and shields.

'The crossbowmen shot and ran,' the blonde man said, watching Maynard's horse jump the pile of bodies and disappear towards Cailly.

'He's going to run into the back of the enemy,' Richard said.

'You can't help him now,' Bowman shrugged. 'And we can't help these men, either.'

A tear ran down De Cailly's black cheek, cleaning a trail through the dust as it went. 'What do I tell their families? That man was Tancred, and there Luc, they were brothers. Their father fixed your sole yesterday, Richard. How do I tell him of this?'

Richard had no answer. 'We should get back to Cailly,' he said.

'They will not siege it,' de Cailly said, 'they have no supplies.'

'No,' Richard said, 'but we also left but a few men to hold the gates.'

De Cailly's face whitened. 'Ride,' he said, 'ride fast.'

Richard didn't need telling twice, because his family was in the castle. The blue roan jumped over the pile of bodies as Maynard's horse had done, and he cantered hard the rest of the short distance to Cailly.

Where they arrived too late.

CHILDREN

A crossbow bolt spiralled through the air from Cailly's gateway before the defenders realised who approached.

De Cailly's horse foamed around its saddle and frothed at the mouth as it halted at the bridge over the boundary ditch. The nervous looking crossbowmen who guarded it lowered their weapons and braced for a telling off.

'I hope your eager lever fingers kept the Tancarvilles out?' de Cailly shouted at them. His horse stamped on the wooden bridge so hard one of the thick planks bent in the middle.

'The walked around us,' the bravest crossbowman said, 'they only had a few horses.'

'I know,' de Cailly said, 'you can thank us for that.'

A sigh of relief escaped Richard's lips. He'd been holding himself in tension because he worried the Tancarville force was easily big enough to force its way into Cailly.

De Cailly relaxed in his saddle and looked to the sky, which was absent of smoke and flame. 'Praise the Lord.'

The brave crossbowman bit his lip and looked at his fellows. One of them nodded at him and another shrugged.

'Yes?' de Cailly walked his horse up to them and peered down its shoulder at them.

'The ones with horses went around,' the brave crossbowman said.

Richard looked up to the keep on its mound, but no flames poured from its roof or windows. The church bells weren't ringing and no dogs barked.

'Did they get in?' de Cailly asked.

'Not into the castle,' the crossbowman said.

'Good,' de Cailly nodded, 'are they gone? Did they kill anyone?'

The crossbowman swallowed. 'They are gone, my lord.'

'Did they kill anyone?'

Richard rode the blue roan onto the bridge, which creaked under its bulk.

The brave crossbowman turned to face him. 'They didn't kill anyone,' he said, 'but they took some people who were near the village gate when they broke in.'

'How did they break in?' de Cailly's voice rose.

'They rode round to the northwest bridge. Only a few of them had horses.'

'Yes, yes, you've said that,' de Cailly pushed through them.

'Tell him,' one of the crossbowmen hissed to the brave one.

They both had their eyes on Richard. 'Tell me what?' he asked.

Another crossbowman elbowed his comrade. 'He's going to find out.'

Richard's pulse quickened.

De Cailly entered his village and turned back. 'Spit it out, man.'

'The Tancarvilles didn't kill anyone,' the brave crossbowman wilted under their attention, 'but they did take someone.'

'Who?' Richard asked.

The crossbowman's face had pity in it. 'Your wife, sir.'

'My what?' Richard choked on the words.

Bowman crossed the bridge, his horse's head hung low and its hooves almost dragged along the planks. 'Sophie?'

The crossbowman shrugged. 'We don't know her name.'

Richard felt a pit open up beneath him. 'But they didn't kill her?'

'A Tancarville knight with blue and yellow diagonal stripes punched another one when he tried to.'

'What colours had the knight who tried to kill Lady Sophie?' de Cailly asked.

The crossbowman conferred with his companions. 'We think it was the Tancarville colours themselves.'

'The Little Lord,' Richard said under his breath. 'I'll kill him.'

'See to your children first,' Bowman said, 'let's not make any hasty moves while you're angry.'

The brave crossbowman raised his hand and then snatched it down.

'You have to tell him,' one of his colleagues said.

Richard's eyes, wide with anger, glanced down at the fidgeting bridge guards. 'Tell me what?'

'They didn't just take your wife,' the brave crossbowman took a step back.

'Did they take my children?'

The crossbowman turned his weapon over in his hands. 'Two of them.'

'The twins?'

'The younger pair,' the guard nodded, 'the one with the foul face is still in the castle.'

'You can't say foul face in front of his father,' another crossbowman elbowed him.

Bowman raised his eyebrows. 'You're not wrong about the face. Did they take anyone else?'

All the crossbowmen shook their heads.

'Come, Richard,' de Cailly said, 'see to your other child and we shall discuss our options.'

Richard walked on over the creaking bridge and into the sprawling village. 'We only have one option. I'm going to kill him. I'm going to follow him back to Castle Tancarville, rescue my wife, and kill him.'

De Cailly stood still as Richard rode past. 'I remember when I punched the Little Lord, I rather enjoyed it. Although I cannot remember why anymore.'

'Don't think about it too hard,' Bowman reached him, 'no need to remember.'

De Cailly wrinkled his face. 'It was gold, wasn't it?'

Maynard followed the blonde knight. 'Gold? Why does everyone keep talking about gold or silver around us?'

'I said don't think too hard on it,' Bowman growled at him.

Richard left them to it and thundered through the village and into the castle. He found Sarjeant and Brian leaning on Solis's stable door, and they both turned to face him when his warhorse clattered into the bailey. Neither looked happy.

The former Templar pressed his hands together and held them up to the sky. 'Thank you Lord,' he said, 'I knew so much ill fortune could not be heaped upon us in one day.'

Richard jumped down from his horse, which snorted at Solis. 'What happened?' he asked.

'The wheel of fortune must surely be at its lowest point,' Sarjeant continued, 'the only way must assuredly be up.'

'What happened?'

Sarjeant lowered his hands. 'The twins wanted to walk around the village. Cailly is the largest settlement they have ever seen. They were in the wrong place at the wrong time.'

'The Red Child is only safe,' Richard said, 'because Sophie won't have wanted his company.'

'Yes,' Sarjeant replied, 'he is in the keep. I must say, this is all very confusing for him.'

'It's confusing for me,' Brian said. 'When the church bells rang, I wondered what fresh misery could be about to befall us.'

'Well, you have your answer,' Richard said.

'What do we do?' Sarjeant asked.

Richard shook his head. 'They aren't going to give her back, are they?'

Sarjeant winced and shook his head back in reply. 'I'm sorry I wasn't there for them.'

'It's not your fault,' Richard said, 'it's the guard's fault for not blocking the entrance, or my fault for leaving them here in the first place.'

'Don't blame yourself,' Brian said.

'If you say it was God's will,' Richard raised his voice, then regretted it. Brian frowned.

'I'm sorry,' Richard said. 'I didn't want any of this. I just wanted to go home and sit by my own fire.'

'What will we do now?' Brian asked.

'Now?' Richard sighed. 'What we always do. Try to protect someone we care about and try to avoid dying in the process.'

Bowman arrived and dismounted with a dark look on his face. 'We need to start getting better at that last part.'

'If you have any bright ideas, then we're listening,' Richard said.

The blonde man patted his exhausted horse as it drank from a wooden trough. 'You can't talk your way out of trouble here, young lord,' he said, 'we'll have to use violence or cunning, but either way we're going to Castle Tancarville.'

De Cailly led his surviving men back into his castle. 'We cannot lay siege to Castle Tancarville, it is impregnable,' the lord of Cailly said. 'You know that. Besides, they left Cailly intact so I must continue to defend it. The Chamberlain could even return with those mercenaries to wreak revenge on us.'

'I'm not asking you to come and help us,' Richard said, 'you don't exactly have an army here.'

'My heart aches for you,' de Cailly said, 'and I wish I could do more.'

Richard handed his horse to Maynard to put away. 'You have done enough for me, and you should ensure Cailly isn't raised to the ground as Yvetot was.'

'We shall round up the horses by Yquebeuf, and with the proceeds of their sale I can hire enough mercenaries of my own to man my walls for a while. My offer to you to become the lord of Yquebeuf still stands.'

Bowman's shoulders slumped. 'I'll follow you anywhere, young lord, except to be lord of that place. I'm not living in a village I cannot pronounce.'

'I can't think about it now,' Richard said, 'I need to get my family back before the Little Lord kills them.'

'Sir John prevented him from doing so here,' de Cailly said, 'and I believe his father will forbid it in his castle. Lord Tancarville is an angry man, but he sees himself as righteous. You, on the other hand, he may not be so lenient with.'

'I'll take my chances, we need to leave as soon as the horses have recovered enough to travel,' Richard said.

'What will you do? The walls cannot be forced.'

'We will find a way into the castle,' Richard said, 'this time I think we'll have to use our heads.'

'Of course,' de Cailly said, 'take anything you need with you.'

Richard pleaded with his eyes. 'Maybe a few spare horses? Then we can leave right away. We might even catch up with them on the road.'

The Lord of Cailly managed a grin. 'They are a gift to you, we shall soon overflow with horses.'

'We'll have to find a small one for the Red Child, he'll just have to learn to ride,' Richard said.

De Cailly stretched himself out, and his hunchback almost disappeared. 'The kindness you show that child astonishes me,' he said, 'many others would have left him in the woods at dusk on a frozen winter's night.'

'He is still of Sophie's blood, and officially the King's bastard. I can't kill the son of the King.' Richard waited for a joke about killing kings, but none came.

'But he isn't actually the son of the King, is he?' De Cailly replied.

Richard shook his head. 'I'm beginning to learn that the truth means little, it is only perception that matters. Would you foster him or Alexander in a year or two when they reach the proper age?'

'Indeed,' de Cailly said, 'although I would prefer not to have the Red Child as my ward. That might invite too much unwanted attention from Castle Tancarville.'

Richard wondered if the Red Child would ever be wanted by anyone. 'Thank you,' he replied.

Brian's fingers played with the cross that hung around his head. 'I heard stories about Lord Tancarville at Corbie. The monks said he's a murderer.'

Bowman's dark face cleared and he laughed while looking at Richard out of the corner of his eye.

'I wouldn't worry about that,' Richard said, 'it was just another argument with a nobleman that went wrong.'

'No,' Brian said, 'they said he had an English devil throw a monk from a tower.'

Richard's face dropped.

Bowmen kept laughing and had to wipe a tear from his eye. 'Trust me, Irish monk, you don't need to worry about the man who did that, you're quite safe from him.'

'So it wasn't a devil?'

The blonde man gave his horse to Maynard. 'Depends who you ask,' he grinned. 'But a monk flew from a tower alright.'

Brian furrowed his brow. 'What was your inn called again?'

'Never mind that,' Richard said, 'we need to go. With fresh horses we don't need to wait. Maybe we can even catch up with the Little Lord if he's on foot.'

'Ah yes,' Sarjeant said, 'before they are safe behind their tall walls.'

'So that's the plan?' Bowman cleared his throat. 'Ambush a small army with two knights, a sarjeant, a monk, and an angry dog?'

'I think we should leave Judas here with Solis,' Richard said, 'Solis can't go fast enough and the dog would be recognised by the mercenaries if we run into them.'

'They are welcome to stay,' de Cailly said, 'they will be looked after. As will your sick man.'

'Thank you,' Richard said.

Bowman frowned. 'The mercenaries will undoubtedly recognise me, too.'

'Do you want to stay here?' Richard asked.

The blonde man chuckled. 'Not a chance, I want to see what stupid plan you come up with to get your family back.'

De Cailly shook his head at the disrespect.

'I'll think of something,' Richard said. 'As long as we can cross the river at Lillebonne without trouble and get ahead of the walking Tancarvilles, something will work out.'

Standing at the edge of the wood that gazed upon Lillebonne and the river its castle straddled, Richard realised that nothing was going to work itself out. Not this time, because in the meadow between the river and the wood was a sea of tents, tents coloured in green and gold.

'I don't think Lillebonne's castellan is letting them cross,' Bowman said.

Their small party stood on the road that ran west towards Castle Tancarville, the road that crossed a river that flowed south into the Seine. Lillebonne's castle sat on the far side of the river, but the bridge ran into the castle itself, so the castellan could indeed close the crossing.

'Can we cross somewhere else?' Brian asked.

Richard sighed. 'Somewhere further north probably, but I don't know where the road goes, so we'd be guessing. We would lose much time.'

'We can't overtake the Little Lord unless we cross here,' Bowman said, 'and cross now.'

Richard squinted into the distance. 'But we can't get to the castle without Sancho's men seeing us.'

'Might not be a problem,' Bowman patted the grey horse de Cailly had leant him. 'There are carts along the road, travellers queuing to be allowed to cross. Sancho isn't robbing and murdering them, so maybe he won't rob or murder us.'

'This is friendly land to him,' Richard said, 'if Sancho serves the Young King and Lord Tancarville is a part of his rebellion, they are on the same side. He can't burn and pillage his ally.'

Bowman snorted and pointed a finger at the bridge. 'See there? I think he is extorting the merchants. He has men taking a toll to cross the bridge.'

'The cheek of it,' Brian says, 'he has no right to do that.'

Richard gripped the hilt of his sword. 'This gives him the right.'

'That's not honest,' the monk complained.

'I didn't say it was,' Richard shrugged. 'It's just how things work.'

'I hate mercenaries,' Brian went to cross his arms, but then decided it would be better if he didn't let go of his reins. De Cailly had given him an old horse with grey hair above its eyes, but Brian had still yet to fully trust it.

Richard looked down at the monk's old chestnut horse with its drooping head. Its bottom lip flapped as it dreamt. 'We look very different from when we last met Sancho. We have twice as many horses and half as many people.'

'I know what you're thinking, young lord,' Bowman said, 'and I don't like it. If Sancho bothers to look at us, he'll recognise us. Remember what the child did.'

Brian frowned and looked back at the Red Child, who tottered on a pony. 'What did he do?'

'Nothing you need to worry about,' Richard said, 'but we do need to keep him out of sight. And you, Bowman, you probably left an impression on them.'

'What about you?' the blonde knight replied. 'And the monk. You both spoke to him. This plan only works if Sancho never looks hard at us. And if his men have poor memories.'

'I hate mercenaries,' Brian said again.

'You didn't hate us when we landed on your beach,' Richard replied.

'Can you tell me about that?' Maynard said from the rear of their group. He led their actual warhorses from yet another borrowed mount.

'No,' Bowman didn't bother to turn back to the squire.

Richard scratched his chin. Stubble grew now more than it had when he'd last looked upon Lillebonne, and he hadn't had his weekly shave.

Which was fine by him. 'I think we can get through the camp,' he said, 'surely the Lord will favour our mission.'

'Have you been drinking?' Bowman asked.

Richard rubbed the pommel of the Little Lord's sword. 'No, but there's not much else to help us, and after Nicholas I think the Lord owes us.'

'You can't say that,' Brian said.

Bowman scrunched up his face and stared into the camp. 'I don't know, young lord, there might be one thing.'

Richard couldn't help but chuckle when his eyes spotted what Bowman had. Then he led his companions out of the woods and along the road. Mercenaries with shields and spears watched them approach the camp, while others hung around with unstrung bows, but their eyes were on the newcomers.

'It would be more strange if you didn't look concerned,' Richard said to Brian and Maynard, who both strained in an effort to look unafraid.

Brian gulped and pulled his brown cloak around his robe. His eyes darted from one Navarrese guard to another, but his horse plodded on without interest.

'I suppose we should look aloof?' Bowman said as they reached the camp boundary and came to a halt.

'Not all knights are aloof,' Richard said.

'If you say so.'

Two mercenaries looked the party up and down. Dark skinned and dark haired, they eyed up the horses for longer than Richard would have liked.

'What are you doing here?' Richard asked in the most lordly voice he could muster.

Bowman turned his smirk into a cough.

The guards spoke to each other in their language, then turned away and lost interest.

Richard gently squeezed his calves onto his horse, and the borrowed palfrey advanced into the camp.

The camp brimmed with bored men. Hundreds of bored men with nothing to do except gamble, drink, and annoy each other. Their shouts floated over the meadow along with the smoke from their fires and the smell of damp canvas and cooking meat. Eyes watches them pass from around the fires where the mercenaries congregated, eyes which lingered on the blue roan and Bowman's black horse.

Richard had to attempt to keep his eyes raised, to show the confidence a knight should show, the disdain for men who were beneath him. Or that's what he thought he should do, he knew he was in reality he was really little better than the men around him.

But his eyes spotted the cluster of the carts in the centre of the camp, drawn up in a wide circle to form a last line of defence. One of the carts was the one Bowman had spotted from the woods.

Richard halted his horse by the cart and knocked his stirrup against the wooden side of the cart. Nothing happened, so he knocked it again, more forcefully this time.

The canvas peeled back and a blinking Nicola emerged into the light. She rubbed her eyes. 'What are you doing here? Are you seeking your death?'

'I'm looking for the Little Lord,' Richard said. 'He has taken my wife and children.'

'Not all of them,' Nicola glanced at the Red Child with raised grey eyebrows.

'Have you seen them come through here?'

Nicola checked no dogs of war stood close enough to eavesdrop. 'I have. And you are very close behind them.'

'They crossed the river then?' Richard asked.

'Obviously,' she replied, 'it doesn't take a star-reader to work out where he was going.'

'Did you see my family?'

Nicola shrugged. 'I noticed their banners, their numbers, and that they had only half a dozen horses between them. I remember nothing more.'

Bowman grinned. 'It pleases me that those turds had to walk all this way.'

Nicola's weathered face cracked into the smallest smile. 'I see,' she said. 'I saw no women or children. Just angry men in a hurry. Sancho tried to force a payment from them to cross the bridge.'

Bowman snorted with laughter. 'I admire the balls on him, I'll tell you that. Taxing the son of the lord who owns the crossing.'

'There was nearly a fight,' Nicola said, 'there was much swaggering and name calling.'

'But the Little Lord clearly got through,' Richard said. 'I see no bodies littering the meadow, and no graves.'

The old woman nodded. 'He garrisoned men in the castle to make sure the mercenaries would not cross.'

'That's probably the first sensible thing the wretch has ever done,' Bowman said.

'Quite,' Nicola said. She propped herself up in her cart and remained tightlipped as a mercenary strolled by with a chicken held by the neck. It flapped its wings and tried to squawk, but its fate was sealed. Bowman's borrowed horse jumped back from the flapping wings and Brian curled up into a ball in anticipation of his horse doing the same. His old horse simply fell asleep again.

'Sancho is personally fleecing the merchants,' Nicola said, 'he is by the bridge himself. That's the problem you need to solve.'

'We can't just ride through,' Bowman said, 'he knows our faces.'

Richard glanced back at the Red Child. 'That's the one we need to hide. The rest of us can talk our way through.'

'What are we going to do?' Bowman asked. 'Let the boy go into the forest to live with wolves?'

The Red Child grimaced, his sword making his small body look even smaller.

'I can't believe you were stupid enough to bring him into the centre of their camp in the first place,' Nicola said, 'your arrogance is an unpleasant surprise.'

'I just need to get across,' Richard said, 'I don't have time to think of everything.'

'Well, you need to think about that,' Nicola pointed at the boy's sword, 'I saw what he did with the blade. That boy's blood is cursed, you'd do well to leave him with the wolves.'

The Red Child contemplated the old woman with a stern expression. 'I've never seen a wolf,' he said in his high voice.

'You will soon enough,' Bowman sniffed.

Nicola shifted around in the cart and lifted her driving whip. 'Get him out of the camp before someone recognises him,' she said.

Richard studied Nicola's cart. 'How attached are you to living with these mercenaries?' he asked.

The old woman spat onto the ground.

Richard nodded. 'Would you help us?'

'Why would I do that?' she asked. 'I'm here for a reason.'

'Can we borrow your cart?'

The old woman rubbed her chin and watched Richard for a moment. 'I remember how you saved Queen Eleanor at Niort,' she said, 'and I suppose you saved me, too.'

'Is that a yes?' Bowman asked.

Nicola glared at him. 'Your manners have somehow worsened.' Then she noticed his golden spurs. 'Ah, I see.'

'We'll only need help to get across,' Richard said, 'then you can come back to whatever you're doing here.'

'Mostly sleeping from what I can see,' Bowman said.

'Stop antagonising her,' Richard said, 'we don't have time for it.'

Nicola stretched her limbs and clambered out of the cart. 'Castle Tancarville is only a third of a day from here,' she said, 'and I wouldn't mind a quick visit to weigh the mood there.'

'You mean to see if the Chamberlain has grown bored with the rebellion?' Richard asked.

Nicola looked away from Richard and towards the Red Child. 'I suppose your plan is to hide him in my cart.'

'Get under the canvas,' Richard told the boy, 'and keep that sword sheathed and your mouth shut.'

The Red Child rubbed his unkempt red hair. 'I'm the son of the King, I shouldn't have to hide in a cart.'

Bowman backed his horse up a step and clipped the boy around the ear. 'You're a boy, a troublesome one, and whoever your father is, you should learn it means little.'

The boy rubbed the side of his face and turned bright red.

'Just get in,' Richard said, 'it's only until we're over the bridge.'

The Red Child dismounted, kept an angry eye on Bowman, and climbed into the cart. Nicola furled the canvas over him and tied it down.

She retrieved Two-Legs, hitched the mare up, and they made their way towards the line of carts Sancho was taking his toll from.

The blue roan let out a loud call to the small mare, so Richard had to make Maynard wait further behind them. The squire tried his best not to look at the mercenaries who coveted the horses he led, but he fooled no one.

The afternoon wore on as Sancho worked his way through the carts, each time stacking a few more coins onto a wooden table set up by the side of the road. A dark-haired clerk marked on parchment each time a cart went on its way.

Bowman yawned. 'This is taking forever. And I can't believe even mercenaries are keeping accounts these days.'

'We have to wait,' Richard said, but he didn't like it anymore than the blonde knight did. He looked up at a flock of birds wheeling in the sky beneath fluffy grey clouds. A bird of prey hovered closer overhead, its light coloured outstretched wings lined with a darker brown. Richard thought it was a buzzard. Sancho waved on the cart ahead of them, and Richard swallowed. He nodded back to Bowman, who eyed the mercenary with contempt.

Nicola rolled the cart towards him and stopped her pony with a whistle.

'Leaving us?' Sancho flashed a toothy grin at her.

The woman nodded. 'Not for long, I'll be back tomorrow.'

'You still have to pay the toll,' the mercenary captain said.

Nicola spat next to his mailed foot. Sancho grinned up at the old woman and laughed. 'Me like you,' he said.

'I'm not paying you anything, and you know it,' Nicola clicked her tongue and the pony pushed into its harness and the cart moved off.

Sancho slapped his belly as he chuckled, but the grin fell from his face when he saw Richard.

Richard moved his horse on and walked behind Nicola.

'Stop,' Sancho shouted, and Richard had to halt because there were too many crossbowmen nearby and he could never outrun them. He turned to face the captain. 'Can I help you?' Richard asked. 'I have somewhere to be.'

'You killed my man,' Sancho said, 'why shouldn't I kill you?'

'I didn't kill him,' Richard said, 'and the boy who did isn't here. It is none of my concern.'

Bowman turned his horse to face the mercenary. 'To be fair, your man allowed himself to be killed by a child not yet old enough to begin training for war. The fault belongs to your man, or maybe even yourself for allowing your men to be so lax in their own care.'

Sancho's eyes narrowed. 'Blood needs blood.'

Richard sighed. 'If you find the child, you can have it,' he said, 'but he isn't here.'

'Where is he?'

'Rouen,' Richard answered. He couldn't see Brian or Maynard behind him, but he hoped they weren't dumb enough to stare at the cart.

'I shall take one of you as a hostage for the child's return,' Sancho waved his men towards Maynard.

The squire's eyes flicked between the three mercenaries who approached him.

'Wait,' Richard shouted.

It was a loud shout and the dogs of war halted and looked back at their leader.

'You say blood for blood,' Richard said, 'but your kind will just as readily take money for blood. What is your toll to cross the river?'

Sancho's grin returned. 'We speak same language now.'

'You can't pay this creature,' Bowman said, 'but if you do, it's coming out of your tournament pay, not mine.'

'A livre,' Sancho said.

Richard groaned.

'Per man,' the captain added.

'That's an outrage,' Bowman cried, then settled down. 'How much is a livre?'

'Parisian livre or Tournois livre?' Sarjeant asked.

Sancho shrugged. 'Just give me silver coins.'

Richard reached under his tunic and withdrew his pouch.

'I thought you didn't want to spend that,' Bowman said.

'I don't.'

Sancho waved his men back from Maynard and walked up to Richard's horse. He held his hand out.

Richard looked down at the outstretched and mailed arm and wondered if he could draw his sword and slice the hand off fast enough.

'You should just give him the Red Child,' Bowman said.

'But we'd have to go to Rouen to fetch him,' Richard said through gritted teeth.

The blonde man shrugged. 'If you're sure.'

Richard tipped a few silver coins into his hand and dropped them into Sancho's.

The mercenary counted them, then held the hand back out. 'That enough for you. Not enough your men.'

Richard peered into the pouch. He'd just tipped out his earnings from Lagny. He picked out half of what remained and gave them to Sancho.

The captain checked the coins. Then shook his head. 'That enough one more man.'

Richard fought an urge to swing his stirrup out and break the captain's jaw. Instead, he tipped the pouch upside down and his fee from Corbie fell into his palm. 'This is everything I have,' he surrendered it.

'Young lord,' Bowman urged, 'that is all the money you have in the world, we need that to feed ourselves.'

Sancho shrugged. 'Still only enough for one more man. Two men left.'

Bowman's face glowed a dark shade of crimson.

Richard put his empty pouch away, but he had to cross the river and nothing else really mattered.

The mercenary captain moved to Bowman and held out a hand. 'You golden spurs, too. You pay for you and the monk.'

'I'm not paying for him,' the blonde man snapped. 'We don't even need him where we're going.'

'Pay him,' Richard said, 'it's just money.'

'That's easy for you to say,' Bowman replied, 'how am I going to earn this much again?'

Sancho wiggled his fingers at Bowman to request his coins. 'If you serve Young King, more coin come,' he said.

'Hand it over,' Richard said, 'we don't have time for this.'

'But it's mine,' Bowman said, 'and why should I have to pay for the monk, what use is he going to be? Is he going to make the guards fall asleep by reciting the Holy Book to them?'

Sancho frowned. 'Why you need guards fall sleep?'

'Give him the coins,' Richard said, 'please. You know where we're going.'

Bowman howled in grief and threw his pouch at Sancho's head. It hit the unsuspecting captain square in the nose and the heavy coins drew blood from his nose.

'Let's go,' Richard wheeled his horse and followed Nicola, who had kept going and already spoke to the Tancarville guard on the bridge.

Sancho scooped up the pouch as blood dripped from his nose onto the road.

'Consider that the blood for your blood,' Bowman growled and spurred his horse away from the counting table.

Sancho threw the pouch to the clerk as Richard's company left them with haste.

The Tancarville guard opened the gate to Nicola and she drove through it.

Richard clattered onto the bridge. 'Keep that open,' he shouted at the guard who began to shut it.

The guard wavered.

'Keep it open or I'll push you into the river,' Richard ran his palfrey up to the guard, where it snorted in his face.

The guard saw anger in Richard's face and stood aside. Richard entered the castle, recognised the bailey, but followed Nicola straight out of it and into the town itself. Bowman rode beside him with a grim expression as they rode past the empty alleyway that had once contained the homeless crippled veterans. Richard even saw the boy who he had bought horsebread from with the promise of future payment, a promise he'd never kept, and now still had no coins to give him. The boy was now a young man and looked up without recognition at Richard's scarred face with fear.

Richard closed his eyes. He'd become what he'd feared without even realising it. The party relaxed as they travelled past the enormous stones of the ruined Roman theatre, and then up the valley side to the ridge which the road would follow until it reached their destination. The ride was peaceful. Bowman went ahead but returned without having sighted the enemy. Richard's hopes of getting ahead of them were dashed, and he sank into his saddle and wondered how he was going to gain entrance to the castle.

The round tower at the sharp end of the castle's triangular footprint loomed up above the treetops and brought Richard to a halt.

'We need to decide what to do,' he said.

The town of Tancarville lay ahead under the castle on its high rock, a cluster of houses, but the forest lay on its edge and ran right up to the castle.

'Can we hide in the cart?' Sarjeant asked. 'It worked at Lillebonne.'

'They might check it,' Richard said.

Nicola sat on her stationary cart and nodded. 'The Chamberlain is paranoid, all carts are checked on the way in. You could smuggle in the odd sword or knife, but not a man.'

'Send the squire or the monk in,' Bowman suggested, 'at least then they will have been of some use.'

'We can't send Brian in,' Richard said, 'he's too foreign. And Maynard is too cowardly. He'll confess the plan within moments.'

Maynard looked offended but didn't dare speak up.

'I can go in,' Nicola said, 'they'll check my cart but not look twice at me.'

Richard nodded. 'If you can find out what things are like inside the castle, and where my family is, we can form a plan. Just tell me what stands between me and my family.'

'You don't ask much, do you,' Nicola grinned.

'I'm sure you'll manage it,' Richard tried his best to smile, but the weight of his task was wearing him thin.

'Where will you be?' she asked.

Bowman nodded towards the trees. 'Right opposite the castle gate, but deep enough into the woods that we cannot be seen.'

Nicola winked back and clicked her tongue at Two-Legs.

Richard watched them enter the town. 'Fine,' he said, 'let us make our camp.'

Their camp was not a luxurious one. Castle Tancarville sat on white cliffs overlooking the Seine, but to its north the land rose up under a blanket of forest, and it was in that forest that they hobbled their horses and gathered wood for a fire.

Bowman took Maynard and pointed at the wood he wanted, then ordered the squire to light a fire. The elms and sweet chestnut trees had lost most of their leaves for the year, but Maynard hauled over several large branches, which he overlaid on each other and hung above the fire. The smoke drifted upwards in the still air and dissipated in the mesh of branches.

'There,' Bowman stood back in triumph. 'No one will see the smoke from the castle or the road.'

Maynard sat down against a tree and rubbed his shoulder.

Richard and the Red Child cut branches from trees and used them to cover their colourful saddles and shields.

'How long are we going to be here?' Brian looked up at the empty branches above him and shivered.

'As long as we need to be,' Richard said.

Large nests built by crows were dotted amongst the tall trees, and the birds called out as the evening light faded.

The company sat around their fire that night as the cold crept in around them and darkness cloaked the forest. Richard ignored two owls hooting to each other overhead and said a prayer for his family. He prodded the fire with a stick and watched the end of it slowly burn. The stick grew smaller and smaller as fire consumed it, and Richard wondered if the same thing was happening to his soul.

'We'll get them back,' Bowman had his hood tucked over his head and his words came out as steam in the night.

Richard didn't reply, instead he gazed into the fire and staved off more painful thoughts by thinking of ways into the castle.

Brian kept turning around and looking out into the forest.

'Calm down, my boy,' Sarjeant said, 'you're making me nervous.'

'The fire will keep the beasts away,' Bowman said, 'although no wolves will venture this close to the castle.'

The Red Child threw a stick at the fire. 'I'd like to see a wolf.'

'The castle was never well guarded,' Richard said, 'not really.'

Bowman looked over. 'Have you had an idea?'

Richard poked the fire, and orange embers flew into the canopy of branches that thinned the smoke. 'Perhaps,' he said. 'We know the entranceway is guarded. That long tunnel through the gatehouse always had two men outside it.'

'And probably men in the tower to drop rocks on anyone they trap in the tunnel,' Bowman said.

'Yes,' Richard agreed, 'but how many men did you ever see on the walls?'

'None,' Bowman replied, 'but there were always men in the towers.'

'The castle is a long triangle with the halls and chambers on the short side. There are no real towers apart from the gateway along the long sides until the point of the triangle, which does have a tower.'

'So?' the blonde knight asked.

Richard looked up through the bare trees and to the night sky. 'Clouds cover the moon. No one would notice a ladder placed far away from a tower or the entrance.'

'Do we have a ladder?' Bowman looked around in a mock search.

'There's no need to be sarcastic,' Richard said, 'but ladders are made from wood and we're surrounded by trees.'

'We aren't siege engineers,' Sarjeant said, 'we have axes but no other tools.'

'It doesn't need to be pretty,' Richard studied the tallest trees that swayed above them. 'It just needs to be long enough.'

Bowman groaned, but when the sun rose the next morning, Maynard warmed himself by swinging an axe at one of the tall trees. Richard winced at the noise it made, but it was a risk they had to take.

Richard rubbed his hands together over the fire and waited for them to finish, but he knew it would take them all day at least. He went to watch the castle gateway so he could see if anyone left, and so that he could intercept Nicola quickly to save her from spending an age searching for them in the woods. Richard huddled in his cloak next to a cluster of bushes and watched the castle gateway for most of the day. Two men stood guard outside and after a while, as the day warmed to a less uncomfortable temperature, he fell asleep.

He awoke to the sound of hooves on the road. The rider was tall and thin and dressed like a priest. Richard looked closer and realised it was his Priest. He entered the castle without difficulty, and Richard cursed Sir Thomas for not holding him back for very long at all. That man's arrival could hardly be good news, but then a cart rolled out of the castle and Nicola threw a bottle at one of the guards. He caught it and cheered.

Richard pushed his way back through the bushes until he was out of sight of the castle, then he walked onto the road. He waited for Nicola, who nodded solemnly at him when the cart rumbled around the corner and into view.

Trees flanked the road on both sides, which kept it cool as well as private.

'Did you see my family?' Richard asked.

Nicola whistled and the cart ceased moving. 'Of course not,' the old woman said.

'Do you know if they are alive?'

She nodded. 'They are being held in the tower at the far end of the keep.'

'Away from everyone else,' Richard said.

'Indeed. The bailey is full of armed men putting up shelters and lighting fires.'

'The Little Lord's army,' Richard said. 'Is Lord Tancarville there?'

'He's given your family to his son Raoul to guard. The Little Lord has been forbidden from entering the tower,' Nicola said. 'Both your Priest and the castle's priest have both been with them, although I can't think why.'

Richard frowned, but then he looked back towards the castle because he could hear hooves. He looked back into the bushes.

'Don't run,' Nicola said, 'just put your hood up.'

Richard slipped his cloak's hood over his head and turned his head toward the town just as the first rider cantered past the cart. His horse wore a red caparison, and the second rider held the Tancarville banner. Neither gave a second thought to the cart or the man standing by it, and nor did the fifty riders that flew with them.

Richard waited until they rounded the next corner and half of their dust had settled back down on the road.

'I suppose Lord Tancarville isn't in there anymore,' Nicola grinned.

'That's good,' Richard pushed the hood back down, 'I think, anyway.'

'None of this is good,' Nicola sat back on her cart. 'Raoul is angry at being given such a menial task, which puts him away from the knights and nobles at the castle, and now the Little Lord doesn't have his father there to restrain him. You will want to avoid him.'

'Trust me, until my family is safe, I want nothing to do with him.'

Nicola chuckled. 'But once they're safe,' her knowing words trailed off. Richard nodded.

'The good news,' Nicola said, 'is that if you can get inside the walls, you'll blend in with the hundred men already there. But leave your horses outside if you can, they will mark you out.'

'Thank you,' Richard said, 'this means a lot to me.'

'I'll be in the town today and tonight,' she said, 'so if you have any cargo to transport back through Lillebonne, any children for example, meet me there. But if you're getting inside, I suggest you do it today.'

Richard watched Nicola drive her cart down the road to the town, then went back to check on his siege ladder.

Bowman stood with his hands on his hips as Maynard and Sarjeant used a stone to hammer a rung into the ladder.

'Everyone has made this look easier than it is,' the blonde knight said.

Maynard had stripped to the white linen shirt under his tunic, and wiped sweat from his forehead. 'I think it's a sturdy ladder though, it will take our weight.'

It certainly was a long ladder, and the rungs looked secure. 'It will have to do,' Richard said, 'Nicola said we should enter tonight. My family is in the far tower.'

Bowman took a drink from one of the two bottles of cider he had left. 'That's a good plan, even if only because we've run out of food. Do you think we could sit at the old man's table and eat his food before we left?' Bowman grinned.

'I think we shouldn't push our luck,' Richard said. 'But if you can find a bow and some arrows I wouldn't complain.'

'Good idea,' the blonde man looked up at the grey sky. 'It will at least be a dark night.'

A formation of geese flew south as Richard scanned the treetops. It was so dark he couldn't see the trees or the geese themselves, he only knew they were there by the sound their flapping wings made.

'I saw a crane fly south yesterday,' Bowman said as they crouched in the bushes outside the castle. 'When you see the cranes fly south, you know winter is coming.'

'I don't need a bird to tell me that,' Richard rubbed his hands together. He moved to pull his cloak around himself, but it caught on brambles and ripped a few new holes.

They all wore their mail, except for Brian of course, and held the siege ladder between them. Their breath clouded in the cold air and from within the castle erupted the sound of a dozen hounds barking and yelping.

'Feeding time,' Bowman said, 'which is good because they'll be barking until they're fed.'

'Let's do this now, then,' Richard swallowed and gazed up at the walls. They seemed taller now that they intended to climb them.

Everyone picked up the long ladder and they tried to walk softly up to the white wall. The far tower was lost in the night to their left, and to their right the entrance tower could just be made out in the gloom only as a light shadow.

'Lift it up,' Richard said and they raised the siege ladder.

'Gently,' Bowman hissed as they let its top slowly fall onto the castle wall.

Richard went around to climb it. He tested the bottom rung, which was nothing more than a thick branch. It flexed under the weight of one foot. 'If this breaks,' he looked at Maynard, 'I'll break your neck.'

The squire glanced at Bowman. 'I just did what he told me to.'

Richard reached for a rung and squinted up to the top of the ladder. 'You idiots,' he whispered.

The ladder only reached two thirds of the way up the wall.

Bowman scratched his chin. 'I could have sworn it was long enough.'

Richard stepped back onto the ground. 'Well it isn't, is it?' His blood boiled. He crashed down his heel onto the bottom rung and snapped it in two. Fortunately, the hungry hounds still barked inside the castle and masked the sound.

Maynard winced at the snap but Bowman intervened. 'That won't help us, young lord.'

'What will?' Richard's hands made fists and he raged within. 'What are we going to do now? The Little Lord will get to my family when his brother grows bored of guarding them. What if he grows bored tonight?'

'We'll make the ladder longer,' Maynard said with hope in his voice.

'It'll snap in the middle when I'm halfway up,' Richard said, 'but at least then I'll be dead and everything will stop.'

'Don't talk like that,' Bowman said.

Richard wanted to kick in the second rung, but fought the urge and scuffed his new leather sole on the road instead. 'Fine,' he said, 'make the ladder longer. I'll drink that last bottle of cider and try to think of a plan that doesn't involve your ladder killing me.'

'That's it,' Bowman's eyes lit up, 'that's what we'll do.' The blonde knight ran through the bushes that lined the road and disappeared into the woods.

'What's he doing?' Maynard asked. 'He can't be that excited about lengthening the ladder.'

'I have no idea,' Richard looked back up to the ladder and shook his head. 'Idiots,' he muttered.

Sarjeant put a hand on Richard's shoulder. 'They did their best, my boy.'

'I'd hate to see their worst,' Richard heard voices from the gateway. He motioned for the others to be silent and crept along the wall towards the voices.

'Where are you going?' Brian hissed behind him.

Richard ignored his worries and walked slowly until he could make out the voices. The two guards spoke to a third person.

Who laughed.

They laughed back, and there was a sound of glass ringing on glass.

Richard realised what was happening and straightened himself up. He walked down the middle of the road towards the conversation, where he found Bowman finishing off a bottle of wine.

'There you are, young lord,' the blonde man held another bottle over, 'you said you wanted a drink, have this one.'

Hope welled up within and Richard claimed the drink, which his parched lips were thankful for. Only once he'd quenched his thirst did he recognise the two crossbowmen who now shared Bowman's last cider.

One had a short brown beard, the other had curly hair, and both looked much older than when Richard had last seen them.

'You remember Rob and Jean, don't you?' Bowman grinned.

Rob looked at Richard and pointed down at Bowman's spurs. 'Look, this one's a knight now.'

'I know,' Richard replied.

Rob scratched his beard. 'Fancy the two of you both appearing again at the same time like this.'

'It is a miracle,' Bowman said, 'and it is another miracle that you are yet to drown yourselves in drink.'

'Us?' Jean threw an empty wine bottle into the trees. 'You drank more than us that night when the monk flew from the tower.'

'What?' Brian asked as he and the others appeared behind Richard.

'Don't worry about it,' Richard said.

'You all keep saying that,' the monk said.

Rob pointed at Brian then up to the tower. 'Don't go up there,' he said, 'up there monks seem to have trouble with their footing.'

Brian went to speak but gave up.

'What would it take for you to let us in?' Richard asked.

Jean shrugged. 'The usual.'

'I would be happy to pay,' Bowman narrowed his eyes at Richard, 'but I have no coin left.'

'Stop complaining,' Richard said, 'he gave you our cider, isn't that enough?'

Rob and Jean burst into laughter. 'One bottle?' Rob grabbed his friend as they wiped tears from their eyes. 'We drink ten bottles a night, one bottle just stops us telling anyone you're here.'

'Why would you tell anyone we're here?' Richard asked.

'That is more or less our job,' Jean said. He burped.

'You can tell whoever you want if you wait just a while after we've gone in,' Richard said.

'Oh, Lord Tancarville won't like that,' Jean said.

'No, he won't,' Rob agreed.

'He's not here though, is he?' Richard said. 'So you can just tell him when he returns.'

Rob tugged at his beard. 'I can work with that. To be honest with you, our lord has been troubling us of late. He never paid us for fighting off all those knights back at Neufchatel the other year, and now he's said we can't be drunk on duty.'

'You're doing a great job sticking to that,' Bowman said with a smile and held up a wine bottle to toast them.

Rob toasted him back and chucked the resulting empty over his shoulder. It smashed against the wall. 'You know what, the pox on the old man. We'll let you in.'

'Really?' Richard blinked in guarded relief.

'Fine,' Jean sighed, 'just bring me something to eat when you leave, because it had better be before sunrise.'

'Don't worry about that, boys,' Bowman said, 'all you have to do is avoid telling anyone who Richard is.'

'Why?' Rob scratched his head. 'Who's Richard?'

'Exactly,' the blonde knight laughed, clapped Rob on the shoulder and marched into Castle Tancarville.

Richard shrugged and followed, not wanting to overstay his welcome at the gate. The tunnel through the gatehouse was as dark as he remembered, but this time it reeked of urine. However, it opened out into a very different world from the one outside the castle.

Richard's memory of the substantial courtyard was one of mock mounted combat and young men and horses, so what he saw came as a shock. The modest army the Little Lord had marched back with him from Yquebeuf had joined the men Tancarville himself had kept there. They filled the yard so that hardly a blade of grass could be seen, except at the bottom of the triangle where a dozen paddocks had been fenced off.

'They were your idea, weren't they?' Bowman noticed where his eyes went.

'Didn't do me much good though, did it?' Richard admired the fine horses Tancarville kept in them. It seemed he'd expanded his stable of foreign horses in the past few years, but Richard wasn't back at Castle Tancarville to dredge up old memories.

'The far tower is to our left, all the other buildings are to our right or ahead,' he said.

'There are so many men we might just fit in,' Sarjeant said. 'But I never liked it here.'

'We've got a squire to do all those jobs now,' Bowman grinned.

'We're only here to do one thing,' Richard said, 'and that's getting into that tower.'

The hounds in the kennels barked still, but servants went in their direction carrying meat, so that sound would soon be gone.

'Follow me,' Richard started to walk along the inside of the wall towards the far tower.

'Richard,' Bowman whispered, 'the Little Lord.'

Richard's blood ran cold. The nearest tents were but a stone's throw away, and only just beyond them, the Little Lord shouted at a man. When Richard stilled, he could hear their words.

'You cannot have Edith,' another voice shouted.

'That's Sir John,' Bowman hissed.

'I can have what I want,' the Little Lord said, 'I'm the heir to Tancarville.'

'You are a spoiled brat,' Sir John shouted and some nearby soldiers gasped.

The Little Lord, always quick to draw his sword, flashed his blade into the air where orange firelight reflected from it.

'Marry the Yvetot whore if you wish,' Sir John ignored the sword, 'go and live in that godforsaken village. Just leave my daughter alone.'

Richard remembered Edith from their hunting trip, she had been a nice enough girl then, and he wondered what she was like now.

'I'll take my village back once I've disposed of those children,' the Little Lord shouted, 'but I'll have Edith first.'

Bowman snorted quietly. 'I suppose your wife might not have cut all of him off after all.'

'She's my daughter,' Sir John said, a hint of desperation creeping into his voice.

'So?' the Little Lord replied. 'It will be her honour, not mine.'

'If you lay a finger on her, I'll tell your father.'

The Little Lord laughed and a crowd gathered around them. 'Is that the best you can do? Run and tell my father? You were supposed to be a strong and respected knight, but now you squeal like a piglet.'

Sir John said something in a hushed tone that Richard couldn't hear.

The Little Lord lunged and struck him in the face with the hilt of his sword. Sir John fell backwards, tripped over and bumped onto the earth. He sat up and touched his lip.

'Things have changed here,' Bowman whispered, 'we should be going.'

'But some things haven't,' Richard said as the Little Lord spat on to the ground beside the old knight and strode off towards the castle's chambers.

Sir John wiped his mouth and swore at the men who gawped at him.

Bowman tugged on Richard's mailed sleeve. 'You started that, you know. You were the first to defeat him.'

'The Little Lord started it when he came to Yvetot and forced Sir John to do his fighting for him. But you're right, we should move on. We might only have until the Little Lord is finished with Edith.'

Bowman shook his head ruefully. 'The world moves in circles, doesn't it? I still want to stop him from doing what he tried to do to Matilda the last time this happened. Edith's another innocent girl.'

Richard remembered what had happened then, the incident that had opened the rift between de Cailly and Tancarville, but today his heart was cold to Edith's plight.

'No one is innocent,' Richard replied. 'But if you need to save her, feel free. Do what you must, but I must see to my family.'

Bowman frowned, frustration etched on his face. 'Once upon a time you'd have tried to save Edith as well as your family,' he said.

Richard sniffed and took a deep breath. 'Not anymore.'

'Probably for the best, young lord,' the blonde man said, 'you'd have only messed it up, anyway.'

Richard searched within himself for remorse for turning his back on

Edith, but he found none. He couldn't save her. His feet started to walk towards the far tower and his companions followed.

The paddocks separated the tower from the army camp, and the sound of horses eating piles of hay and swishing away flies with their tails took over from the sounds of drunken and bored men. Richard knew which of the sounds he preferred.

But a guard stood at the bottom of the tower, leaning on the wall playing a flute. Its notes were high, mournful, and sounded like they should accompany a funeral.

The guard lowered the flute when he saw Richard. 'What do you want?' he asked in a gruff voice that contrasted with his playing.

Richard paused for a moment. He hadn't thought this far ahead. 'We're here to relieve you,' he said.

The guard thought about it then pushed himself off the wall. 'Good, I thought you'd never come,' he walked off, giving Brian a questioning look on his way.

Richard let out a breath.

'Good thinking, young lord,' Bowman grinned and opened the wooden door. 'Although that was almost too easy.'

'I'm not complaining,' Richard followed Bowman into the tower.

Inside it was dark, no fires lit the staircase that spiralled in an anticlockwise direction. Richard's staircase at Yvetot had turned the other way, and he was sure it made his legs uneven. Bowman had once told a story to a woman that all staircases went the same way to help knights defend them, but he knew Bowman was making it up, and shook his head because he also knew his mind was distracting itself.

The first chamber up the staircase had two men in it, dicing over a table lit by two candles, but Richard couldn't tell if they were martial men or some sort of servant. He went on, past the doorway to the second floor chamber that was just a storeroom full of baskets of stones, javelins, crossbows and other siege equipment.

Bowman nipped in and came back out with a bow and two sheaves of arrows.

That left Richard to climb the stairs in the lead, and he almost bumped into the man that guarded the closed doorway on the third level.

The guard had a sword belted around his waist, no mail but a leather jerkin over his tunic. Light poured down from the floor above, but this doorway was shut so the light was dim and flickering.

'Who are you?' the guard asked.

Richard put on his best smile. 'We're here to relieve you.'

The guard tipped his head to look behind Richard, and could see he was far from alone. 'No, you're not.' He stepped backwards into the door with a thud and his hand went for his sword.

Richard went for Sir John's dagger and he rushed at the guard who took more time to draw his longer weapon.

Bowman was at Richard's shoulder, a blade in his hand, and the two of them pounced on the guard, driving both of their points into his chest and neck.

The guard never reached his sword and cried out as his eyes bulged in recognition of his death. Richard smelled wood smoke on his clothes.

A key turned in the lock. Bowman pulled the guard to one side and pushed his body down the staircase.

The door handle rotated, and Richard and Bowman nodded to each other.

The wooden door opened a fraction, and both of them rammed it with their shoulders. It flew backwards, opening the room up, and hit the man who'd opened it in the face. He cried out and staggered backwards into a poorly lit chamber.

Bowman jammed a foot behind the man's already unsteady legs, and Richard pushed him.

He toppled down, hit the floorboards and groaned.

Richard raised Sir John's dagger, but the light from a small brazier flickered across the face of his victim and he stopped. 'Raoul Tancarville?' he asked.

Raoul squinted from his painful nose. 'I've seen you before,' he mumbled. Then he saw the sharp and red dagger before him and groaned. 'Not like this. No, I can't die because of my wretch of a brother.'

Richard stayed his hand.

'My brother can rot in hell, curse him and this dishonourable job I'm going to die for.'

Raoul looked like a younger version of his father, short and with a barrel-like chest, but his eyes were softer. 'I don't have to kill you,' Richard said, 'I'm only here for my family.'

Raoul frowned. 'It is your family I'm guarding? My father would send others to rescue me, he'd never go himself. How did you get into the castle?'

'You have no idea who you're dealing with,' Bowman stood next to him, ready to drop down if the Tancarville moved too much.

Raoul shook his head. 'No, I don't, I have only heard stories. I just want you out of my castle.'

'It's not really yours, is it?' Bowman mocked.

'Not yet.'

Richard lowered the dagger. 'I'll happily lock you in this chamber when we leave. Someone will let you out eventually. I'm not here to spill blood.'

'Tell that to my guard,' Raoul said, 'but this must make you Richard. The Richard. After everything I've heard about you, why are you offering to spare me? Many here tell that you killed Simon Martel and hurled a monk from this very tower.'

Brian groaned behind Richard. 'That's what you're hiding,' the monk said.

Richard grimaced for a moment. 'Look, we wouldn't have got through the locked door if you hadn't opened it, and I think you hate your brother as much as we do. If you mean no harm to my family, I will gladly spare you.'

'I care not for your two children,' Raoul said, 'it's the bastard child I want. Kill that one and I can inherit Tancarville without trouble.'

Bowman scoffed. 'The Red Child is a bastard, he cannot inherit while you live.'

'No,' Raoul said, 'but anyone who doesn't like me can still back him and challenge me. I may have to waste months stamping out the flames of a pointless revolt.'

'It almost sounds like we're on the same side,' Bowman grinned.

Raoul gestured with his eyes to a door at the back of the chamber. 'They're in there.'

'You kept them in there?' Richard asked, for the room looked like nothing more than a tiny storeroom in the corner of the tower.

'It was not my doing,' the Tancarville said, 'and it could be worse, it could be full of hanging meat or urine for the tanner. It is only full of clean sheets and blankets.'

Sarjeant picked up the long iron key from the floorboards and made for the locked door.

'Maynard,' Richard got to his feet, 'go back down to the courtyard and tell us if anyone approaches.'

The squire nodded and descended the staircase, stepping gingerly over the body in their doorway.

Sarjeant opened the door and revealed a pitch-black storeroom, out of which a blinking Sophie emerged.

'Richard?' she asked, her voice rasping and rough.

Lora erupted from the darkness and flung herself at Richard, hugging his mailed legs tightly. Her face was pale.

Sophie joined her and the knot in Richard's stomach loosened ever so slightly. 'I didn't think I'd see you again,' Richard said.

'My hope had gone,' Sophie said, 'I was ready for the end.'

Alexander loitered in the doorway before Sarjeant picked him up and nearly crushed him in his embrace. 'My boy, it is good to see you again.'

The boy didn't react, his face was sunken and haunted.

'They haven't fed us,' Sophie looked down at Raoul with utter hatred, who sat up. 'Give me the dagger,' she said.

'We're not killing him,' Richard said.

'He's one of them.'

'But I'm not like them,' Richard said. 'The killing has to stop somewhere.'

Sophie's eyes pulsed. 'The Little Lord is starving us, starving our children, until I agree to marry him.'

Brian shuffled towards the brazier to warm his hands. 'He can't marry you, you're already married.'

'Both of the priests who are here will do whatever their lord bids them to,' Richard said, 'they are both worms.'

Sophie's face, already angered, flushed redder. 'The Yvetot Priest has been leering over me, enjoying my suffering. He told me if I repent the sin of marrying you, God will forgive me. The Tancarville priest is planning a trial by ordeal to check if the devil has possessed me. He said he'll perform the ritual on the roof so we're closer to our Lord's view.'

Brian looked around the gloomy chamber. 'That's not how the ritual is done.'

Richard's hands flexed involuntarily. 'I know. The ordeal seems to be the Tancarville priest's passion. Had he touched you, I would kill him.'

'Hush,' Sophie said, 'don't speak of such things in front of the children.'

Richard shrugged. 'It is the way of the world, you can't hide them from it. My mother shielded me from the harshness of life and it cost me much to learn the truth of things.'

Sophie kept her eyes on the Tancarville knight, who rubbed his nose. 'Very well, can we leave?'

Richard nodded. 'Of course. We'll lock Raoul in this chamber and we'll leave the key with the guards at the gate on our way out.'

Raoul's face looked surprised. 'That is honourable of you, but the guards will stop you from leaving.'

Bowman coughed. 'You leave that to us.'

'I thought you didn't want to spill blood.'

'Oh, we won't,' Bowman grinned.

'The guards are our problem,' Richard said, 'and I have no ill will towards you. I hope you can remove your brother, he is a stain on your family that I hope you can clean.'

'Even our father hates him.'

Richard had a thought. 'Does the Little Lord ever eat pottage?'

Raoul frowned and shook his head. 'No, never.'

'Just ask him why,' Richard smiled.

'Why?'

Footsteps came from the staircase, the rapid slap of leather soles on bare stone took Richard's attention.

Maynard appeared, leant on the doorframe, and caught his breath. 'Men,' he said, 'men are coming.'

'Who?' Bowman asked.

'How many?' Richard added.

The squire swallowed. 'The Little Lord, I'm sure of it. He had men with him, I didn't count them, they were still far away.'

'Useless,' Bowman grumbled.

Brian's face drained of colour. 'We can't get out of the gate now, can we?'

Lora looked up at Richard, her big round eyes seemingly understanding the danger they were in.

'I'll get you somewhere safe,' Richard stroked her hair, 'I promise.' He looked up to Bowman. 'We can run along the battlements to the gatehouse and descend the staircase there.'

'There are guards in the tower,' Raoul said. 'You'll never get out of here alive.'

'You would say that,' Bowman hadn't put his knife away and kept it in the knight's eyeline.

'Suit yourself,' Raoul shrugged.

Richard looked at Sarjeant. 'We left the ladder on the wall, didn't we?'

The older man nodded back. 'But it was not long enough.'

Richard looked into the dark storeroom. 'Clean sheets and blankets, was it? Tie them together, make a rope long enough to reach the top of the ladder. Then we can tie it round a crenellation and climb down.'

Sarjeant put Alexander down and peered into the storeroom.

Richard looked around at the nervous faces that surrounded him. 'Brian, Sophie, Maynard, start tying sheets together. Bowman, go and see if we can reach the gatehouse and get down it.'

Sarjeant looked tired. 'What shall I do?' he asked.

'We're going to stop the Little Lord from entering the tower, follow me.'

Richard didn't have time for niceties, so he pushed Lora away as gently as he could. He rushed down the stairs, over the body of the guard and towards the ground level. He could hear Sarjeant's footsteps above him as he turned and turned in the dark, his feet aiming for steps he couldn't see and hoping they were there.

Richard reached the tower's door without falling down the staircase, but reached it only a heartbeat before the Little Lord. The two men locked eyes for a moment, and the young Tancarville's widened with shock even as Richard pushed the oak door shut.

Except a blade appeared between it and the doorframe at the last moment and the door rammed into it, stopping it from shutting. The heavy wooden door bent the sword, but it didn't snap.

Sarjeant flew down the staircase and threw his weight at the door. It juddered loudly, its hinges rattled, but the sword didn't give way.

'We only need to give them time,' Richard said, 'as long as we can.'

Sarjeant gritted his teeth and pushed. 'I'll stand by you.'

Richard knew he would.

Shouts from outside leaked through the not-quite-shut doorway, and the Little Lord's high voice cut through. 'Open the door and I promise not to kill you,' he said.

'I'm not falling for that,' Richard said.

A scraping noise sounded like someone was scratching at the stone, and then a spear tip wormed its way in next to the bent sword, and someone started to lever the door open.

Richard strained all his muscles to counter it, he wedged his heels onto the first step and tried to lock his body between the step and the door. Sarjeant grunted with effort, but the spear was joined by another and the door just wouldn't shut.

Sweat dripped down Richard's face and it stung one of his eyes. One hand slipped on the rough door and impaled itself on a splinter before he could find a piece of ironwork to grab. He felt a muscle in his arm start to wobble. 'We don't have long,' he whispered to Sarjeant, 'you go up first and I'll hold them here as long as I can. We'll make a stand on the roof.'

'My duty is to your children,' Sarjeant said.

'Why does everyone want to be a hero?' Richard asked.

'That's not what I meant, I don't want to be a hero,' Sarjeant said, then turned and leapt up the stairs two at a time. Richard didn't watch him, instead he pushed with everything he had left as the spears took it in turns to lever the door open bit by painstaking bit.

His legs started to burn and his lungs stung from the exertion, and Richard knew he had moments before the door was prised open.

So he ran.

His already burning legs threatened to cramp as he darted up and around the spiral stairs. Richard wished he had a shield as he jumped up past the floor with the two gambling men. They had left their table but Richard caught movement in the corner of the room as he sprung past. If the men were guards, they were also cowards.

Someone had locked Raoul's chamber and Richard bounded up towards the roof.

The stairs exited through a doorway onto the round tower roof, and immediately to its left was the entrance onto the wall back to the gatehouse. In the centre, a brazier roared away with a stack of logs beside it. A solid metallic looking bar grew a dull red in the centre of the flames.

But all around it were people.

Maynard stood pointing a sword at two priests on the back wall. Sophie and the children stood nearer, but Bowman was gone, hopefully along the top of the wall.

Sarjeant, red in the face, tossed a spear to Richard and grasped one himself. 'I wish we had more time to loot that storeroom,' he said.

Richard lowered the spear towards the staircase doorway and Sarjeant joined him. Footsteps and shouts echoed up from below.

'Where's Bowman?' Richard asked without turning away from the door.

'Not back yet,' Maynard shouted.

Richard felt a hand on his waist, a delicate hand, and then Sir John's dagger was drawn from its sheath. Sophie took it and approached the Tancarville priest.

'We don't have time for that,' Richard shouted, 'where's Brian?'

'He's gone to tie the sheets to the wall,' the squire answered.

'Wait,' Richard said, 'you actually found enough?'

Maynard made a strange laughing sound. 'Maybe, but then we thought the ladder would be long enough, didn't we?'

'This is no time for jokes, boy,' Sarjeant said, 'they're nearly here.'

The footsteps slowed as they ascended, taking their time in fear of an ambush in the dark.

Sophie waved the dagger at the priest who had tormented Richard years ago. Richard hadn't seen him since, but his wife seemed to have found a strong hatred for him in a much shorter time. 'Pick up the iron bar,' she cried, 'or I'll saw your hands off here and now.'

The Tancarville priest's eyes darted between Maynard's sword and the enraged woman with the sharp dagger. 'You are mad, utterly mad,' he cried, 'I don't need to put you through the ordeal, you are spawned from the burning depths of hell.'

'So are you,' Sophie said, 'you drove me to this. My eyes ache from thirst, my belly rots from hunger, and my soul yearns to make you pay for putting my children through so much. Pick up the bar.'

Spear points appeared into the doorway, followed by a hesitant guard who resented being made to advance first. He halted in the doorway as Richard and Sarjeant both lunged at him with their spears. The second guard, still below on the stairs, could wave his spear up past his comrade's waist and aid his defence, and the four spears fenced for a moment without inflicting harm.

Bowman sprinted back onto the tower roof from the wall. His new bow was strung and hooked around his shoulder. 'Do you want the good news or the bad news?'

'Bowman,' Richard shouted.

'Alright,' the blonde man said, 'I can't see any guards in the gatehouse, but then the door into it from the wall is locked, so we can't get in. I suppose that's why they can't be bothered to guard the wall.'

'So we can't get down to ground level?' Maynard's voice wavered.

Richard batted one spear aside and Sarjeant tried to lance the guard, but his companion behind him managed to parry the thrust just in time.

'We'll be taking your stupid ladder then,' Richard swung his spear across and blocked a stab aimed at Sarjeant's legs.

Brian appeared from the wall. 'The sheets are tied,' he said, 'I suppose it's ready.'

Yvetot's Priest, who looked like a younger version of the older relative he hid behind, pointed at Brian. 'You're a monk, how can you work with these abominations?'

The Irish monk looked at Richard. 'Quite easily really, and I don't work for them. I don't even say mass for them.'

'No mass?' the Priest cried. 'Pagans. Heretics.'

Sophie stepped forwards with the dagger raised just as the spearmen made their move and charged up the steps.

Richard stepped to one side, Sarjeant the other, and the lead guard could only block Richard as Sarjeant stabbed him through his side. He staggered sideways and the man behind pushed past, the Little Lord on his heels.

'Sophie,' Richard's spear gashed the guard on his arm but didn't stop him, 'stop mutilating worthless priests and get the children away.'

Sarjeant's waving spear forced the Little Lord to think twice, and the young Tancarville stalled in the doorway.

Richard couldn't see his wife, but he heard her. 'I will not be the pawn of weak men any longer,' she said.

'If you want to be my squire,' Richard shouted, 'save my children.'

Richard's leather breastplate took the full force of a spear thrust, but he heard the rush of footsteps behind him, so maybe Maynard was doing something useful for the first time in his life. The squire fled from the tower, pushing Lora and Alexander before him.

A rushing sound flashed past Richard's ear and Bowman's arrow found the face of the spearmen in front of him. The missile cracked his jaw, but Richard helped him on his way by stabbing his spear into his shoulder. It found the seam between body and sleeve, and the man yelled as he reeled backwards and slumped against the doorframe.

But another guard took his place, rushing up the steps with his spear lowered and a war-cry on his lips.

Sarjeant stabbed again and again at the Little Lord's face, too far away to reach him, but the knight dared not close the distance. Sarjeant was safe, but only while he still had strength for such violent thrusts.

Bowman loosed another arrow which dug into the next man who traversed the staircase, catching in his leather jerkin without harming him, but slowing him down.

Maynard came back. 'The children won't go down the rope,' his voice was desperate.

'For the love of God,' Richard ignored a stab which gouged a chunk of his leather armour off. 'Put one on your shoulders as you go down. Bowman, take the other one. Don't mess it up.'

'I never mess things up,' Bowman whirled around and pushed the squire back the way he'd come.

Sophie watched in fear for her children for just a moment, but it was enough for Tancarville's priest to make his move.

Yvetot's priest went to join him, but Brian howled and leapt at him before he could reach Sophie.

Sarjeant's ferocious stabs slowed down and the Little Lord flashed a knowing grin. 'You're too old for this,' he pushed the next attack aside and stepped inside the range of Sarjeant's spearpoint.

Richard couldn't help because the guard Bowman's arrow had inconvenienced attacked him, and he now faced two spears at once.

The Little Lord struck Sarjeant and cut through the tunic on his arm.

Richard swung his spear down like a quarterstaff and bashed one guard on his unprotected head.

Tancarville's priest cried out as Sophie drove Sir John's dagger deep into his shoulder. Brian fumbled with the Priest behind them, their fight all nails and fingers. The Irish monk stepped back, remembered his heroics at Baginbun Head, and swung a punch at the Priest, whose head snapped back. His opponent stunned, Brian turned and attacked the man Sophie looked to kill. Sophie brought the dagger down again, this time it scraped down his chest and dug a painful gash over his ribs. She grabbed one of his hands and pulled him towards the brazier. Brian took the other and twisted it behind his back.

Sophie plunged the unwilling hand of her overwhelmed victim into the flames. The priest's scream seared the air.

'What are you doing?' Richard shouted as he parried a spear thrust. 'Get out of here.'

Sarjeant sprung away from the Little Lord and out of danger, but it meant the Tancarville knight was free to chop at Richard. Richard tried to bring his spear around to block it, but the sword cut down on his wooden shaft and hacked the iron tip clean off.

Richard, for one brief moment, admired the sheer strength needed to do that. The Little Lord wasn't a youth anymore.

Sophie held the holy man in the fire as his flesh boiled and peeled. 'I know what he did to you, Richard,' she shouted above his screams.

Richard could smell the roasting flesh. 'Our children need their mother.'

That snapped Sophie out of her rage, but Yvetot's Priest regained his senses and his arms appeared around Brian's neck and started to strangle him. The Irish monk let go of the howling and suffering priest, who freed, snatched at Sir John's dagger with his unburnt hand.

As the remaining spearman stabbed Richard in his abdomen, Richard pushed his broken spear at the Little Lord and charged. He gritted his teeth and pushed, pushed his enemy backwards and towards the staircase. There was a pain in his stomach but he was only dimly aware of it.

The last guard aimed a stab at Richard's back as he drove the Little Lord on, but that meant he didn't see Sarjeant stab him through the throat.

Richard stopped. 'Hold him here,' he said to Sarjeant.

Sarjeant advanced and used his spear to keep the Little Lord in the doorway.

Richard left them and ran to the priests. He snatched the dagger which Sophie and the priest wrestled over, and reached over to stab the Priest who tried to strangle Brian. Sir John's dagger caught him in the eye.

Yvetot's Priest screamed a high-pitched yell as his eye disappeared, and Richard marvelled that his dreams had finally come true.

Brian, crimson-faced from lack of air, spun around to his attacker. 'I'll kill you,' he shouted. He pushed the Priest, who clawed at his bleeding socket, back to the edge of the tower. The Priest thudded into the stone, oblivious to anything but his pain, and Brian pressed up to him. 'An eye for an eye,' the Irish monk snarled. He put one hand around the back of the Priest's leg and tipped him up and back. Then Brian hurled him from the tower.

Sophie watched open-mouthed, and Tancarville's priest cried out after his relative. Then he shrieked in grief and stumbled away waving his toasted hand in the air.

The last guard wasn't the last guard. More advanced, and the Little Lord again attacked Sarjeant.

'Sophie, go,' Richard shouted.

Sergeant tripped over backwards and sprawled into the brazier. Burning wood and one glowing hot iron bar spilled over the floorboards, embers exploded high into the air in a great crackle.

One spearman left the doorway and took a step to his left to block the escape route out onto the castle wall. Another guard stayed in the doorway, but with the carnage around him he hesitated.

Sarjeant scrambled on his knees, his spear gone, then stood up. His chest heaving, he drew a dagger. It was all he had left.

Richard glanced at his broken spear as Brian looked down the outside of the tower. 'What have I done?' he whispered.

The Little Lord sensed victory. 'You made a mistake by coming here,' he sneered, 'I'll rid myself of you and your children, and take what is mine.'

'I'm not yours,' Sophie whispered.

Richard eyed the guard who blocked their escape onto the wall. 'Our children have gone so you've already failed,' he said. 'Let us go and no more blood needs to spill.'

The Tancarville priest held his scolded fingers up to his eyes. Red, white, and blistered, he screamed.

Sophie kicked him between the legs in an attempt to silence his wailing. The priest bent over in agony, dropped to his knees, and whimpered.

The Little Lord watched. 'You have even done me a favour by doing that,' he said, 'that priest deserves it for what he once did to me.'

Richard almost smiled at the thought of what the Little Lord might do when his brother asked him about the pottage.

'Lay down your arms and surrender to justice,' the young Tancarville said.

Richard shook his head in disbelief. 'What do you know of justice? Stand aside and I won't show you what it means.'

The Little Lord's round face twisted up into a grin. 'You're in no position to threaten me, I think I'm going to kill you slowly, Richard. I haven't forgotten the gold you hid from me.'

Brian snapped around from the battlements. 'Gold?'

'I'll peel your fingernails off one by one,' the Little Lord said, 'slice you open and pour salt into the wounds. And once the fingernails stop hurting, I'll chop the fingers off, but you will tell me what you did with that gold.'

Brian frowned with thought. 'If Richard had gold, why would he risk everything by coming to Ireland as a mercenary?'

'Listen to the monk,' Richard said, 'there is no gold, I swear that on my eternal soul as well as that of my children.'

'Those are just words,' the Little Lord said, 'we shall see how pain changes the song you sing.'

Echoes burst up the stairwell. More feet on stone.

Richard gulped and glanced back at Sophie, whose face was nervous.

'It's over,' the Little Lord stood tall.

Tancarville's priest crawled towards the guard blocking the wall while Richard considered his options. There were three ways off the tower. Down the staircase, along the wall, or to jump.

The priest vanished behind the spearman who brandished his weapon at Richard. The staircase wasn't an option, and Richard was not yet ready for death, so he chose the wall.

'Now,' he shouted and charged the spearman.

Richard tried to bat the spearpoint away and twist around its thrusting attack, but his body obeyed him only slowly and the point ripped into the leather breastplate and he felt the tug of his mail as iron rivets popped open and then the burning sensation of the point piercing his skin.

It didn't save the spearman though, Sir John's dagger claimed another victim and Richard raced over his body despite his wound.

Sarjeant reacted to his charge, but so did the Little Lord, and they clashed at the entrance to the wall.

Brian slipped around them and joined Richard, but the Little Lord cut Sarjeant's arm, and the backswing of his next attack caught Sophie on the chin as she tried to follow Brian. The blow knocked her off her feet and the Little Lord turned around to see what he'd hit.

Sarjeant took his chance to kick the Little Lord and then squeezed around him to get onto the wall.

A guard picked Sophie up and the Little Lord was joined by another and faced Richard.

The Little Lord held his sword out in front of him, warding Richard away. 'Come on,' the Tancarville cried, 'test your dagger against my sword.'

Richard didn't want to, but his wife was trapped behind his red-faced enemy, so he attacked. There was precious little space to wield a sword in the entrance to the wall, stone on either side of them, but the Little Lord still parried Richard's first strike. He countered and cut some mail rings from Richard's forearm.

Richard sprung back. Except it was more like a stagger. He didn't look down, but he knew two stomach wounds now drained his strength.

The Little Lord grinned. 'This time, after all the others, you can't best me.' His eyes found his old sword at Richard's waist. 'You've got my sword.'

'You've got my wife,' Richard replied, 'I'll trade.'

'I'll have both,' the Little Lord said, 'I'll claim it from your bleeding body once I finish you.'

Sophie struggled, but a second guard grabbed her and held her still.

'We'll marry now,' the Little Lord said, 'it will be done, then our son will be the rightful heir to Tancarville. My blood will rule here, my child will be the Chamberlain of Normandy and I shall command ninety knights. My name will be written into history, but you, Richard, you will die forgotten.'

That couldn't happen. Richard summoned his energy and slashed at his opponent. The dagger cut through air, scraped off the castle wall, but spear points from yet more guards appeared around the Little Lord to defend him.

'You can't cut through five of us,' the Little Lord said, 'lay down the dagger and you can die in peace.'

Richard looked for Sophie but couldn't see much of her through the men that jabbed at him with their spears.

'Or,' the Little Lord said, 'maybe I'll promise to only torture you a little, until you give up the gold.'

'Sophie,' Richard shouted, despair mixing with the pain from the wounds in his belly. A darkness was closing in and he could feel his limbs slowing down.

'Richard,' his wife cried back, a cry that sliced through the night air. The light from the spilled brazier died and gloom cloaked the tower.

'Don't pretend you care for each other,' the Little Lord scoffed, 'you didn't pick each other, did you?'

'Look after my children,' Sophie shouted.

'I'm not leaving you,' Richard put a hand on the wall to steady himself.

'You already have,' the Tancarville knight said. 'Someone grab a crossbow from the storeroom, we'll shoot him from here.'

'Save yourself,' Sophie said, 'you can't save me.'

Richard shook his head. He couldn't abandon anyone again, that was a promise he'd made to himself.

'That monster is right,' Sophie said, 'we never chose each other. I know you never wanted me, you were just a boy. Run while you still can.'

'This is tiresome now,' the Little Lord said as one of the guards holding Sophie disappeared down the staircase to fetch a crossbow.

Richard gritted his teeth. He remembered the pain of leaving his sister behind at Keynes, the guilt and shame that dogged him even though he knew he'd had no choice. 'I'm not running away and leaving someone behind,' he said. 'Never again.'

'Richard,' Sophie's voice was fraught, intense, 'you came to me a boy, but now you're a man. A good man. I can't let you die for my sake. No woman should be the instrument of such a poor excuse of a man, either, and I will not let that abominable child rule here. You will not die for me and I will not leave my children without both parents.'

Richard felt something warm on his upper leg and he knew he was bleeding more badly than he'd realised. He had to attack now, he could dodge the spears and then only needed three or four good stabs to rescue Sophie.

Sophie clawed her fingers at her captor's eyes and he stumbled away with red lines down his face.

'Goodbye, Richard,' Sophie said, 'you did your best.' She ran away from the guard, but not down the stairwell. She didn't choose the wall either, as one of the spearmen blocking Richard turned towards her. Sophie chose the third exit from the tower, jumped up onto the battlements, and without a glance backwards, hurled herself off.

The swoosh of air from her falling body was the only sound that rose above the last crackles of the spilled brazier wood. The fire died with pops and cracks that sounded to Richard almost like a chuckle.

Richard's breathing overtook him. It sped up and threatened to overwhelm him.

The Little Lord blinked as he gazed at the now empty crenellation. 'What? Now nothing will work.'

Richard felt sick.

A loud noise burst through his malaise from behind him and he snatched a look to see a crossbow bolt bounce off the wall, its iron head snapping off and spiralling up into the night air. Down in the courtyard, guards who had heard shouts and screams aimed their crossbows up at Richard.

But the noise focused his mind, there was nothing left for him on the tower anymore. His children were still alive, and he had to reach them. So he turned and ran towards the makeshift rope that should be somewhere behind him along the wall.

A bolt flew overhead with a whistle.

'Come on,' the Little Lord shouted and Richard knew he didn't have much of a head start.

He found the rope made from knotted sheets, but with it he found the Tancarville priest frantically cutting at them with his one good hand. 'You'll die here,' the priest cried, spit flying from his mouth.

He'd half cut through the sheet.

'Not you,' Richard cried and lunged, 'you will not be the death of me.'

Richard brought Sir John's dagger down across his wrist and the priest dropped his knife. Richard used his other hand to pick the priest up.

'This is for the iron bar,' he tipped the priest up and onto the wall. Richard's stomach tore and pain exploded inside, but he pushed the struggling priest off the wall as if he were a throwing stone.

A crossbow bolt slammed into the wall near his face and threw up a cloud of powered stone, which coated his face and sent grit into his eyes.

He heard the Little Lord's footsteps.

In the back of Richard's mind, he wondered if the rope would break having been cut in half, but he didn't have time to think too much about it. He flung himself over the wall with the rope in one hand, and before he knew it, he was hanging down the wall and bouncing off it. Richard let himself down the sheet hand by hand, his dagger getting in his way. He looked up when he saw the Little Lord's red face stick out over the wall.

How he hated that face, Richard thought.

Then the sheet tore.

It ripped loudly and the rope fell from the battlements. Richard fell too. His foot hit the top of the ladder and snapped the rung. Then the next rung snapped, then the next, and he clawed the air to grab on to any part of the ladder he could. His dagger was gone. His head hit the wall and a white flash burst across his vision.

Richard's leg caught on a rung which amazingly didn't break, and that spun him upside down and he smashed his head on the rungs below.

He was upside down, but the ground was now close. He clenched his core to haul himself up, but the pain was almost unbearable and he cried out. Richard righted himself and climbed down the last three rungs of the shattered ladder. Except the bottom run was already broken, and his foot tried to stand on it and it wasn't there. Richard fell off the ladder and thudded onto the earth below on his back, hitting his head yet again.

Bowman stood over him. 'That's what your tantrum earlier got you.'

The blonde knight held out a hand for him and pulled Richard to his feet. His children both stood still nearby, struck dumb by the body of the priest with a seared and blistered hand who lay next to the ladder.

Bowman looked up. 'Where's Sophie?'

Alexander, water in his eyes, looked up from the priest. 'Why did you do that, father? You will go to hell.'

Richard couldn't answer him because a blackness he'd never known before engulfed him. 'Sophie is dead.'

Bowman's eyes froze and there was silence.

No one spoke, no one moved, and Alexander glanced towards his sister.

Richard felt dizzy.

Shouts from inside the castle broke the quiet.

Bowman, his expression pale in the darkness, grabbed Richard and shook him. 'We need to get to the horses and ride away from here. We don't have much time to make ourselves scarce.'

Richard felt the wetness of tears roll down his cheeks, but his mind was numb. 'We can't take the road east along the wall,' he said.

'Why not?' Bowman asked.

Richard glanced along the road and down the wall to where he knew his wife lay. 'We just can't.'

WOUNDS

Sir John's dagger had fallen from the wall when Richard did, but it had landed on the Tancarville priest and embedded itself in his chest as if the blade itself knew its purpose. Richard stared at it, then blacked out.

His senses returned as Bowman and Maynard together lifted him up into the saddle of the blue roan, surrounded by trees and the icy blackness of the night. He cried out from the pain in his stomach and Bowman shushed him. 'They will have men on foot searching the woods soon,' the blonde man said, 'scent hounds probably. I know you're hurting, but we must be swift and silent, young lord.'

Branches snapped to the south and Richard panicked for a moment before Bowman told him it was just Sarjeant returning from finding Nicola.

'She says to meet her at the chapel of Saint Jean in the morning,' Sarjeant whispered. 'It's north, do you know it?'

Bowman nodded and passed Richard his reins. 'We rode by that chapel when we hunted here years ago,' Bowman said. 'If we pick our way north through the forest, I'll find it. Not straight away, but we'll get there.'

Maynard threw up in a dense thicket of thorns, but the rest of the party rapidly readied their horses. Bowman dropped the canopy of branches that had dissipated the smoke from their fire onto the ashes of it, in the hope it would conceal the remains of the fire from any pursuers. Then the knight took the lead heading north.

It was slow going. More than once Bowman had to double back because of a wall of thorns or such dense, low trees that the horses simply couldn't get through.

It was dark too, and branches and twigs struck faces. Many curses were aimed in the direction of the foliage that night, but after a seemingly endless slog, a faint ray of light illuminated the cloudy sky above.

Bowman nodded at the faint glow. 'Good,' he said, 'we've been going north.'

'What do you mean, good?' Maynard asked. 'You mean you were guessing our direction the whole night?'

'Aye,' the blonde man said, 'no stars and no sun, what did you think I was doing?'

Brian had a long branch of thorns stuck in his cloak. 'Are we near the chapel?' He ripped the thorns off, ripping his cloak and cutting his finger.

Bowman shrugged. 'Once we find a sign of life I'll answer that. But Lillebonne is probably only a short way east of the chapel.'

'Yes,' Sarjeant said wearily, 'she is sending us the back way towards Lillebonne.'

'Mounted pursuers will take the road,' Bowman said, 'and get to Lillebonne before us.'

Sarjeant looked back behind him into the trail of broken vegetation they'd left behind. 'Although we won't be hard to track.'

'We don't have much choice,' Bowman stood next to his horse and patted its neck. He noticed something on the woodland floor and bent down to scrape something into a linen bag. He went to Richard and unlaced the mangled leather breastplate.

'This thing is done now,' the blonde man tossed it to Maynard. Then Bowman took some of the moss out of his bag and stuffed it into Richard's stomach wounds.

Which hurt.

Richard cried in pain but stifled it with his hands over his mouth. He gritted his teeth and tears flowed out of his eyes, which at least cleared the dust which had been scratching his eyeballs all night.

'There,' Bowman said, 'this moss is a special sort, young lord. It stops corruption.'

Richard knew of it, everyone knew of it, but his world swam and it took everything he had just to remain upright in the saddle. He was thirsty and his thoughts were slow and jumbled.

Bowmen left him and continued to take the company north.

They trudged ahead in silence as the dawn chorus chimed around them. The light grew brighter and filtered down to the earth and the horses stumbled less. Their eyes were stung by fewer unseen branches.

Soon after, Bowman emerged onto a narrow track, but for the first time it was a track used by people rather than animals. The going improved and Richard could close his eyes and stop looking out for low branches. The blue roan's mood improved too, now he didn't have to watch his feet, and his walk smoothed out which Richard was glad of.

The chapel of Saint Jean was a modest wooden structure with a sloping roof of thatch and a golden cross shining above the doorway. It was the size of Yvetot's church, but at least it didn't have a lump of stone blocking the entrance. It was surrounded by trees instead of a village.

Nicola's cart stood next to the building, her small pony hobbled amongst the trees looking for some leaves that were still green.

Bowman sighed. 'You'll want to go in, won't you,' he said.

Richard nodded. 'I need to lie down,' he said. 'And I need to pray.'

Brian walked over. 'Me, too.'

Bowman groaned. 'This one time I'll go into the church,' he said, 'but only to help you.'

'No one cares,' Sarjeant said, 'just get him inside, he needs to rest.'

They helped Richard out of his saddle, and he limped into the chapel. His legs weren't wounded and he didn't know why he was limping, but inside it was dark and cool.

Richard lay himself down near the altar that Nicola inspected.

'There's not much here,' she turned and studied Richard. 'But you look terrible.'

'I feel terrible,' he clutched his side, then let his body melt into the floor as he lay on his back on the flagstones.

Brian knelt down, put his hands together, and started praying. 'Forgive me Father for my sins, forgive me for the base desires that drove me to take the life of a priest.'

Richard looked up at the old beams of the chapel's roof. They were not of uniform sizes, but they were robust and covered in a thicket of cobwebs, each strand enlarged by a layer of dust.

'If you hadn't killed him,' Richard said, 'I'd have done it, so don't feel too bad.'

'And if he hadn't done it,' Bowman added, 'I'd have surely done it. But I cannot believe you really said an eye for an eye, not when it was the young lord who stabbed him in it. What is wrong with you?'

'Something foul came over me,' the monk sniffed and clenched his hands together so tightly his knuckles turned white.

Nicola raised her eyebrows.

'Don't ask,' Bowman said. 'And don't ask where his wife is. She won't be coming with us and only the Lord can rescue her now.'

Richard could see Sophie's face up in the grey cobwebs, but that was most likely an effect of his wounds. He'd seen his wife's face in his daughter's too, as they pushed through the woodland, and the sight of Lora's face had haunted him. He didn't know if he'd ever be able to gaze upon his own daughter properly ever again.

Nicola sat down next to Richard and inspected his injuries. She prodded the deeper wound with a long, bony finger and wiggled the moss around. 'Not bad,' she said, 'it's been packed well.'

Bowman crossed his arms and nodded. On another day he might have grinned.

'How deep is it?' she asked. 'If he cannot travel, then you shall have tough decisions to make.'

'I'll travel,' Richard said, 'I'd rather die from the journey than a Tancarville noose.'

'I don't think the Little Lord would go for a noose,' the blonde man said, 'I think he'd come up with something more creative.'

'As long as he doesn't kick me with my own horse,' Richard groaned. His head hurt and lumps had swollen up on his skull where'd smashed it against the outside of Castle Tancarville.

'You never said how deep it was,' Nicola said.

Bowman coughed and beckoned the old woman to him.

'No one ever thinks of my knees,' she pushed herself up and shuffled to the tall knight.

Bowman whispered something in her ear. Then they both looked at Richard.

'What? Is it that bad?'

'No, young lord,' Bowman said. 'It's just not that good.'

'We can wait out the sunlight here,' Nicola said, 'give him some time to start healing. The Tancarvilles will ride east from the castle now dawn has broken, and they will make straight for Lillebonne. We want to cross after them.'

Bowman nodded. 'Anyone they send into the woods will take longer than a day to find us. Unless they stumble onto our trail.'

'Pray they don't think you'll flee north,' Nicola said. 'But then, why would you flee north? There is nothing that way but the narrow sea.'

Brown let out a deep breath and shook his head. 'We can't move fast with a party of children and that cripple lying on the floor. We'll bump into a Tancarville rider at some point.'

'We only need to be on the road where it crosses the river at Lillebonne,' Nicola said, 'after that there are tracks only locals know.'

'I suppose you know them all.'

Nicola held up her hand, the blue veins clear under thin skin. 'Better than these lines,' she said. 'We'll disappear. The greatest danger lies at the crossing, and here. If a scout rides here, well,' she shrugged.

Bowman patted the bow he held still strung over his shoulder. 'I'll sit on the cart all day,' he said, 'and greet anyone I don't like the look of with an arrow.'

Nicola shook her head. 'It's always violence with you, isn't it?'

'I keep telling them that,' Brian turned from his prayer. 'One day it won't work out well.'

It hadn't worked out all that well in Castle Tancarville, Richard thought, it had killed his wife. He had killed his wife. She jumped because he'd refused to leave. Painful thoughts bubbled up in his battered head, and Richard was glad when the fuzziness of sleep encroached on his unruly mind and enveloped him.

At least Richard didn't dream of poking the Yvetot Priest's eyes out anymore. His welcome sleep broke when Bowman shot back into the chapel short of breath and with a wild face.

Richard couldn't feel any part of him that was still lying on the cold floor. He opened his eyes and then the agony of his stomach hit him.

'We need to go,' Bowman rushed over and crouched down.

'Why?' Richard groaned and tried to push himself up.

The blonde man picked the still mailed Richard up with a great heave and carried him out of the chapel as if he were a child. Twilight had already set in, and a fox's bark echoed in the distance.

Everyone saddled horses and gathered belongings.

Sarjeant threw a pile of bedding into the cart, collected Richard's belongings and threw his in too. 'Lie on that, my boy,' he said. 'We can't have you riding, you'll tear your insides apart.'

Bowman lifted Richard into Nicola's cart, and that's when he saw a new horse amongst them. It had a wooden war saddle painted red, and a thick leather breastplate across its chest. It sniffed at the blue roan and got a hoof in its face for its trouble. The new horse shook its head but the new shoe-shaped outline remained.

'Where did that horse come from?' Richard squeezed his side as he wedged himself up in the corner of his new transportation.

Bowman nodded down the road.

A body lay sprawled half on the track and half on a bush, one arrow in its chest and another in its neck.

'The old woman was right,' Bowman said, 'they did send scouts.'

Richard groaned and sunk back into the cart, the wooden sides hiding the road and chapel and leaving him to gaze up at the tops of the bare trees that swayed gently in the evening breeze.

He watched the treetops when the cart moved and the sky above them grew yet darker.

The company rode in silence. Everyone avoided meeting Richard's eyes when he tried to look out, and soon those riding on horses all grouped together far ahead of the cart.

'They are afraid they might say the wrong thing to you,' Nicola said after the cart hit a hole in the road which jarred Richard's back.

Richard didn't mind because he didn't want to speak to anyone anyway. His children were scared of him and Sophie was gone. His village was gone. Soon his life might be gone, too, and he'd go to the next world as badly off as Sir Rob had in the abbey at Lagny. He shivered.

The moon snuck out from behind a cloud. Owls hooted somewhere and Richard cursed them, then tried to doze as the cart bumped along the uneven track. The wheels creaked and wobbled, but it settled into a rhythm and Richard slipped once more into sleep.

They reached Lillebonne and the main road so late that all three children slept next to Richard when the halting of the cart woke him up. Lora lay near Richard, but none of them woke up. He couldn't imagine what the past few days had done to them, he wasn't even sure how many days it had been.

Nicola leant back. 'I can see the shadow of the wall of the castle up ahead. We'll cover the cart now. Try not to make any noise.'

Richard didn't need to be told, he was sure the castellan was on the lookout for them. He was certain that the castellan would have given orders to check everyone crossing to the east, and a cart arriving at night, which was most unusual anyway, wouldn't be spared a search.

But he couldn't move, let alone think of anything better to do, so he closed his eyes as the canvas rustled over the cart and cocooned him and his children inside.

Soon the cart rumbled on. Then it parked again and muffled words were exchanged. Someone laughed. Nicola's reins cracked and the wooden wheels moved again with a great squeal, on a smoother surface this time, and then onto the noisy bridge. The whole cart bounced up and down on each plank, and the screeches and moans of the bridge seemed to last forever. The children woke up and Lora clung to Richard. He held a finger to his lips and hushed and they understood. They shouldn't have had to understand, not at their ages. Alexander and the Red Child found opposite corners of the cart and glared between each other with tight lips.

Richard had no idea how he could resolve whatever their problem was.

They crossed the river and after only a few moments they stopped. Richard knew they would be nowhere far enough along to be through Sancho's camp, and he fumbled for Sir John's dagger as the canvas was swept off and fresh air washed over his face.

Bowman's head peered down at him and smiled. 'The Navarrese dogs have all gone, young lord. Maybe our luck has changed.'

'Don't say that,' Sarjeant's voice said from somewhere.

Richard pulled himself up by his elbows. Lora released her grasp on him and looked up with uncertain and frightened eyes.

Richard had to look away, his heart ached because he couldn't make eye contact.

Outside the cart, the meadow was empty. Yellow patches of grass marked the spots where shelters and tents had stood, mounds of ashes and semi-burnt wood stood between them. Piles of unused firewood were the largest thing left behind by Sancho's company, and relief swept over Richard.

Bran mumbled a prayer, his lips moving and his eyes closed.

Maynard, leading all their spare horses, relaxed too.

'It will take two nights to reach Cailly,' Nicola said.

'We need to avoid Cleres,' Bowman remounted his horse.

Nicola clicked her tongue and Two-Legs pushed into her harness and began to walk again. 'I shall not bother to ask why,' she said. 'There are other routes, other villages to go through which do not lengthen the journey.'

Richard collapsed back into the cart and his eyes watched the mottled grey and black clouds overhead. He wondered why Nicola was helping them, said a quiet prayer for a safe journey, then again fell asleep.

His dreams were of his ruined village, tortured beams sticking out of the earth still smouldering, winged demons soaring overhead, and his daughter tugging at his tunic and looking up at him with her big round eyes. A tune danced over it all, the mournful tune of the flute-playing guard outside the tower at Castle Tancarville. Then he heard the rush of Sophie's dress as it flew from the top of it.

He woke up with a start, covered in sweat and breathing quickly. He could smell smoke in the air. The cart was stationary and he wondered if they'd made a fire.

Richard clambered up the sides of the cart and the outside world appeared. Ahead of him, the riders of his small group sat on their horses looking down at the village of Cailly.

Or what was left of it.

Houses on the edge of the town had collapsed and buildings in the centre still burned. Bodies lay in the streets and dogs looked for their families or sated their hunger on the dead. Ash floated through the air on the breeze. The sun had risen, and it felt like it might be mid-morning, but that didn't matter because his refuge was gone.

Bowman turned his horse around very slowly and walked towards Richard. 'Ah, you're awake,' his face was glum and dark circles ringed his eyes. Richard didn't think he enjoyed being responsible for everyone.

'The castle still stands,' Bowman nodded towards the keep on its mound, 'no smoke comes from it and I'm sure I can see movement on the walls. Gerold and your horse may still live.'

Richard's heart wobbled and he swallowed down the mix of emotions that plagued him. 'We need to find out.'

The party crossed a bridge over the ditch in which two crossbowmen lay floating, and Richard decided to lie back down in the cart. He didn't need to see another burning village. His mind was full of burning villages. Lying on his back and with Lora huddled on his chest, he had no choice but to watch the plumes of smoke roll overhead. They kept stopping so bodies could be cleared out of the cart's path, but eventually they reached the castle's wall and Richard once again heaved himself up.

Bowman rode forwards and waited for men to appear on the wall by the gate.

They soon did, with loaded crossbows. One of them was the brave crossbowman who had almost shot de Cailly when they last entered the village. 'It's only them,' he shouted back down into the bailey.

'Good,' Bowman said, 'so you can let us in now. I'll even say please.'

The brave crossbowman frowned. 'We aren't letting anyone in, not after what happened.'

'Fetch your lord then,' the blonde knight said, 'he'll let us in. Can't you see we have a wounded knight to care for?'

'Sir Roger isn't here,' the crossbowman replied. 'No knights are here. I think I'm in charge now.'

'In charge of what?' Bowman asked. 'Where did Sir Roger go?'

'To join the king.'

'Which king?'

The crossbowman put his crossbow down and leant on the wall. 'He didn't say.'

Bowman groaned. 'Give me strength. What happened here?'

'The dogs of war came back,' the crossbowman said, 'I think it's clear what happened.'

'Can you let us in, we have come a long way and need to rest.'

The crossbowman shook his head. 'We've agreed to keep the gate barred until Sir Roger comes back.'

'We?'

'We had a meeting and it was agreed.'

'So you won't help us? Even though you know exactly who we are,' Bowman asked.

'We don't trust you.'

'Can you at least give us some food? We haven't eaten for days,' Bowman said, 'my belly feels like a rabid dog is clawing at it.'

'We'll discuss it,' the crossbowman disappeared back into the bailey.

Bowman rode back to Richard. 'I don't know what's going on in there, young lord, but the world is going mad. Maybe the priests are right, maybe the end times are coming.'

Brian shook his head. 'This is just men being men,' he said, 'it's no different to what you did in Meath.'

'It is,' Bowman said, 'this time it's being done to us, not by us.'

The monk frowned, but didn't have time to reply as the crossbowman reappeared and dropped a linen blanket onto the ground outside the wall. It spilled open and a few loaves of bread rolled out.

'Cowards,' Bowman muttered under his breath.

'We should take what we can get,' Richard said, 'ask if Gerold, Solis, and Judas are well.'

Bowman did so as Sarjeant scooped up their new hoard of food.

'The old man is sitting up now,' the crossbowman answered, 'I don't know about the horse, but the dog keeps jumping out of the stable and nobody can catch him to put him back.'

'Find out about Solis,' Richard asked. He tried to shout, but his throat was so dry he croaked instead.

The crossbowman sent someone to check on the palomino.

'Will you let them out?' Bowman asked him.

'Of course, we don't want them here.'

'Wait,' Richard said, 'it's already bad enough you have me slowing us down. Gerold could ride in the cart, but that's hardly fair on Two-Legs. I'd rather we left the children here behind these walls.'

'Why?' Bowman asked. 'Where are we going now?'

'Isn't it obvious?' Richard asked.

'Not really, young lord,' the blonde knight said, 'we came here for safety and rest. We have nowhere else to go.'

'We'll go where Sir Roger went,' Richard said, 'and we need to go as quickly as we can.'

'Can we leave the children with you?' Bowman shouted up.

'No,' the crossbowman replied, 'what do you think we are, some kind of church?'

'They are merely children,' the blonde man said, 'they can't hurt you. They won't open your gate at night.'

'If we open the gates for them now, you might try to come in. You might be tricking us, besides, we have agreed not to.'

'You know who we are,' Bowman's voice strained. 'We are friends of your lord.'

'It still could be a trick,' the crossbowman said, 'we can't risk it. There are supplies for months here, but too few of us to fight you if you get inside.'

'Sarjeant,' Richard said, 'would you stay here and protect the children? Maybe act as the steward of the castle while we're gone?'

'Whatever you need.'

Richard raised his voice. 'We'll leave my steward and my children with you. They can stand outside your gate, then we'll ride off. You can let them in when we're too far away to trick you. Will you take them in then?'

'We'll have to talk about it,' the crossbowman's head vanished behind the wall again.

'This is ridiculous,' Bowman said, 'if you talk everything through you never get anything done.'

The crossbowman came back after what seemed like a very long time. 'We have decided Sir Roger would be upset if we refused your request,' he said. 'But we'll only open the gate once you're out of sight.'

'Are you leaving us?' Lora asked.

'I'm sorry,' Richard kept his eyes on the castle, 'you're safer behind the walls, and you know Sarjeant better than you know me.'

The Red Child cradled his sword. 'I'll man the walls with the guards,' he said. 'I'll learn to shoot a crossbow.'

Richard believed him, not that he was tall enough to see over the walls. 'I need all of you to look after my horse and my dog,' he said, 'and speak to Gerold, he was my father's man and he can tell you about your family. All the things your mother didn't know.'

Lora started to cry.

'What about us?' Bowman asked.

'Find Sir Roger.'

'I know, but we don't know which king he's with.'

'We do,' Richard stroked Lora's hair, 'he'll be with the older one. The Tancarvilles are searching for us, and they are on the Young King's side. So we go to Old King Henry.'

'You want to switch sides again?'

'We're still on our side,' Richard replied. 'We've only ever been on our side.'

Maynard looked uncomfortable at the sight of a crying child. 'We should go to the Young King,' he said, 'he will take you back, and then we can earn bags of coins.'

'I'm not earning anything for a while,' Richard winced at the gashes in his stomach.

Bowman silenced the squire with a look.

'Rouen,' Nicola said.

Everyone looked at her.

'Rouen,' she repeated, 'that's where we need to go. In the city someone will know where the king is. And we shall reach it before nightfall.'

Richard didn't have a better idea, so he agreed. Then he prised his daughter away from him, which hurt his stomach, and Sarjeant lifted her out of the cart. Alexander started to cry too, and only with great cajoling could they get the twins to walk with Sarjeant to the castle gate. The Red Child hoped down happily, his sword hitting the ground and leaving a line in the earth behind him.

Richard couldn't watch as the cart rumbled away, he knew he didn't have to leave them behind, but he couldn't take them with him either. He couldn't look at Sophie's eyes, they both had Sophie's eyes. He prayed for forgiveness for his weakness, and that his yellow horse was doing well. The answer to his condition never came, but Richard decided it was for the best, for he couldn't tolerate more bad news. Instead he covered himself in blankets, now alone in the cart, and cursed the Little Lord. Richard clutched the linen strip on his tunic that had once been his crusading cross. He'd promised to take the cross and journey east at least two times in his life so far, and now he did so again. If his children, horse, and Gerold all recovered, then he would go east. He'd reclaim the silver and leave everything behind. Not that there was much left to leave.

They reached Rouen with the sun still in the sky, just as Nicola had predicted, and found a church that would allow them to sleep in a hall they maintained for poor travellers. None of the impoverished men and women who slept in it had ever shared a hall with the likes of Richard before. Their eyes followed the golden spurs as Bowman moved around, and everyone shuffled away from the unusual visitors, but Richard didn't care about any of that.

Nicola woke him in the morning with news. The old woman handed him a bowl of pottage with her wrinkled hands. 'Limoges,' she said.

'What's that?' Richard asked.

'You mean, where,' she replied, 'it's a place.'

'Is that where King Henry is?'

Nicola nodded. 'Unfortunately.'

'Why? Is it a bad place?'

'I've never been,' Nicola said, 'but it's probably as far south as La Rochelle or Niort. It could take us ten days to reach it.'

Richard groaned, the cart was less comfortable than a saddle.

Bowman took Richard's blankets away from him. 'We had better get going then,' he grinned, 'I can't wait to find out how angry this king will be with us.'

KNIGHT OF THE CART

As it turned out, they needn't have bothered going to Rouen for directions. Richard watched from his cart as it trundled through village after village that had been raised to the ground.

'Sancho,' Bowman said with distaste at the first devastated settlement they'd found. 'But all we need to do is follow the smoke and we'll find both kings.'

Some larger villages and towns had spared themselves Sancho's wrath by paying him off, and those men's eyes followed Richard with disdain as they continued their journey south.

'Have they never seen a knight in a cart before?' Richard asked when the laughing burghers of Chartres threw mud at him as they traversed the city's gleaming streets.

'No,' Nicola said, 'knights do not ride in carts. There is a new story going around about a knight who has to ride in a cart to save a queen, and the whole point is how riding in a cart is beneath a knight. I think the men of Chartres have heard it.'

'I don't really care,' Richard muttered. Chartres ran along a wide river and had many buildings with white walls and red roofs. It seemed somehow cleaner than London. Luckily it had plenty of holy houses and churches, and they found adequate refuge in the city for a night.

The journey towards Limoges was arduous, but the weather was warmer, the sun brighter, and the clouds smaller than in Normandy. Maynard started to whistle in the mornings and Brian stopped spinning his neck around to see if they were being followed.

Bowman rode ahead to scout from time to time, but they had plenty of horses now, so he could afford to use their strength to check the mercenaries were not over the next valley or through the next forest. Each time he reported back from the road ahead it was a tale of another shattered village or ransom paid, but the mercenaries still led them.

'If anything, I think they're pulling ahead,' Bowman said, 'which is hardly surprising given the speed of that wheeled contraption.'

'I'll ride soon,' Richard said, and he hoped it was true.

'You had better,' Bowman said, 'no disrespect to the old woman, but we need to be moving quicker.'

'Why?' Richard asked. 'So we can catch up with Sancho sooner and get captured by him?'

'No,' Bowman said, 'because we need to see how things are looking as fast as possible. If one side outmatches the other, we need to be on the winning one.'

'I just need to reach the king and Sir Roger. He needs to know what happened to Cailly,' Richard said, 'and maybe the king will grant me Keynes.'

'Hadn't you given that up?'

'I don't know,' Richard sank back into his cart. 'I need somewhere safe for my children to grow up, I don't much care where it is anymore.'

'There was a deal concerning Keynes,' Bowman said, 'and I think you might struggle to argue that you upheld it.'

'Cailly then,' Richard said, 'maybe I'll take Sir Roger up on his offer of Yquebeuf.'

'We've been over that,' the blonde man said, 'I know you hit your head, but if I need to explain things to you again and again, we're going to have a problem.'

'We already have a problem,' Richard said, 'or more than one. There's two in my stomach right now.'

'I'll change the moss later,' Bowman said.

Later came and went. Chateauroux came and went too, a town in the picturesque valley of the River Indre. The air wasn't as sharp at night as it had been outside the walls of Castle Tancarville, and in the day the sun was strong enough to warm Richard's face. The air grew only more pleasant as they journeyed south, the land greener, but the villages were all torched and they saw more and more dead travellers in the ditches and hedges as they drew near to Limoges.

Bowman raised an alarm with a great shout, his horse cantering back down the road towards the cart. He arrived so fast that Sarjeant's horse reared up and spun to get away from him, but he stayed where he was and didn't bolt.

'What is it?' Richard asked.

'A company heading this way,' Bowman puffed.

'How long do we have?'

'They'll crest the ridge before we turn the cart around,' the blonde man replied.

Sure enough, fifty horsemen swept down the road, rapidly followed by a great cloud of dust that engulfed everyone and made Richard cough.

The horsemen arrived, but the dust had to blow over before either party could work out who the other was.

Richard wiped fine grit from his face and studied the red and yellow quartered banner. He knew it, but couldn't place it in his memory.

Bowman coughed next to the cart. 'I'll be damned if we haven't seen that banner before.'

'I know,' Richard said, 'and I can just hear Sir Thomas chiding me for forgetting whose it is.'

The owner of the banner spat onto the side of the road as the yellow cloud from his hooves settled.

He squinted at Richard, then his eyes narrowed at Bowman. 'The men who helped me take Conan of St-Malo's castle,' he smiled. 'Am I right?'

Richard nodded, and his recollection of Brittany came back to him. 'Sir William,' he said, 'do you still have the hammer you used there?'

William Mandeville, Earl of Essex, grinned. His smooth, clear face was covered in dust, but the curly brown hair under his yellow and red painted helmet was something Richard recognised. 'I still have the hammer,' Mandeville replied, 'although I've left it at the siege.'

'Who is besieging who?' Richard asked.

'We have cornered the rebels,' Mandeville said.

Bowman frowned. 'You're going to have to be more specific,' he said. 'And you'll have to name whatever kings might be involved, I've had enough of being confused.'

'You were the rude one,' Mandeville half smiled, 'but you Richard, your face is mangled and you seem to have forgone travelling by horse.'

'I was wounded fighting the Tancarvilles. Did you hear about the siege of Neufchatel?'

'You were wounded there, were you?' Mandeville frowned. 'To still be this unwell after so long you should seek a bishop.'

'I have to make do with a monk,' Richard said. 'Is King Henry here?'

'He means the old one,' Bowman added.

Mandeville nodded. 'We have his son trapped inside the abbey of Saint Martial.'

'I heard King Henry was at Limoges,' Richard said.

Mandeville laughed. 'You ignorant country knights. Saint Martial could be described as one half of Limoges. There is a settlement around a bridge over the river that people call Limoges, but closer to us the abbey stands in the centre of another urban area. It has its own walls, they are the height of two men, and the king's son is fortified there.'

'Good,' Boman said, 'it seems we're on the right side for once.'

'The king's side is always the right side,' Mandeville said with as much enthusiasm as he could.

'You would say that,' Nicola grinned at him, 'seeing as your father was no better than the Tancarvilles.'

Mandeville's face darkened, and his smile retreated. 'I do not recall asking a woman's opinion.'

'No one ever does,' she replied. 'But it is no mere opinion that your father died in rebellion to the king you serve.'

'That's enough, Sir William is our friend,' Richard said, 'can you take us to the king?'

'I am scouting in search of the Marshal,' Mandeville said, 'he led a raid somewhere north and we must stop him.'

'The Marshal?' Bowman scratched his nose.

'If the rebellion is a warship, he is its figurehead. He strikes out like lightning, raids monasteries and shrines, then brings the spoils back to his master at Saint Martial. The ill-gotten plunder is used to pay for their mercenaries, without which their rebellion would crumble.'

'How can the Marshal ride out if Saint Martial is under siege?' Richard asked.

'Ah,' Mandeville rested his lance on his foot, 'this is more of a standoff. King Henry cannot order an attack on an abbey, you see. Do you remember the Becket problem?'

Richard nodded. 'So he can't attack the Young King while he's in a holy building.'

'The boy is a coward. I remember the Marshal too, and who his friends were. I knew he was a bad one from the start, when he pestered me for food.'

'He's a prancing peacock,' Bowman added, not having to fake his opinion in the slightest.

'And that is why I cannot escort you to the king,' Mandeville said, 'but I have two squires I can spare to show you the way. Not that you should struggle, he is on this very road, camped on the north side of Saint-Martial's moat.'

'What kind of abbey has a moat?' Brian asked.

Mandeville raised his eyebrows. 'Your monk is speaking to me, Richard.'

'He's from Ireland,' Richard said, 'he's yet to learn proper manners.'

'I see,' Mandeville replied, 'my men will guide you. Speak to the king if you wish, find someone to treat your wounds. But stay away from the king's mercenaries, they are from the Brabant and are distasteful. They'd steal the dressing from your wound.'

'Thank you,' Richard said.

'I hope you catch the peacock,' Bowman shouted behind the earl as he took his company back north in pursuit of the man Richard had previously called a friend. He had no idea what to call him now, probably a threat considering Bowman had aimed a crossbow bolt at him. The peacock was not likely to release that grudge in a hurry.

They travelled behind the two squires through land that didn't appear all that different to Normandy. Although strangely, Richard thought, it had more ferns.

'Even his squires have surcoats.' Bowman said as they found their first village that had been neither devastated nor rinsed for a ransom. 'Why don't we have surcoats?'

'Because I don't have any money to pay for them.'

The blonde knight snorted. 'And whose fault is that?'

'I needed to pay Sancho,' Richard said, 'are you suggesting that I should have spent the money on new surcoats instead of rescuing my children?'

'Your wife would still be alive,' Bowman said.

'Don't you dare,' Richard shouted but caught himself before he lost his temper.

'Stop it,' Nicola said as the cart bounced in the air after hitting something. 'You'll need your wits about you where we're going, and you'll all need to stick together.'

Richard went to cross his arms but his stomach twinged and he couldn't.

'Why do we need to worry about where we're going?' Sarjeant asked.

Nicola laughed. 'Your young knight perhaps hasn't quite told you everything about his adventures.'

'There hasn't been time,' Richard said.

'You are running to your old friend Sir Roger,' Nicola said, 'and to the Old King in the hope he'll have forgotten most of what recently has passed between you. On that account you may be lucky, but what sort of company do you think King Henry keeps?'

'His knights?' Richard replied.

'And who else?'

Bowman swore. 'Him. The root of all of it.'

Richard groaned and closed his eyes. 'Maybe we'll be able to avoid him, but if we don't, you can't start any trouble with Geoffrey Martel.'

'Start it?' Bowman laughed. 'He started it when he kidnapped my mother. Mark my words though, young lord, I'm going to end it.'

'Not before we find somewhere for the children to live,' Richard said, 'your revenge will have to wait.'

Bowman clenched his fingers around his sword pommel, rubbing the disc as if the motion would relieve his anger.

'I'm sure we can move around the king's camp unnoticed,' Richard said, 'it'll be a vast camp. We can speak to the king, find Sir Roger, then leave.'

'What, go back north and live like a hearth son?' Bowman said. 'That sounds like giving up to me.'

'Why shouldn't I give up?' Richard asked. 'Trying to make things better has just cost me more. Every time. We at least need somewhere to live until this war is over.'

The royal camp rolled into view. The plain beyond the abbey of Saint-Martial's moat bustled with activity, but not relating to the building of siege engines. Instead work parties chopped wood or rode out to gather food. At its heart, the king's tent was large, occupying more land than Richard's own keep, and so tall he wondered how anyone could transport it. It was white with vertical lines of gold all around it, which seemed to make it even taller.

'The bastard's here,' Bowman pointed to the tent Geoffrey Martel had erected for himself at the Corbie tournament. But it wasn't the only other tent. Hundreds of tents littered the landscape, not in one huge camp, but in clusters around banners spread out far and wide.

'I suppose we're heading for the big tent,' Richard said.

Two-Legs pulled him onwards behind Mandeville's squires.

'Do you want to get on your horse for this part?' Bowman asked.

Richard did, he didn't want to look like he wasn't a real knight, but equally he didn't want to look like he cared how he looked. 'I'm fine where I am,' he said, 'a knight doesn't care what others think about him.'

'That's not how all the knights I've met have acted,' Bowman said.

Sarjeant chuckled in agreement and Richard stayed in the cart all the way up the lines of horses that took up as much space as the royal company's tents.

Line upon line of horses were tied to makeshift wooden railings, piles of fodder to eat in front of them, and a small army of boys engaged in a never ending battle to remove their droppings from the camp. A dozen carts worked in a rotation to be loaded with horse dung and then ferry their steaming loads off to somewhere else.

'There'll be a bumper crop next year around here,' Sarjeant mused. 'That's what we lacked in Yvetot.'

'That and a lord,' Richard stood up. 'Amongst other things.'

Sarjeant helped him down and Richard's feet hit the earth with an uncomfortable thud. He still wore his mail, which rusted orange both around his midriff and where he'd bled onto his legs.

'If you had a surcoat, no one would see that mess,' Bowman said. 'But you look to be able to walk more easily than before.'

Richard grimaced with the pain of walking, but the pain had faded to a dull ache, which only became more intense when he moved. Bowman and Nicola had stopped whispering behind his back about him, too.

'Will you be waiting for us?' Richard asked the woman before he tried to gain entrance to the royal tent.

The old woman shrugged. 'I'll rest my pony here for a couple of days,' she said. 'If you happen to be leaving then and want to go the same way, we can carry on together.'

'Thank you for your help,' Richard said, 'I'd have bled to death without you.'

'Don't thank me,' she said, 'just don't go after the silver. It will kill you more quickly than your stomach wounds could.'

'Silver?' Maynard spun around even as he tied his horse to a space on a railing.

'Shut up,' Bowman clipped him around the back of the head and tied his own horse up.

Richard nodded to Nicola instead of answering her and limped into the tent.

Bowman alone followed. 'Why are you limping?'

'Because I have to,' Richard said, 'but try to be quiet. If Geoffrey Martel is here, I'd rather you left before he noticed you.'

Bowman snorted and waved the question of a guard away. One of Mandeville's squires spoke to them before they could raise an alarm, and Richard entered the tent in search of the king.

Richard expected to find a vast audience as he had back at Canterbury Castle the last time he'd spoken to the monarch, but the scene he found couldn't have been more different.

A man in a striped red and blue cloak waved a stick at a brown bear which danced on its hind legs and howled into the musty air of the cavernous tent. The bear had a black iron collar around its neck, but its owner had taken off a thick metal chain that lay coiled on the rushes beside him. The handler twirled the stick and the bear twirled too, then dropped to four legs and roared at the handler.

He reached into a pouch and threw a fillet of fish through the air. The animal batted it out of the air with its giant paw, sniffed it on the ground, then ate it.

'Impressive,' King Henry clapped. Two dozen men stood around him and clapped along. There was no crowd of nobles or important locals.

The bear wasn't the only animal in the tent, a white pony, stockily built, knelt down on two knees and bowed to the king.

'That's what I like to see,' King Henry cried, 'this horse has more respect for me than my own sons do.'

The pony's handler bowed to the king himself. 'Your majesty, would you like the horse to point out the most venerable, courageous, and magnificent man in the tent?'

The King slapped his leg. 'Go on, I don't know how you'll make a horse do that.'

The handler appeared to do nothing, but the pony got back up onto four legs, then waved a white foot at the King. He roared with laughter and clapped again. 'I grant you a village somewhere. I don't know which one, but my clerks will sort it out for you.'

The handler bowed and both animals were led away.

'Quite impressive,' Bowman nodded.

'If you say so,' Richard said. 'I'm sure it's not too hard to train that.'

'You,' the king flashed a finger with a blue-jewelled ring at him. The canvas rippled around the tent as a gust of wind moved around the structure. A rank of fine birds of prey were perched around the edge of the tent in the background, and some fluttered their wings as they sensed the movement of the canvas.

Richard approached and bowed, although he only made it halfway before he clutched his wound with a gasp.

'What have you done to yourself this time?'

'A spear,' Richard said. 'Well, two different spears really.'

Henry's laugh boomed across the empty tent. 'I suppose you are but a country knight, it's hardly a surprise that you would allow yourself to be skewered by the common folk.'

A handful of the men with him sneered and chortled. One did not, a tall man of a distinguished age with piercing green eyes and a surcoat with a red and yellow chequerboard pattern.

Bowman clenched his jaw beside Richard.

'This is not a time for jokes,' Geoffrey Martel said to the king, 'nor is this a time for dancing bears and sycophantic ponies. This is a time for war, and what is more, these are the very men who killed and butchered my son.'

Richard sighed. So much for a quick conversation, the return of some land, and a peaceful exit.

'My son,' Geoffrey bellowed, 'these men tore off his jaw.'

'I know,' Henry waved a hand at him. 'Everyone knows. But we aren't speaking about it, are we?'

Geoffrey bristled.

The king rubbed his forehead. 'Your son tried to kill mine, and now he's dead, so the matter is settled.'

'Settled?' The Martel lord raised his voice. 'It was a murder, clean and clear. Eustace never wanted to kill your son, but merely to capture him. It was a tournament, after all.'

'Do not speak to your king so rashly,' Henry roared back, 'reliable men have told me of the numerous graves of the fallen. When two men die in a tournament, it is a tragedy, when a hundred die, it isn't a tournament.'

Geoffrey tapped his mailed foot hard on the rushes that lay scattered across the tent. Most had not yet been trampled on. 'Regarding these two, these two criminals, tell me then, whose banner did they serve under?'

Henry glanced up to the top of the tent, which already crawled with winged insects and spiders, locked in their own fight for supremacy in their new canvas battlefield.

'Need I remind you that the same banner flies above the abbey, while we watch bears and horses dance,' Geoffrey said. 'The abbey where everyone who opposes you flocks. The banner of your enemy.'

'He is my son,' the king shouted, 'he is not my enemy. He is my heir.'

'He is under arms and fighting against you,' the Martel lord said. 'Did he not lure you into an ambush just yesterday? Did his men not shoot at you?'

Henry's top lip twitched, the hair on his ginger beard flecked with white hairs. He looked older than the fifty years he'd lived.

'Why are you here Richard?' the Angevin king asked.

'He is a spy,' Geoffrey said, 'it is known that your rebel son sent a spy west to Neufchatel, as it is known he sent spies both south and to your court. Richard is one of them. His companion is known to me, he is a poacher and a criminal. A base man.'

'A base man?' Bowman frowned. 'What does that even mean?'

'Precisely,' the Martel said. 'These are your enemy's spies.'

'Do not call my son my enemy even one more time, so help me God if you do,' Henry turned to Richard. 'Are you a spy?'

Richard hesitated because he was supposed to be King Henry's spy.

'It is not a difficult question,' the king said.

'He is struck dumb by his own guilt,' Geoffrey said. 'He rode in your son's company, therefore he is your son's man.'

Richard licked his lips. 'I believe you will remember the agreement we had when we met in Canterbury?'

Henry narrowed his eyes and a black-robed monk filtered through from the back of the king's attendants.

'Not you,' Bowman groaned.

Brother Geoffrey shook his head at Richard. 'I'm sure our king does remember the deal,' the monk said, 'but he also knows you didn't keep it.'

'Do I?' Henry replied. 'I cannot keep up with every scheme and plot swirling around. I don't remember what we agreed on.'

'This boy double crossed you.'

'I'm loyal to the crown,' Richard said.

The king raised his hand for silence. One bird of prey squawked loudly and flapped its long brown wings.

'My king,' Geoffrey Martel said, 'hang him like the common criminal he is. There is no reason not to, hanging him would be a wise precaution.'

'You can't hang someone as a precaution,' Richard said, 'can you hear yourself?'

'Do not speak to me,' the Martel raised his nose, 'you are beneath me.'

'Everyone's beneath you,' Henry muttered, 'sometimes I look at you and think you expect me to bow to you.'

'Of course not.'

Bowman snorted. 'He thinks he's better than a king.'

Geoffrey stepped forwards and grabbed his sword. 'One more word from you and I'll remove your head myself. I should have done so years ago.'

'Draw that sword and I'll be the one removing heads,' Henry's face darkened.

The Martel saw the change in his face and withdrew, his head bowed.

'Coward,' Bowman mumbled under his breath.

The king ran his hands through his red hair. 'I am sick of bickering and fighting amongst my people. I have a mind to punish everyone in this tent just to make a point. I cannot trust you anymore, Richard.'

Richard opened his mouth, but the king's eyes had changed, he held his mouth differently and something told Richard he needed to be quiet.

'His village,' Brother Geoffrey whispered in the monarch's ear, 'by your agreement with him, he should lose his village.'

'What village?' the king's voice had a steel to it, a harshness that hadn't been there before.

'Yvetot,' the monk hissed.

Bowman coughed and had to raise a hand to his face to cover his smirk.

'Very well,' Richard said, 'I accept that, I'll leave Yvetot.'

The king frowned and stroked his chin. 'Most men wail or shout or threaten when I take something away from them,' he said, 'they don't accept it and remain unaffected.'

Richard swallowed. 'I humbly request that I could be given some land somewhere else. My loyalty to the crown has never been questioned.'

Both Geoffreys shouted accusations or insults at Richard and the birds of prey screeched in response.

'Silence,' the king shouted.

'He is a rebel,' the Martel lord said, 'treat him like one. Kill him, set an example to the others who hide behind the abbey's walls or ravage your land.'

Brother Geoffrey rubbed his hands together. 'There was another village, Keynes,' he said, 'do not give it back to him.'

'I wasn't going to,' the king said, 'I didn't even know it existed.'

Richard sweated down his back and his palms were clammy. 'Keynes would be a quiet place for my children to grow and me to improve. It is a worthless place, and you could be rid of me if you grant it to me.'

'This boy is the spawn of Satan,' the monk said, 'witness the impudence of what he asks.'

'I thought he'd been found innocent?' Henry asked. 'Or have I got that mixed up, too?'

'Perhaps,' Brother Geoffrey said, 'we speak about many, many people, perhaps this slipped your mind.'

The king growled, a low growl that Judas could have made. 'I have half a mind to execute you here and now, just to be sure.'

'Yes,' the monk said, 'very sensible.'

'Very wise,' Geoffrey Martel nodded.

'If you remove our heads,' Richard said, 'who will trust you then? Why are the reeds in your tent untrodden? Why are there not hundreds of knights here?'

'They are busy,' the Martel lord said. 'This is a siege.'

Richard didn't have much to lose. 'This is no siege, no one builds ladders or screens or rams. Your lords pitched their tents up on the hills around, why are they not fighting to camp as close to the royal tent as possible? Why do men still follow your son now that you no longer pay him the upkeep of his company?' Richard guessed the last part, but it hit home because the king's eyelids twitched.

The Angevin grabbed his own beard and tore out a small clump of hair with a great effort. 'No one dares speak to me like this,' the king roared, 'I rule more land than any man since Charlemagne, earls tremble in fear at my name, and I have crushed every single man who has raised a sword against me.'

Richard swallowed. 'And yet men flock to your son.'

The king jumped to his feet. 'If I draw my sword, do you think anyone will come to your aid? I am above the law, I wrote the law, I am the law.'

'I have no ill will towards you,' Richard bowed his head, 'I am loyal to the crown and wish nothing more than to help you.'

Henry seethed and even Geoffrey Martel backed off.

Bowman nudged Richard. 'I don't think what you're trying is working, young lord.' The blonde knight knelt down before the king. 'If I may speak,' he continued without waiting for an answer, 'Richard here is the most loyal knight you could wish for. He lost a finger for you in Brittany, captured one castle by himself, another almost by himself, saved your life at least once that I saw, and most recently, defeated the Young King in battle.'

Uncertainty replaced the darkness across Henry's face. 'What battle? Speak.'

'Don't listen to him,' Geoffrey Martel sneered, 'he is spinning lies.'

Bowman looked up at the monarch. 'You have heard of the siege of Neufchatel, have you not?'

The king nodded.

'What is Neufchatel to you?' Bowman asked.

'The lynchpin of eastern Normandy's defences,' the king said, 'the gateway into the duchy.'

Bowman smiled. 'And what happened when your son gave up the siege and marched away from it?'

'His rebellion was broken,' the king said, 'he had to slither his way down here, where he fights simply because he refuses to back down. He has already lost.'

'Do you know why your son left Neufchatel in your hands?' Bowman stood up.

Henry waited.

'Because Richard here ordered me to shoot one of the rebel leaders. Count Robert of Meulan, you must know him?'

'Another rebellious snake,' Brother Geoffrey interrupted, 'but your story is just that, a story.'

Bowman shook his head. 'Ask any man who was there who shot the crossbow that broke the siege. And it was this knight who ordered it.'

King Henry raised his eyebrows.

'It is a tall tale,' Brother Geoffrey said, 'for the men who say it was you, are in the pay of the Young King.'

'Ah,' Richard said, 'so others have heard said it was us?'

Henry's face cleared and he bellowed a booming laugh. 'Monk, I do love it when you're proven wrong. It is one of the few pleasures I have left. I am going to spare Richard, it seems he has done what none of the rest of you could, and defeated my son.'

Bowman grinned so hard his face could have shattered.

'But,' the king looked at him, 'that is as long as you did not aim at my son?'

'No, God help me, no,' Bowman said quickly. 'I can promise you I did not.'

Richard nodded. 'He most definitely did not aim at the Young King.'

'And those wounds,' Bowman pointed at Richard's body, 'those unsightly wounds, those he gained while fighting against the

Tancarvilles.'

The king picked up a cup resting on the arm of his throne and hurled it across the tent. 'Those renegades, how could they turn on me?'

'The Chamberlain has always been his own man,' Geoffrey Martel said.

'He can consider that privilege revoked,' the king rounded on a clerk who sat nervously off to one side. 'Write that down.'

Brother Geoffrey approached the king. 'If you wish to spare this man, then it is assuredly a wise idea.'

'Spare me your honeyed words, what do you want now?'

'Banish him,' the monk said, 'before the swells the ranks of the rebels.'

King Henry chuckled. 'Look at him, he's not swelling anyone's ranks. He can hardly stand up.'

'I have no wish to fight,' Richard said, 'my fighting days are behind me.'

Geoffrey Martel snorted. 'One cannot simply quit knighthood.'

The canvas flap that acted as a door to the tent was pushed aside and de Cailly entered. The knight stopped in his tracks. 'Richard?'

'Sir Roger,' Richard said, 'I have news for you.'

'What are you doing here?' de Cailly asked. 'Where is your family?'

Richard told him, although he left out the part about how they got into Castle Tancarville, and how reluctant de Cailly's men had been to admit his children. He especially left out what had happened to the two priests.

'I am so very sorry for your loss,' de Cailly said.

The king turned very slowly to face Brother Geoffrey. 'And you wanted me to kill this man as a traitor? I have heard a great many lies in my time, and this tale was not so tall as you suggested.'

De Cailly shook his head. 'Such an unnecessary tragedy,' he said, 'but I would be more than happy if you returned with me and helped to rebuild Cailly. You and your household are very welcome there.'

Geoffrey Martel watched de Cailly closely. 'Your majesty, you should not allow this, Sir Roger's lands are close to Rouen, do not allow this young knight and his unreliable loyalties to ferment rebellion in your heartlands.'

Brother Geoffrey wasn't done yet. 'My king, before you decide if you allow this, ask yourself, who is Sir Roger's lord?'

Henry groaned. 'I honestly don't remember.'

'Lord Tancarville,' the monk said triumphantly.

'I see,' the king drummed the armrest of the ornate throne that had travelled with him from Canterbury. 'I cannot allow your scheme Sir Roger, you must see that? I cannot trust you as the vassal of a rebel.'

De Cailly's eyes widened. 'I am here, am I not?'

'He could be another spy,' Brother Geoffrey said.

'The rebel mercenaries destroyed my village,' de Cailly said, 'do you take your king for a fool to suggest I am allied with those same men?'

'He has a point,' the king said, 'but I cannot risk Richard staying there. Richard, you are forbidden to seek refuge with any lords of the realm. I have too much to worry about to add you to the list.'

'This is madness,' Richard said, 'let me go to Cailly, there I shall never draw my sword in anger again. I just want to live in peace.'

All the king's confidants laughed.

'If we all took the path of peace, the world would fall apart,' Geoffrey Martel said, 'your ignorance is painful to hear.'

Richard's shoulders slumped. 'What am I supposed to do now, then?'

'Go home,' the king said.

'Home?' Richard's hands trembled. 'You've just ensured that I don't have one, that I can't have one.'

'Mind your tone,' the king said.

'This is exactly why men are riding to the abbey and your son,' Richard said, 'you should think about that.'

Four of the men behind the king drew their swords and advanced.

King Henry raised his hands to stop them. They paused.

'You need to give the sort of men you punish as you're punishing me another option than rebellion,' Richard said.

The Martel lord shook his head. 'Young men these days do not know how to speak to their elders.'

King Henry stared at Richard, his eyes burning a hole in him. Then the king tapped his armrest with his knuckles. 'They boy isn't wrong though, is he? Richard, I heard Count Philip of Flanders abandoned the rebellion at Neufchatel. He is normally happy to play me off against my son and never really favour either, you could try him. You must know him from your tournaments?'

Richard nodded.

'Good,' the king said, 'join his company, then at least you shall not harm me. But I do not wish to hear or see you ever again, is that clear?'

Richard ground his teeth. 'Very clear.' He turned to de Cailly. 'Goodbye Sir Roger, I shall retrieve my children and leave you free from the suspicion of harbouring me. I've caused you enough trouble, and I am truly very sorry about your village.'

De Cailly sighed. 'That was not your doing, and it is the way of the world. While there are men who would steal and harm the innocent and defenceless, the privileged of the world must live under arms. And there will never be an end to the sort of men who prey on the weak, so my village will not be the last to burn.'

'On that we can agree,' the king said. 'How else can the world work other than to revolve around the wars of noble men on noble horses?'

Richard, who now felt himself to be more of a Knight of the Cart, didn't know, but he was sure there was a better way.

KNIGHT OF NOTHING

Flanders was north. Far to the north, and Nicola drew her cart to a halt at the bottom of a gentle slope that was surrounded by woodland a very long time before they reached Count Philip's lands.

'This is as far as I'm taking you,' she tapped her driving whip across her legs.

'I don't think I can ride yet,' Richard said. 'And we're less than a day from Limoges.'

Bowman's gaze followed a fork off the road that made its way up the slope and into the trees. 'Do you know what's up there?'

'Why do you think I stopped you here?' Nicola replied. 'Just for the fun of dumping the cripple in the middle of nowhere?'

Bowman grinned. 'I would.'

'It's an abbey,' the old woman said, 'Grandmont. They are a poor order, but they will treat a poor knight. And no one will come looking for you here.'

'I suppose you have business back in Limoges?' Richard asked.

'I'll need to find someone to buy wool from,' she winked. 'But I know the Corrector here, he's the one who is in charge.'

Richard hauled himself out of her cart and tentatively lowered himself onto the ground. 'I'll miss the cart,' he said.

'Now you're not even the knight of the cart, you're the knight of nothing,' Bowman grinned.

Richard frowned at him but didn't have anything to counter with.

'Do they have manuscripts?' Brian asked.

Nicola shook her head. 'They do not approve of property, be it lands, cows, or books.'

Bowman groaned. 'Do they at least approve of making wine or brewing beer?'

'You are not here to feast,' Nicola waited for Maynard to dismount and unload their bedding from the cart.

Brian grunted.

'Or read,' the old woman turned Two-Legs around and clicked her tongue. Nicola never looked back.

The blue roan watched the pony and her cart trundle back towards Limoges and the Angevin civil war. He whickered softly.

'Don't tell me the warhorse is capable of something other than violence,' Bowman said.

'I don't want to use him again for war,' Richard said, 'so it's probably for the best. We could breed horses using him and Solis. Perhaps that's how we make our fortune.'

'There's always a new plan with you, young lord. How about we concentrate on the current one?'

Richard grimaced. Spending any length of time in an austere abbey wasn't what he wanted to do. That would give his mind time to think about the things he was trying not to think about. He needed the silver hidden in Abbot Anfroy's tomb, then he could do anything he wanted.

The abbey nestled within the woods, the trees now devoid of branches, but so dense their limbs looked like a wall of brown trunks. The buildings were arranged in a square with an open courtyard in the centre. They were of stone, but plain and lacking the expressive craftsmanship Richard had seen elsewhere. A large wooden stable, almost as large as the abbey itself, stood off to one side, and pigs rummaged around in the woods, penned in by extensive wooden fencing. There were vegetable gardens and a small fenced herb garden, and the Corrector was not nearly as harsh as Richard had expected a man with his title to be.

The Corrector was a thin man, with skin drooping from his cheeks like wax running down a melting candle. Bowman helped Richard walk up the slope and told him to look as sick as possible so they weren't turned away.

Richard didn't have to pretend, each step up the slope shot a pain through his stomach and by the time they reached Grandmont Abbey's entrance, he was puffing and panting.

The Corrector's language was understandable, but he used different words for things and sometimes Brian switched to Latin to avoid a discussion over what he meant.

'He says we can stay,' Brian pointed down at Richard's ankles, 'but the spurs have to come off.'

'Gold,' the Corrector shook his head. 'Pride.'

'I'm not bending down,' Bowman grinned as Maynard came back from stabling their horses. 'Squire, remove our spurs for us.'

Maynard frowned but obeyed.

Brian exchanged Latin with the Corrector. 'He says the food is simple and the bedding rough, but if the Lord blesses you, you may recover here. All our weapons and belongings have to be kept in the stables.'

'I don't like that,' Bowman said, 'someone could creep in and steal everything we have left.'

Richard smiled and looked at Bowman. 'Perhaps one of us will have to spend the night in the stables.'

The blonde man grinned and beamed at the squire.

'Really?' Maynard groaned. 'This is going to be bad enough as it is. Can't we go and find the Young King?'

'He'll hang us,' Richard said. 'Just sleep in there at night. If someone steals our weapons, we'll be defenceless.'

The Corrector nodded. 'Better leave your weapons here. Leave war behind.'

'That's what I'm trying to do,' Richard said, 'it really is.'

The Corrector bowed and led them to the guest wing of the abbey, where the floorboards were not covered by rushes or even straw, and only simple undyed linen hung over the few windows. The gentle breeze fluttered the window covers now and then, but they were almost the only furnishing in the whole wing. There were sacks of straw to serve as beds on the floor, but no fire. At least it was so warm this far south that Richard didn't miss having a hearth.

Richard spent the rest of the day in the chapel, because that would endear the Corrector to him, and afterwards they were fed bread and water. Bowman was served only frowns when he asked for cheese and wine.

They spent a few days resting, which did their aching limbs some good, but boredom settled in quickly. Bowman took to exercising the horses one at a time for great rides that would last a whole day. Maynard suggested a few days later that he rode south to check the situation at Limoges. Richard didn't see why not, so let him leave.

Bowman took his bow out on his rides and smuggled in the results for Richard under his cloak. 'There,' he said, 'you need something better than bread, young lord.'

Richard agreed. Bowman smuggled his copy of Eric and Enid in for him next, which at least gave him something to do during the long days. When he unwrapped the book, his father's spurs fell out of the linen and landed in his lap. He turned the golden spurs over in his hands, ran his fingers along the cool metal and the dents in the smooth golden bars. He wondered where those dents had come from and daydreamed answers to pass the time.

Another few days later and Bowman wondered where Maynard had got to. 'It is barely a day back to Limoges,' the blonde man said, 'he's had plenty of time to see if the siege still holds.'

'I don't really care,' Richard said, 'I don't want a squire, anyway.'

'Certainly not that one,' Bowman paced up and down in the otherwise empty guest wing.

Richard tried to ride the following day, and the blue roan took him on a gentle walk to the nearest village, which sat in a beautiful valley. The mornings were cooler now, and the days shorter, and the climb out of the valley on the way home nagged at Richard's healing wounds.

'How are they?' Bowman asked from his black horse.

'Good enough,' Richard said, 'I could amble now if we wanted to travel north again.'

'Do you want to wait for the squire?' Bowman asked.

Richard thought about it. 'One more day,' he said, 'then we leave the morning after.'

'Good,' Bowman yawned. 'Try a canter on the flat tomorrow, if you can do that, then we can at least flee from trouble.'

'I'm blaming the squire for this,' Bowman said the next morning, when trouble found them first.

Richard walked through the refectory and out of the abbey to where the Corrector confronted a group of riders outside his gate.

'There nothing steal,' the Corrector told them. 'We no riches, barely anything else eat than bread. Our order forbids money. You find none here.'

Richard and Bowman stopped at the gateway and peered out at the riders.

'Blue and white stripes,' Bowman said, 'I'm guessing you haven't forgotten those colours?'

'Of course not,' Richard said, 'but what is Guy doing up here?'

'He's not alone though,' Bowman said, 'he's got red shields with him.'

'Do you think we can get to the stables without being seen?'

Bowman didn't answer.

A red-shielded rider approached the Corrector and Richard saw something green hanging from his shoulders. 'Is that?'

'Oh, no,' Bowman stepped back out of view and pressed himself against the inside of the wall. 'What's he doing here?'

'I thought he hated Guy?' Richard asked. 'The Marshal would never ride alongside him.'

'Well apparently he is,' Bowman said, 'I really think we need to leave.'

'Obviously,' Richard said, 'but our horses are not saddled, and they can see the stables from where they are, how do we leave? I'm not walking.'

The Marshal pushed his horse right up to the indignant Corrector and peered down at him. 'You have animals though, do you not?'

The Corrector didn't flinch even though one of the warhorse's iron shoes pressed down on the end of the holy man's leather shoe.

'We not have animals destined you steal,' he said, not hinting whether the horseshoe crushed his toes or not.

The Marshal sighed. 'You do have animals though, don't you. I can see the fencing in the woods, I know what that's for. I'll wager you have some livestock hidden elsewhere in the trees. I have mouths that need feeding.'

The Corrector pressed his lips together and folded his arms.

The Marshal's horse snorted in his face and its long iron bit jangled in the thin man's stoic face.

'Do you know how big an army is?' the Marshal asked. 'How many mouths gape open twice a day demanding to be fed? Do you have any idea what it's like to be responsible for filling them?'

The Corrector fixed his gaze up to the Marshal's frustrated eyes and gave him no response.

Guy of Lusignan groaned and walked his horse closer to the entrance. 'Marshal, your job is rather simple. I don't know why you insist on making it so difficult for yourself.'

'What would you do then?' the Marshal lifted his chest and his horse backed up two steps.

The Lusignan knight frowned, leant his arms on the tall pommel of his saddle and considered the Corrector. 'You see, Marshal, one look at this man and our approach is clear. You can see his face, can you not see he will not willingly help us?'

The Marshal shrugged.

'You are blind to men, aren't you,' Guy said, 'look harder. He will resist us. His life itself he will throw away, so threatening him with your horse or even sword will be fruitless. Instead, think about what this man does value.'

'His God?' the Marshal suggested.

'His abbey, you fool,' Guy said, 'he will die for his abbey. But he will protect it. He will crumble if we light torches and approach his precious and dull buildings.'

The Corrector uncrossed his arms. 'You not dare.'

Guy laughed, a laugh that told the Corrector that he most certainly would dare.

'Your choice, man of God,' Guy said to him, 'be helpful to us and your rightful king.'

'No kings here,' the Corrector said, 'only Lord above.'

'Is that treason?' Guy asked the Marshal. 'I'm never quite sure.'

The Marshal shrugged and rubbed one of his eyes. 'Serve your lord and you can't go wrong, that's what I do.'

Guy chuckled. 'Simpleton.'

'We need food,' the Marshal said, 'and ideally some gold for the Navarrese. I wish we didn't need them, but they are our infantry.'

'No gold,' the Corrector said, 'no money.'

'You've said,' Guy groaned. 'But the Marshal is right, once the pigs of war have stuffed their bellies, they hold their purses up and expect us to stuff those, too.'

The Corrector shook his head. 'Not gold cross church. We poor.'

'All monks are poor,' Guy sneered, 'when knights knock on their door.'

The Marshal looked at the plain walls. 'I don't know, I think these ones do actually look quite poor.'

Guy sat up in his saddle and took a deep breath of the warming morning air. There was still dew on the grass, and probably mist in the nearby valleys. 'The monks will plead poverty, but monks are liars. Who can trust a man who trusts only in a god? My men will search for their hidden gold. Marshal, your men can round up their pigs.'

Bowman would have laughed, but he was so concerned the Marshal would find him, his humour evaded him. 'We should hide,' he whispered instead.

'Guy will turn this place inside out,' Richard said, 'if we hide we'll show fear, and then Guy will attack. He's like a wolf. Stand up to him and we might survive this.'

The Marshal faced his horse at Guy's. 'I am in command here,' he raised his voice. 'My men will hunt for gold, and Guy, your men will wrangle the swine.'

Guy laughed. 'My blood is purer than yours, you're a trumped up stablehand.'

The Marshal drew his sword. 'Stablehand? I'll remove your head and cast it into a stable.'

'Now or never,' Richard said to Bowman and then stepped out into the entrance.

'Don't,' Bowman hissed from his hiding place.

Richard walked out next to the Corrector, put his hands on his hips and looked up at the feuding knights. 'What is going on here? This is a holy place.'

'You!' Guy whirled his horse towards Richard.

'Richard?' the Marshal lowered his sword. 'What are you doing here?'

'I could ask the same thing,' Richard said, 'this abbey has nothing. They've been feeding me bread and water. Take a few pigs from the woods if you must, but I can assure you, this is the most austere place I have ever spent the night.'

'Where is Bowman?' the Marshal asked. 'He tried to kill me.'

Guy laughed. 'That? Marshal, you are being overly sensitive. Your pride is as ugly as that ridiculous cloak you insist on wearing.'

'He must be here,' the Marshal said, 'the two of you are never apart. I'll kill him for what he did to me.'

'Get over it,' Guy said, 'the bolt missed you. Your lack of courtesy is not becoming of a knight.'

'Lack of courtesy?' the Marshal's voice raised in pitch. 'You're the one who killed captives at a tournament. That's downright murder.'

Richard bristled at the memory. But he didn't want Guy to remember the ransom he might technically still owe the Lusignan. 'Marshal,' Richard said, 'you have told me many times to act like a knight. Perhaps you need to live up to your own words. The bolt didn't hit you, and Bowman will not shoot at you again. Forget the whole thing, and forget this abbey, too.'

The Marshal let nothing go. 'I'll find him and drag him back to Saint Martial. The Young will swing him from the nearest gallows. You can hang next to him, Richard, you did not stop your man from attempting to murder me.'

'Nothing?' Richard couldn't believe his ears. 'I pushed the damned crossbow away just as he squeezed the trigger lever. If it wasn't for that, it would have hit you in the neck. If anything, I saved your life and you owe me for it.'

The Marshal pointed his sword at Richard. 'Oh, so you're the one to blame for Count Robert being shot? He liked you, do you know that? This will disappoint him greatly.'

'I was trying to save you,' Richard said, 'I didn't re-aim it towards the count on purpose.'

'It doesn't matter if you meant it, he was shot because of what you did,' the Marshal frowned. 'If that doesn't make it your fault, I don't know what does. Did you know he still hasn't recovered from it?'

'Recovered?' Richard scratched the back of his arm. 'We thought the wound had killed him. We thought his death was what drove everyone away from Neufchatel.'

Richard wondered if Bowman was breathing an enormous sigh of relief inside the abbey.

'He's alive, but it's no thanks to you,' the Marshal said.

Guy raised his eyebrows at his companion. 'You are taking it awfully personally. They could have hit me just as easily as the Count, but you don't see me blabbering like a spoiled child. Richard is right, you really must calm down.'

'I'm very calm,' the Marshal advanced on Richard at a walk, 'I'm not the one who is going to swing from a rope.'

Richard sighed. 'I wish I was surprised, but after the way you reacted to me freeing you from your captivity, I'm not. After that, after everything we've been through, are you really happy to drag me and Bowman off to be slaughtered?'

'We haven't been through all that much,' the Marshal shrugged.

'Does Castle Peacock mean nothing to you?' Richard asked. 'I saved your skin there. Or was that not all that much?'

The Marshal frowned. He lowered his sword and rested the pommel on his thigh. 'But I evened you up for that, at Neufchatel when you tried to flee.'

'What are you talking about?' Guy asked.

'Nothing,' the Marshal answered. 'But we're even Richard, so I don't actually owe you anything. If anything, Bowman's attempt to murder me has swung things very much the other way.'

'Life isn't a ledger,' Richard shouted, 'what is wrong with you? What are you, a Templar?'

Some of the knights behind the Marshal sniggered and laughed. He whirled around and shouted at them to remain silent.

'Heaven forbid it,' the Marshal said, 'I am a man of honour.'

Guy laughed. 'You're a man of complaints and self-righteousness.'

Henry the Northerner flew out of the woods below and up the slope to the abbey. 'Great Marshal,' he said, 'someone is coming. There's a dust cloud to the south.'

Richard entertained a fleeting thought about how he wished Bowman's bolt had accidentally clipped Henry instead.

The Marshal barely acknowledged the news. 'Most likely some locals who are fleeing the war.'

'It was quite a large cloud,' Henry pleaded.

'Maybe you should just get back to keeping watch,' the Marshal turned away from his man.

Guy rubbed his forehead. 'No wonder you walked into my ambush at Niort,' he said, 'you are an idiot. You cannot just dismiss a dust cloud because you don't want it to be the enemy. It is probably a royalist company. Possibly looking for us.'

'You can't know that,' the Marshal said, 'but even if it is, we'll fight them off.'

'That's the point, we cannot know,' Guy said.

Some of their company fidgeted and turned their heads towards the road.

Richard stepped forwards. 'I'll do a deal with both of you.'

'Why would we need a deal with you?' Guy asked. 'What could you possibly offer us? You don't even seem to be wearing your sword.'

A wry smile crept across Richard's face. 'Because I know who is ahead of that dust cloud. And I know how many of them there are.'

'You're a reader of the stars now, are you?' Guy asked. He paused for a moment. 'You owe me a horse.'

'There's no yellow horse here, so you can forget about that,' Richard said, 'but I can help you with the problem that is riding towards you.'

'It could be nothing more than a herd of cattle moving towards a market,' the Marshal said. 'But maybe if you give me my blue roan back, then I can forgive the crossbow bolt.'

'Do you not care about your own survival?' Richard looked at both Guy and the Marshal. 'You have no idea who is coming for you.'

The Marshal rolled his eyes. 'Very well, who is it?'

Richard paused for effect. 'William Mandeville.'

The Marshal's face dropped. 'The hammer?'

Richard shrugged. 'He wants you, though, Marshal. And he's got ten more knights than you do, and ten more squires, too.'

Guy shifted in his saddle.

Richard remembered Bowman's complaint. 'They're so well armed even the squires have his red and yellow quartered surcoats.'

'I'm worth the ten knights,' the Marshal said. 'We are on the hill, too, so we have the advantage.'

Guy shook his head. 'You have always been one for haste. Hasty complaints and hasty acts. But between the two of you, you killed most of my company at Lagny, and I have no wish to lose those who remain. Especially not for no reason at all.'

'No reason?' the Marshal waved his sword at him. 'We are on the Young King's business, our expedition is crucial to the war.'

'Crucial to the war? How can this dust-filled abbey be crucial to anything?' Guy asked. 'This has got to be the plainest holy building I have ever set my eyes on. I might burn it just to cleanse the world of such offensive plainness.'

'Blasphemy,' the Corrector said, then realised his mistake and backed away.

'Spare the abbey,' Richard said, 'plain as it is, and I'll hide you from Mandeville.'

'Why?' the Marshal asked. 'I don't owe you anything.'

Richard raised his eyebrows. 'Because I'm not like you.'

'Obviously,' the Marshal said, 'you wield a sword like a drunken child.'

'That's not what he means, you fool,' Guy said. 'I suppose in exchange, you wish not to be hauled back to Saint Martial?'

'Yes,' Richard said, 'and to spare the abbey. I am riding away from the rebellion, it has nothing to do with me.'

'You aren't out of it,' the Marshal said, 'you lost Neufchatel for the Young King. You almost killed the Count of Meulan. You are in this war.'

'You don't have time to argue about this,' Richard said, 'follow me and you'll all live.'

Guy looked up into the sky, sighed, then gazed back at Richard. 'Very well, what is your scheme?'

'Follow me,' Richard turned and walked over the grass towards the stable building. Their horses had been stalled at the far end, and he hoped the blue roan would keep its huge black head to itself.

'Stable your horses in here,' Richard said, 'take them to the back and stay in. Then Lord Mandeville shall not see you. I will speak to him and send him further north. Just keep quiet and you can go back to the abbey at Saint Martial.'

'That's a cowardly scheme for a knight,' the Marshal said even as he rode towards their proposed sanctuary.

'Self-righteous,' Guy muttered, 'like I said earlier.'

Richard had been impressed by the size of the abbey's stable block, but even so, the squires all had to double up and squeeze two horses in each stall. Some horses squealed and kicked at each other, one kicked a squire and there was a shout from a stable where two horses who didn't know each other exchanged bites.

Richard's mind toyed with the idea of simply pointing Mandeville up to the stables if he arrived, a plan which would deal with all his problems in one fell swoop.

Bowman stuck his head around the doorframe. 'Are they all gone?'

Richard shook his head. 'They aren't really gone,' he said, 'but you can come out.'

The blonde man stood next to Richard and watched the stable block. 'You know, young lord, we could just, you know, suggest to Lord Mandeville where he might want to search for the rebels.'

'We can't do that,' Richard said.

'Why not?'

'That's not what knights do,' Richard said, 'if we don't keep our word, we are no better than anyone else.'

'But you aren't better than anyone else,' Bowman shook his head.

'I can ride a warhorse and defend my lands,' Richard said, 'a normal farmer can't do that.'

Bowman laughed. 'Nor can you, have you already forgotten what happened to your village?'

'That's not the point,' Richard said. He squinted over the woods and could see the dust rising from the road. Henry the Northerner galloped up the track and slammed to a halt at the abbey. Small pebbles from his horse's hooves pelted Richard and the Corrector.

'Where have they gone?' Henry's eyes were wide and his horse's nostrils flared.

'They're in the stables,' Richard said, 'but you don't have time to join them, you're too clumsy to do it quietly.'

'Clumsy?' the broad-chested man boomed in his deep voice.

'Yes,' Richard said, 'just gallop off into the trees. Come back later.'

'Much, much later,' Bowman added.

Henry spurred his horse and did what he was told. No sooner had he disappeared into the treeline in a crash of broken wood, the Mandeville banner appeared at the bottom of the slope.

Richard brushed his tunic down, caught the sliver of linen that remained of this crusading cross, and it flew off and landed on the earth.

'I think that's bad luck,' Bowman said.

'Everything's bad luck,' Richard stood tall and waited for Mandeville. His company moved swiftly and their horses pulled their tired bodies up the hill and towards the abbey. They ceased their charge and the cloud of dust that followed them overtook and swamped the abbey.

The Corrector coughed and shielded his eyes.

Richard did the same, and when the dust subsided, Mandeville sat atop his horse scrutinising Richard from exactly where Guy had been not so long before. The Earl of Essex snorted a laugh. 'You again?'

'I'm on my way north to Flanders,' Richard said. 'I'm doing nothing wrong.'

'I never said you were,' Mandeville said. He unlaced his helmet and rested it on his pommel. 'That's better,' he said, 'it was getting awfully warm under that.'

Richard waited.

Mandeville took a breath of the fresh air. 'I heard what the king did to you, and if I am honest, it seemed a touch unfair.'

'A touch?' Richard said. 'He made me a landless knight again.'

Bowman chuckled. 'You never wanted the land. You thought you did, but you didn't.'

Richard wrinkled his face up. Then he realised he felt freer without Yvetot's future shackled to his leg. It had cost him a lot though. It had cost him his wife.

'Don't look so sad,' Mandeville said, 'I saw your village on the way to Brittany, it was pitiful. Either way, the king overreacted, I for one do not doubt your loyalty.'

Richard realised the irony of hiding the rebels from Mandeville, but pushed that thought aside. 'There is nothing to be done about it now,' Richard said, 'I'll be a knight of Flanders by the end of the year.'

'You are taking your time riding north,' the Earl considered the poor abbey, 'why stop here?'

'Because this is as far as I got,' Richard said. 'The journey to Limoges almost killed me, but I'm about to move on now.'

Mandeville nodded. 'Sensible enough,' he said. 'But I am still searching for my quarry. Have you seen or heard word of the Marshal? We have seen signs of horsemen travelling on this road.'

Richard shook his head. 'No, why would anyone tell me anything? We've had no visitors.'

'That's a large stable block,' Mandeville nodded towards it, 'seems the monks are used to visitors.'

'No visitors,' the Corrector said, his folded face stern.

Mandeville looked down beneath his horse at the track. Richard held his breath, but the ground was hard on the hill and there were no tracks visible to betray the Marshal and Guy.

The Earl nodded away to himself. 'I'll comb the countryside. We'll find the prancing peacock, I can almost smell his arrogance on the breeze.'

'It leaves quite a stench,' Bowman nodded in agreement.

Mandeville ignored him. 'Goodbye Richard. If our paths do not cross again, I hope you find what you are looking for.'

Richard wasn't sure what that meant as the fifty red and yellow surcoats turned their horses about and rejoined the road at the bottom of the hill.

'That was the easy part,' Bowman watched them leave.

'I know,' Richard said, 'if our horses weren't in the same stable, I'd run at this point.' He took a deep breath and strode towards the hiding rebels. 'Let's get this over and done with.'

The Marshal's head jutted out of the stable before he reached it. 'Are they gone?'

'Luckily yes, or they would have just seen you,' Richard said.

The Marshal opened his stable door and led his horse out.

Guy exited the stalls next. 'Marshal, you gather the pigs and I'll search for their gold.'

'We had a deal,' Richard said.

'I agreed not to burn it to the ground,' the Lusignan smiled. 'But even so, I'm going to do that anyway.'

'You can't.'

'I think I can,' Guy held his reins out for a squire to take. 'You had leverage before the earl arrived. Now you don't.'

Richard's shoulders slumped. 'You're an animal.'

'Speaking of animals,' the Marshal said, 'I'm not chasing pigs. I'm looking for gold.'

'No,' Guy drew his sword. 'Do not be a halfwit, although I know you cannot help it.' The Lusignan waved at some of his knights and they marched towards the main abbey building.

'I suppose no one will gather any pigs,' the Marshal frowned and stomped off to find a back way into the abbey. He stopped and shouted back to Richard. 'If we don't find any gold, I'll take Bowman back to the Young King. Maybe the hungry mercenaries will be satisfied to watch a hanging.'

'I never hurt you,' Bowman said, 'even though you deserved that arrow in your neck.'

'Be quiet,' Richard said to him, 'but you, Marshal, ride south back to Saint Martial before Lord Mandeville comes back here. He'll soon realise your tracks haven't gone further north.'

The Marshal walked towards Richard, five knights at his back. 'Guy is right, you have no leverage now. I'll take you as well.'

'Have you forgotten your uncle?' Richard asked. 'Uncle Patrick. The man who Guy murdered in front of you. Have you balanced that ledger?'

'I'm a patient man,' the Marshal said.

Bowman scoffed. 'You're nothing of the sort. I know horses more patient than you.'

'One thing at a time, you see,' the Marshal said, 'we need to win the war first. The Young King counts Guy as his ally, so for now I will respect their alliance.'

'You argued with your master in Corbie about that,' Richard said, 'I know you hate him. Fight Guy and not us.'

'I care about the Young King,' the Marshal said, 'he is the future of this realm and will propel me to the heights of the royal court. I shall be Christendom's first knight.'

'Aiming low then,' Bowman muttered.

The Marshal looked off into the air as if an image of his future hung above him. 'I shall marry a rich heiress and be granted lands beyond your imagination. Everyone will know my name, and history shall remember it.'

'I don't know about any of that,' Richard said, 'but it seems to me that the Young King is stuck in a trap, and once he runs out of money he will sue for peace. He'll gain nothing apart from the animosity of his father. King Henry has locked his queen up for siding with the Young King during the last rebellion, you know that? He could lock the Young King up after this one. Then what will happen to your dreams of greatness?'

'What do you know of war or politics?' the Marshal asked. 'Our great campaign is on the verge of a breakthrough, everyone expects us to triumph before long. The Old King will run out of supplies and retreat with his tail between his legs. Mark my words.'

Guy stormed out of the abbey, his face disappointed. 'There is no gold, there was barely anywhere to even search. We'll fire this dismal place and be gone.'

'You can't burn it,' Richard said, 'the monks here have done nothing to you.'

'Their architecture has offended me,' Guy nodded to his knights. 'Torch it.'

'Help us,' the Corrector said to Richard, his eyes filled with terror.

'Why bother?' Richard said to Guy. 'It will only take up time you don't have. Just leave.'

'The monks should have been more helpful. We could have saved the bother of searching had they told us they had nothing to give.'

'They did tell you that,' Richard reached for a sword that wasn't there. 'We all told you that. You're mad.'

'They didn't say it convincingly enough, this abbot or whatever he is should have been better at telling the truth,' the Lusignan snarled at the Corrector. 'This trip was a colossal waste of time.' He stomped off and went to supervise the destruction of Grandmont Abbey.

Richard turned to Bowman. 'Is my book still inside?'

'No,' the blonde man said, 'I wrapped it up ready to travel, we've got nothing in the guest wing except a blanket.'

'Good,' Richard said, then caught the stare of the Corrector. Richard had to look away. 'I'm so sorry, but we don't have our armour on or anything bigger than an eating knife between us.'

The Marshal swore at Guy as he disappeared into the buildings. 'We did get what we came for,' he shouted as his comrade vanished.

'Did you?' Richard asked. 'You haven't found any valuables and you are too proud to round up any pigs. You'll go back to Saint Martial empty handed.'

The Marshal shook his head. 'We didn't ride all the way up here for either of those,' he put his hands on his hips.

A lick of flame shot into the air from the kitchen building and a pair of monks ran out soon after. Guy crossed the courtyard and into the refectory. A moment later Richard heard a scream and didn't need to be told why.

'What did you come all the way up here for, then?' Richard asked. 'If it wasn't to butcher some innocent monks.'

The Marshal's grin worried Richard, but he was more concerned when the swarthy-skinned man's eyes swivelled over to Bowman and rested on the blonde knight.

'Surely not?' Bowman said. 'You didn't ride up here with dozens of men just to find me?'

'And yet here we are,' the Marshal said.

'There's a war on,' Richard said, 'and you're supposed to be busy fighting it.'

'Some things are more important than war.'

'For you, I doubt that,' Richard said.

'Justice,' the Marshal said, 'I must have justice. Your man wronged me and he will pay the price for it.'

Bowman cast his eyes around the abbey grounds where knights tore down walls or mounted horses. There was no escape. 'How did you know we were here?' he asked.

The Marshal's grin widened. 'You do not have as many friends as you think you do.'

'Nicola took us here,' Bowman said. 'But why would she betray us?'

Richard closed his eyes and took a deep breath. 'I don't think it was her.'

Bowman's face flashed with rage. 'The squire. I'll kill him, I'll cut his little lying goddamn throat.'

Extinguished

Brian told Guy of Lusignan four times that God would visit vengeance upon him for burning Grandmont Abbey.

The first three times Guy laughed, but his patience evaporated after the fourth and he snarled at the monk and told him what would happen if he didn't cease. It involved the removal of some fingers.

Brian wisely let the matter drop and spent the rest of the journey back to Saint Martial in silence.

Richard stayed quiet too, there was nothing to gain by speaking to Guy, and the Marshal rode out in front, eager to return and dish out whatever he thought justice was.

The company rode south until it reached the River Vienne, and followed that until they sighted the settlement of Limoges that lay just to the south of the Abbey of Saint Martial. Richard assumed their route served to ride around the royal army, and meant that when they eventually sighted the red-tiled spire of the abbey, it was to their north.

The Marshal led them through a familiar tent encampment with a green and gold banner above it, where he waited for Richard to catch him up.

'Were these mercenaries with you in Ireland?' he asked.

'No,' Richard said, 'I don't know every mercenary.'

The Marshal shrugged. 'These ones are a bad sort, we spend so much time plundering to pay them, I do sometimes wonder who I actually serve.'

'Maybe you shouldn't be plundering at all,' Richard said.

'Then how would we eat?' the Marshal asked. 'We've already eaten all the food in the abbey itself, the monks who wouldn't leave have begun starving to death.'

'You're letting monks starve to death?' Brian's face dropped. 'When does the sin end?'

'They could leave if they wanted to,' the Marshal said, 'but as I said, we need to eat and the war needs to be won. We are one victory away from triumph.'

Richard watched as Sancho's Navarrese danced around a large fire in the centre of their camp. It didn't seem warm enough to justify such a fire, but they played music and threw a handful of women between each other.

'Does the Young King know they are doing that?' Richard asked. 'Those women don't look like they're enjoying themselves.'

The Marshal frowned. 'I think they're dancing, women like dancing.'

The company made its way around the mercenary camp, past their wagon lager and on. Richard thought the wagons looked well stocked, canvas covers securely fastened over loads which bulged out of the top of the carts. 'At least someone is benefitting from all this,' Richard mumbled as they reached the town that had once prospered around the Abbey of Saint Martial.

They found the Young King perched on a lathered grey horse and surrounded by a dozen of his highest ranking companions. A pack of dogs, their tongues out and heads low, were led off towards a barn, and footmen trudged towards the abbey carrying a single deer hanging from a stick held between two of them.

'I thought there was a war on?' Bowman regarded the scene with a shake of his head.

'I don't share the thrill about hunting,' the Marshal said, 'but it does bring food to the tables.'

'Not much food,' Richard said, 'that's a lot of hunting men to come back with a single deer. And it's not a mature adult.'

'They used to bring back more,' the Marshal said, 'but the forests are emptier now. Come, it is time to learn your fate.'

Richard wondered how the young Angevin's mood would be after what Richard considered a failed hunt, but the monarch's eyes were bright when the Marshal greeted him.

The Young King's horse foamed around his leather breast-piece and its coat shimmered as the sun caught it. 'Marshal,' he glanced over to Richard, 'I see you have had more success in hunting your quarry than I did mine. I hope you feel less aggrieved now.'

'Not yet,' the Marshal replied, 'Bowman is still breathing.'

'And so are you,' the Young King patted his horse on the neck, 'you must learn to restrain your temper.'

'Bowman must learn to restrain *his* temper,' the Marshal answered back tersely.

'No doubt,' the Young King rode past his knight and faced Richard.

Richard tried to keep his face still. He knew if he faced the Old King in this situation, he'd only have moments to live.

The Young King sighed. A long, drawn out breath escaped him and for a moment he looked tired. 'What did I do, Richard?'

Richard frowned.

'What did I do to you? What wound did I inflict on you to cause such a betrayal? I gave you arms when you lost or broke your own, then replaced those when you lost or broke those. You ate at my table, drank my wine, and took my coin. I favoured you with my attention, favour which caused grumbling amongst some who had served me for longer. And yet, after all that, you turned your back on me.'

Richard swallowed. 'I have no words to answer you, my lord. You showed me nothing but kindness and trust.'

'I let you into my confidence, Richard, even when I knew you were placed with me to spy. I told you a betrayal would cut me deep and be severely punished. Why? Tell me why.'

Tears filled Richard's eyes. He knew why and stood by his choice, but the Young King's words made Richard question himself. 'You did nothing to me,' Richard said, 'I left your company for my family.'

'No, you left me and then defended a town against me. Normandy was open for the taking, all I had to do was occupy Neufchatel. You didn't leave me and go to your family, you left me and fought against me.'

'We were trapped in the town,' Richard said. Then he told him everything. Except for the priests he and Brian had hurled from the walls of Castle Tancarville, and the skirmish outside Yquebeuf, because that could be seen as siding with the Old King.

'I'm very sorry about Count Robert,' Richard said, 'I liked him.'

'He liked you,' the Young King said sharply. His horse snorted. The bells in the abbey chimed. 'Had you not driven us from Neufchatel, we would have taken Normandy and would now be negotiating with my father. I'd be the Duke of Normandy, and the war would be over. But instead, because of you, we are holed up in the south. As for Count Robert, he knows who your man was aiming at and knows what happened was an accident. He will live.'

Richard was pleased to hear that, but had no other words for his former lord than another apology.

The Marshal sat on his horse close by, following every word, awaiting the sentence.

'I tried to trust you,' the Young King said, 'but such disloyalty cannot go unanswered, otherwise others will think crossing me is of no consequence. That cannot be, can it?'

Richard shook his head. He wished to be anywhere other than where he was, he felt shame and guilt as the Young King's eyes radiated disappointment.

'Count Philip is my cousin, I will not have you serving him. I will send him a message instructing him to bar his door to you if you appear at it begging for a place in his company.'

Richard winced for whatever might come next.

The Young King rubbed his chin. 'But that is because your place is beside me.'

'What?' the Marshal roared.

'Look what happened when you went off on your own,' the Young King said, 'chaos. But when you were beside me, you defended me with your own life and suffered for me.'

'You can't let him get away with it,' the Marshal drew closer, 'it isn't fair.'

Richard nodded because he had indeed suffered greatly. Nicholas was gone, Solis was wounded, Yvetot was destroyed, and Sophie was dead. He sniffed and tried to wipe away a tear without showing what he was doing. He wondered if he had stayed with the Young King, would Sophie still be alive, and would Yvetot still stand? Richard didn't know.

'You can't invite him back,' the Marshal said, 'he fought against. He actually fought against you.'

'Marshal,' the monarch snapped, 'he will pay for what he did, pay by serving me. I don't expect you to understand, but I do expect you to endure it.'

Richard blinked as the sun warmed his neck. 'What about Bowman?'

The Young King half shrugged. 'Sometimes I want to kill the Marshal, too.'

The English knight's face turned red and his breathing deepened.

'I know you perfectly now,' the Young King said to Richard, 'I know that if I keep your family safe, you will be loyal to me. You risked everything for them by leaving me, so if I protect them, in turn you will risk everything for me. We shall bring your children from Normandy and then you will be my most loyal knight.'

'I'm your most loyal knight,' the Marshal cried.

The Young King set his face. 'You pouted in Amiens while men tried to kill me. This is your punishment for that.'

Richard couldn't believe what he was hearing, he'd expected to have his head removed.

'Your man will join you,' the Young King said, 'I know he will be loyal to me if you are. Once I am the one true king, then you will be rewarded with lands. Perhaps not all the Martel lands, but productive lands nonetheless.'

'Your generosity is overwhelming,' Richard bowed in his saddle, 'I cannot thank you enough.'

'Thank me by serving me.'

Richard nodded. Once his children were safely back by his side, he could rebuild his life.

'Not all kings are monsters,' the Young King said, 'and not all kings are consumed with paranoia. Some reward their followers and act justly.'

'Justly?' the Marshal said. 'You are rewarding active disloyalty.'

'I am creating loyal followers,' the Young King said, 'for the coming battle with my father. We need every lance we can muster to achieve our final victory.'

Richard didn't know what to say, an enormous tide of relief swept over him, and when he looked back to Bowman, the blonde knight looked just as bewildered as he himself felt.

Only Brian sat shaking his head.

'What's wrong with you?' Richard asked.

'Grandmont will be punished,' Brian replied, 'the Lord saw the destruction and will punish those who were responsible. And this king is responsible.'

'Holy men keep telling me that,' the Young King said, but his face revealed no concern. 'Come, let us eat this deer, I have an announcement to make.'

The Abbey of Saint Martial was large and more finely adorned than Grandmont had been. Ranges of tall white buildings with tiled roofs populated a bend in a river, with a white wall running along its boundary. Gatehouses led to two bridges over the waterway, and a third to the road south to Limoges. They passed through that gatehouse, stabled their horses, and were returned their possessions.

In the echoing, well lit chamber that the Young King's forces had taken over to use as their hall, knights, counts and the odd duke drank wine and grew merry.

Richard and Bowman found a place at the back of the hall, while Brian sulked outside.

The Young King, once enough wine had been consumed, stood up at his high table and called for quiet. 'We have been welcomed here at Saint Martial for weeks now. We have weathered my father's wrath with barely a loss and subdued the local population. Towns and villages all around bow to us. Our task here is complete. Tomorrow we shall proceed south, for I have a strategy to defeat my father and end this war.'

The hall erupted in cheers and cups were banged on tables.

'We shall bring the Old King to his knees.'

The cheers continued and drunken knights shouted their approval.

The Young King basked in their adoration for a moment, and then waited for them to quieten. 'I will now ask you all to swear an oath. An oath of rebellion against my brother Richard, the Count of these lands, our enemy. He is an unjust lord for those of you who hail from these parts, and must be defeated. But first, lest any of you have misgivings, let us hear from our own troubadour, Bertran de Born.'

The knights cheered again as a knight took to his feet next to the Young King. The knight was unremarkable in appearance, but he wore his mail, and over it a surcoat of black and gold. His nose was large and his ears wide, but when Bertan lifted his head, the hall fell silent. He paused for a moment as no one moved or spoke.

'You have heard many fine songs from me,' Bertran said, 'but these words are my most joyous. Without war, men are selfish, lazy, and lonely beings. Their experiences are meaningless, for what importance can a deed have if it is done at a time of comfort and peace? War brings men together, as you are now, binds them to one another and to our society. We become stronger together, important together, better together.'

Richard could have heard a mouse scurry along the floor in between Bertran's words.

The troubadour looked from face to face. 'The prospect of war stirs my heart. When the time draws near, my bones come alive at the thought of the pennons snapping in the wind, the horses neighing as the sides regard each other. Trumpets shall blare and drums shall beat along with the quickening rhythm of my heart.'

Knights nodded, for Bertran spoke for them.

'War gives men a proper death, born from the tangle of shields, the shattering of lances, and the demonstration of prowess.'

The Marshal wiped a tear from his eye.

Bertran lifted his voice. 'The corpses on the field are a monument to the moral achievements of the victors and the vanquished, the living and the dead. I yearn, as we sit here on the eve of our victory, for the smell of burning villages, the sight of riderless horses crossing the land, the counting of the slain.'

Knights cheered.

Richard frowned. Bertran had lost him at burning villages.

'War improves men,' the troubadour continued, 'without the test of the iron work, what man knows what he is made of? Until he has wallowed in the high bath of honour, what man can call himself full-grown?'

A count jumped to his feet to applaud Bertran and was joined by knight after knight. They howled their approval and stamped their feet.

'We're going to get killed, aren't we,' Bowman muttered.

Richard nodded. 'For sure.'

'Swear the noble oath of rebellion,' Bertran shouted, 'swear resistance to Count Richard, the man I call Yes-and-No because he is torn by two natures, at once seeing himself as both a god and a man, forever ordering one thing and countering it later. Swear the oath and rid yourselves of this unreliable lord.'

The Young King got back to his feet and clasped Bertan's shoulder tightly. He said something to the poet and both men smiled before embracing each other. Then the monarch rode the wave of enthusiasm that crashed around the hall and called for an oath to defeat his brother. The knights clamoured to repeat his words.

'I notice you're not joining in,' Bowman said.

Richard shook his head. 'Nor are you.'

'I've never met this Count Richard,' the blonde man replied, 'it seems awfully rude to swear an oath against a man I've never met.'

Richard crossed his arms. 'I'm not swearing it either, I still don't want to draw my sword again.'

'You do know what serving the Young King means, don't you?' Bowman asked.

The Young King celebrated the commitment of his army by ordering in the last of the wine in the abbey.

A familiar figure floated around the tables in a blue dress and came to a halt opposite Richard. As she recognised him, her face was one of shock.

'Alice?' Richard hadn't expected to see her again. She still wore the silver circlet.

'Richard? I heard you were fighting for the Old King?'

Bowman laughed. 'We change sides every day. A bit like you. Go away, we don't want your kind here.'

Alice frowned. 'You are just as rude as your brother was.'

Bowman's laugh faded and was replaced by sternness.

The Lusignan woman's face softened. 'I heard about your wife. It must be terrible.'

Richard said nothing.

Bowman stole the drink of a knight who stood and shouted his happiness at the oath. 'This woman is nothing but a tart, young lord, send her on her way.'

'I am nobility,' Alice said, 'in this part of France, people know who I am.'

'Why do you keep coming back?' Bowman asked. 'Your brother has no interest in Richard now.'

Alice rolled her eyes. 'I'm not coming back, you came back. I've been with the Young King this whole time.'

'Trying to find a rich knight stupid enough to fall for you?' the blonde knight found another unguarded cup.

'I'm so poor,' Richard said, 'that she couldn't possibly be after me for wealth.'

'You're in disgrace,' Alice said, 'no one at all will hunt for you.'

'And you called me rude,' Bowman downed the stolen wine.

'I really am very sorry about your wife,' Alice said, 'and I hope you can bring your children safely here.'

'Thank you,' Richard said. Apparently news travelled fast.

'Don't speak to her,' Bowman glanced around for more drink, but nothing was within reach.

Alice shot an angry look at Bowman and then floated away.

'I suppose I am in disgrace,' Richard said, 'no one here must trust me. This could be a very lonely time for us.'

'Speak for yourself,' Bowman said, 'we'll harvest a few pouches of coins, and then women will be queuing up to be with me.'

'I don't know,' Richard watched some of the knights sit back down, 'I don't think we'll be advancing on the enemy when we leave here, it feels more like we're fleeing.'

'Too late for doubts, young lord, we're stuck here now. We have literally nowhere else to go.'

Unlike Richard, the Young King's company had somewhere else to go, at least that was what he told them. Before dawn a thousand horses massed to the south of the abbey on the meadows previously occupied by Sancho's mercenaries. Banners flew in the air, although only gently because the morning breeze was faint. Horses, knowing something was happening, pawed the ground while waiting for companies to form up, but otherwise the mood was quiet. The army's departure from Saint Martial was being done in dim pre-dawn light, and as discreetly as possible. If the Old King's army came crashing into them now, the meadow would be the scene of a great slaughter. But the Young King's military machine was buoyed by the oath swearing and motivated to creep away from Limoges with discipline.

Richard mounted his blue roan for the first leg, lest they be ambushed, but near midday he swapped to the captured Tancarville horse and let his warhorse march along unencumbered. No longer trusted with a red shield of the Young King's household, Richard and Bowman were given blue and white striped shields and sent to bolster the depleted ranks of Guy of Lusignan.

'I cannot believe what shields we have,' Bowman said as he slung his upside down on his back so it wasn't in the way or banging on his knee for the entire journey. Most knights simply slung them on their warhorse's saddles, but Richard kept his on his arm. He felt safer with it there. 'They say fate is a wheel,' Richard said, 'I'm sure it will turn again.'

'If it's a wheel, then we're at bottom being dragged through the filthy silt of the river,' Bowman moaned.

'Do you remember when Guy offered you a castle to become one of his knights?' Richard asked.

Bowman coughed. 'I still never thought I'd ever ride under this banner. We've spent much of the past few months fighting against it.'

'I don't like it, either,' Richard said, 'but I think we're being tested. We need to endure this.'

The army snaked out in three divisions and headed towards the sun. Its rays were bright and strong in Richard's face, and the warmth gave him a burst of optimism.

Brian didn't share it, and still sulked as he rode and led their other spare horse. 'God will punish us,' he said, 'we march with heretics.'

'They aren't heretics,' Richard said, 'just evil, I suppose.'

'Then how can you march with them?'

'How can we not?' Richard replied. 'I can't farm for food, I can only fight for pay.'

'I thought you wanted to give that up?' the monk asked.

'Maybe the Lord isn't done with me yet,' Richard said. 'Give me another option and I'll take it.'

Brian grunted in disagreement, then complained it was too warm for the time of year.

Guy of Lusignan's division was in the vanguard and ranged ahead of the others, and after two days they stopped at the top of a series of rolling hills which overlooked a village.

Guy ordered scouts to ride in all directions, then signalled a rest.

Richard dismounted and tried to stretch out his stomach which felt like it had been turned into solid rock. It didn't hurt much anymore, but the muscles felt like they didn't properly work.

Brian took his cloak off and went to refill his waterskin.

Guy walked through his camp and gave orders. His men were in good spirits. The other hundred men in the vanguard took their rest on the previous hill, the mood all around full of optimism and energy.

'Do you know what that village is?' Guy pointed out the church spire to Richard. There was a yellow-stoned tower too, as tall as the spire and dominating the houses around its base.

'No,' Richard said, 'of course not.'

Guy turned to Bowman and grinned, his missing tooth all the more obvious when the sun hit his smile. 'Martel.'

'What?' Bowman almost choked.

'This is where they come from,' Guy waved in the direction of the village, 'I know you ache with revenge against them.'

'Do you think any of their family will be here?' Richard asked.

'Not the important ones,' Guy replied, 'this place may have spawned them, but the foremost ones are all north now, closer to Angevin power.'

Bowman considered the square tower and the trees beneath it. 'I suppose you plan on burning this place and looting it,' he said, 'for once I'm inclined to join in.'

Guy chuckled. 'You'll have to wait,' he wandered off and left the blonde man staring at the birthplace of the family he hated.

The Young King arrived in the evening and the rolling hills filled with camps and horses. Foraging parties set out into the countryside and it wasn't long before smoke rose around the horizon.

'This is hell,' Brian watched black smoke pollute the blue sky.

'No different to Meath,' Bowman shrugged.

'That doesn't make this better,' the monk said.

What made things worse was when the red-shielded company rode towards Martel and the Young King consulted with Guy within earshot.

'It is the strongest tower within a day's ride,' Guy said. 'I think the Old King will take the bait.'

Richard looked twice at one of the red-shields and was sure he saw Maynard amongst them. He decided not to tell Bowman.

The Young King looked happy. 'This will be the place,' he said. 'The site of our great victory. We can use the hills to hide. The tower will hold for weeks, but we'll only need days. We can fortify the village and use it to delay the enemy. They'll push us back into the tower and think they've won a small victory.'

'If you say so,' Guy said, 'but these men are hungry and the Navarrese are already complaining they are due pay.'

'The army needs to move on anyway,' the Young King said, 'it cannot be here when my father arrives, else he may not lay a siege. Take the vanguard south, there are rich shrines at Rocamadour. Take what is there to pay the Navarrese, then I shall join you. We will stay at Rocamadour for a week to regain our strength, then return here to ambush my father. The tower will be our anvil, my army the hammer.'

Guy half shrugged, half nodded. 'Why not,' he said, 'we'll leave in the morning.'

'Burn it, burn Rocamadour,' the Young King said, 'send a message to the local villages that it's better to surrender their goods to use than resist us. If we're willing to destroy the shrines, the threat to their villages will have been well made.'

Richard didn't tell Brian about that conversation, and the following morning they set out, the red banner flying behind them from the top of

Martel's tower.

They reached Rocamadour before midday, a collection of shrines and holy buildings sprawled up the face of the steep north bank of a river. The shrines clung to the cliff-side as if in constant danger of falling, for buildings were built directly into the rocks. The cliff-side complex was hidden as Guy approached from the north, the entrance down into Rocamadour itself guarded by a castle keep with tall yellow walls and a square tower at one end. The castle was the gateway down into the valley where the shrines and riches were to be found. A line of pilgrims snaked up to the castle where a toll was extracted before they were allowed into the sacred areas below. Amongst the pilgrims there were bedraggled families who flinched away from the armed men who approached.

'More refugees,' Bowman said as they pulled up at the foot of the castle. They'd seen and overtaken more and more common people on their journey, the news of an army's approach spreading only slightly quicker than the army itself.

Bowman watched a child cry on the back of a mule. 'Are you sure we're on the right side?' he asked.

Brian grunted scornfully.

'I keep saying,' Richard said, 'we're on our own side.'

'Yes, but is that on the side of the right?' Bowman asked.

'Dead and dying villagers have never affected you before,' Richard said, 'I expect Bertran de Born would sing a song of how wonderful it is to see the crying children.'

'I expect he would,' the blonde man said, 'and I don't care about them. I just don't see who it benefits to have them so miserable. Life is miserable enough already.'

'This doesn't sound like you at all,' Richard said.

Guy and five of his knights dismounted and barged their way into the castle gate, sending pilgrims scurrying out of their way.

Bowman sighed. 'I'm still here, next to you, because you insist on trying to do the right thing, remember? How sure are we that this is the right thing?'

A pilgrim tripped over evading Guy and bloodied her knee on the ground as she fell.

'Not that sure,' Richard said.

'Look at these people,' the blonde man said, 'they'd be at home if it wasn't for the Young King. Some of them probably don't even have homes anymore.'

'Are you saying you don't want to serve the Young King?' Richard asked. 'Or just that his cause is wrong?'

Bowman rubbed the worn pommel of his saddle. 'All I'm saying is that maybe he isn't going about things in the right way. The Irish monk is annoying, but he might not be all wrong, we can't completely ignore the next life. And we all know the Young King is losing. His words are cheery and his plans fantastic, but has he ever won a battle or taken a castle? I don't think he's ever going to grant you any lands at all, so what justifies all this suffering?'

'Have you had a secret bottle of wine on you all morning?' Richard asked.

'I'm being serious,' Bowman frowned.

Richard looked up at the castle keep. It was two storeys high and looked very solid. There was no way around it without jumping off the cliff top.

'Once the Old King dies,' Richard said, 'then we'll be well placed with the Young King. Then the wars will stop.'

'Will they?' Bowman watched the pilgrims reform their patient line.

'They have to,' Richard said but his voice wasn't strong.

Brian made the sign of the cross. 'Bowman is right, and you must act according to your conscience, for that is how you shall be judged in the next life.'

'Is it?' Richard asked. 'I'm not sure that's what the priests say.'

Brian rolled his hood down and looked around at the sun behind them with disdain. 'It is what I believe,' he said, 'we must all choose how to act in response to what fate places in our path. We know right from wrong.'

'Does that mean you're siding with Bowman?'

'I'm not siding with him,' the monk said, 'just agreeing that I think we are on the side of the unjust.'

'I can't think about this anymore,' the blonde man said, 'this is making my head hurt. There must be some monks in this place who will give me a drink.'

Guy exited the castle on his own and waved another group of his knights and squires inside. He squinted in the sun as he approached Richard. 'Have you seen the views from this place? From the other side of the castle it is stunning to look over the valley. It's going to be a terrible shame when we burn it all down.'

A pilgrim placed a flute to his lips and played a slow tune. It dug up the memory of the mournful melody outside the tower in Castle Tancarville. The tune tugged at his heart and Richard looked Guy in the eyes. 'We're not burning it.'

Guy blinked. 'What do you think we're doing here? We aren't here to light a candle in the church and buy a pilgrim badge.'

Brian mopped his brow. 'You can't burn Rocamadour,' he said, 'this is where Saint Amadour's body was discovered in 1166, his body uncorrupted by time. A thousand years of time. That is a miracle and this place is one of the most holy you can find.'

'That was the year the Martels destroyed my life,' Richard said, 'and the year I won my golden spurs. Is that a sign?'

Brian nodded. 'Surely.'

Guy groaned. 'Every town has a saint buried in it around here. Aquitaine can afford to miss one.'

'Saint Amadour arrived in Aquitaine from the Holy Land. Do you know who greeted him?'

Guy looked like he was deciding which part of Brian's body to chop off.

'We don't know,' Richard said, 'and you know it. Being smug is a sin.'

'Saint Martial,' Brian said triumphantly.

Bowman looked at Richard and shrugged.

'So?' Bowman asked.

'Where have we just come from?' Brian asked. 'The Abbey of Saint Martial. The Young King despoiled the abbey and stole everything within it. Did you know they even killed some of the monks? If we attack Rocamadour, then there will be two saints seeking revenge against the Young King. No mortal can survive the wrath of two saints.'

'I can't guess how you know everything about Rocamadour,' Richard said, 'not when we haven't even entered it yet.'

'I spoke to the monks at Saint Martial, they heard where we headed and were horrified. Rocamadour is the Young King's last chance to avoid divine retribution.'

A pair of black kites circled overhead, their wings outstretched and helping them to soar effortlessly through the warm air. They reminded Richard of the crows that had landed on the Corbie Tournament field and pecked at the remains of the fallen.

'I don't like this,' Richard said, 'too many omens and signs. Something bad will happen here.'

'There is no doubt,' Brian said.

'You're right,' Guy smirked, 'it will be bad, for the residents at least, when the whole place is nothing but charred rubble.'

'Oh,' Brian said, 'I nearly forgot, do you remember the Song of Roland?'

Richard did, he'd heard the tale of Charlemagne's doomed knight in halls across France.

'His sword is here. The sword named Durendal.'

'What?' Richard's eyes lit up. 'Where?'

Brian pointed to the castle. 'Down there somewhere. The abbot told me it was driven into the cliff.'

'That's ridiculous,' Bowman said. 'And who is Roland again?'

Richard groaned. 'Do you ever listen to the singers?'

'Well, no.'

Guy scratched his beard. 'It must be worth a fortune. Even if it isn't real.'

'Of course it's real,' Richard said, 'who would lie about that?'

'Me for one,' the Lusignan grinned. 'I think I'll take it, thanks for telling me about it, monk.'

'No, you can't steal it,' Richard said.

'Why not?' Guy laughed. 'Roland doesn't need it anymore, so it doesn't have an owner.'

'That's not the point,' Brian said, 'the point is that you must save Rocamadour to save the Young King. And all your souls. And probably mine, too.'

The black kites drifted down and landed gracefully on the top of the castle. Their feathers were dark but their heads were lighter.

'I couldn't stop Grandmont burning,' Richard said, 'or countless villages in Brittany. In Meath I watched while we destroyed monasteries, knowing it was wrong but not bringing myself to try to stop it. Then Yvetot was reduced to ash as a punishment. Then Cailly fell to flames, and now I wonder where the burning will end.'

All eyes turned to Richard, whose eyes were more resolute than ever before. 'But now I know. Here. It ends here.'

Bowman raised his eyebrows. 'You want to bring an end to the way of life of all of Christendom?'

'I ignored Meath, so Yvetot burned,' Richard said. 'I'm not ignoring Grandmont.'

'Big words,' Guy yawned.

Richard clenched his teeth and considered the castle again. 'If the only way down is through the castle, then barely a dozen men could hold off an army. The walls look strong and the tower is high.'

Guy straightened up. 'I'm sorry, are you talking about taking this castle for yourself and holding it against the Young King?'

'Young lord,' Bowman said, 'let's slow down. You're talking about betraying the Young King right after he let you back in and throwing away everything he can offer you. We had nothing before that, and if you do this and somehow aren't killed, you'll have nothing again.'

'He'll have his soul,' Brian said.

The pilgrim playing the mournful flute coughed and gave up. He tried to have a drink, but his water container was empty.

'What the Young King offers me is hollow,' Richard said. 'How can we accept what is being offered when it is paid for by blood and destruction? Do you remember Sir Rob in Lagny? How he died with wealth but no worth to his name. I will die a worse death than the Scot if I keep standing aside when evil deeds are done.'

'I remember him,' Brian said, 'but I tried to save the baptistry from those mercenaries, and you wouldn't help me then, either. I'm not backing down this time.'

'Don't blame me for that,' Richard said, 'the baptistry was very different, there was no one there at all to defend. I don't think it really counts as a sacred building anymore. But Sir Rob died with nothing to lift his soul to heaven. If we allow Rocamadour to fall, then we will be no better off. But instead of purgatory, we will face hell.'

'What are you idiots talking about?' Guy asked. 'Please turn your backs on the Young King, give me the pleasure of being able to kill you and have you out of my life. You are nothing but trouble.'

Richard shook his head at Guy. 'You do know that King Henry has an actual army, don't you? You have a mercenary company, but he has one too, a company from Brabant. I've seen them, and they look better than the Navarrese. But he also has more lords than his son does. And his men are fed and well equipped. But more than that, they know they are right. The church is behind them, which we cannot say for the Young King, can we?'

'No, not really,' Bowman muttered.

'Until Old Henry is gone they are on the legitimate side,' Richard said. 'Then, they will all shift their allegiance willingly to the Young King, and there will be no need to burn anything at all. I know you are all calling it a war, but to everyone else it is a rebellion. And you're the rebels. One defeat and the rebels will scatter. You'll be left on your own with the Young King because you are so close to home you can't really flee to it.'

Guy sniffed and rubbed his leather sole on the dusty ground. 'I know all this, but I must fight to keep these Angevin snakes from my lands. They will spread like a pestilence until they have consumed everyone smaller than themselves.'

'Just stand aside,' Richard said, 'the Old King will be left with many, many more rebels to face if you bow out now. He may even forgive you if you stand here with me and force the Young King to change his ways.'

'I have barely twenty knights and as many squires,' Guy said, 'the Young King will get into this castle.'

'Don't tell me you've fallen for the golden boy's charms?' Bowman asked.

Guy shrugged. 'He believes in himself so much he actually sticks to his word. This is a novelty to me, especially when I've been dealing with his younger brother. Bertran calls him Yes-and-No for a reason.'

'That is the whole reason men stick to their word,' Richard said, 'so they can trust and work with each other. It is what our entire society is built around.'

'That's why our society doesn't work,' the Lusignan said dismissively. 'I cannot believe you are so stupid as to throw the Young King's generosity back in his face. He's perhaps the only Angevin you can bargain with.'

'I'm not throwing anything in his face,' Richard said, 'there are higher powers than men on this earth, and we shouldn't forget it. I propose we act to show him the error of his ways.'

'You called me mad,' Guy said, 'but you're the one speaking nonsense. And don't listen to the priests, I don't know if they know what they speak about.'

'But you only care for your own survival,' Richard said.

'Who doesn't?' Guy asked.

Bowman nodded. 'I do, and I'm not sure this is a good idea. The best result is that we are left homeless and poor again. Count Philip won't take us in now, that opportunity has been snatched away. What would we have left?'

'Our dignity and our souls,' Brian stared back at the blonde man.

'I care little for either,' the Lusignan took a heavy breath.

'Then you should care that this rebellion will fail,' Richard said, 'I think it has already. The Old King will punish everyone involved except for his son. And Guy, he already hates you. You tried to kidnap his queen, back when he still liked her.'

'True,' Bowman said, 'and when Conan of St Malo tried to kidnap the queen, Old Henry hunted him down like a dog and killed him himself.'

'They say he used Mandeville's hammer,' Guy said.

Richard flashed a knowing smirk. 'We were there.'

'Were you now?'

Richard nodded. 'You should be scared of the Old King. I am.'

'I'm not blind or dumb,' Guy said, 'and the lack of success our war has enjoyed so far has not escaped me.'

'Wait, wait,' Bowman said, 'you're not entertaining this hair-brained idea, are you?'

'We aren't exactly going from victory to victory,' Guy said, 'and I cannot see a way out.'

'Make a stand,' Richard said. 'Here with us.'

Bowman laughed the laugh of a condemned man. 'You're mad. You're both mad. You'll get us all killed.'

'That doesn't matter,' Richard said, 'our souls are eternal. We need to muster everyone here who can wield an axe, spear, or bow. And find out if there are other entrances.'

'Are you sure?' Bowman asked.

Richard grinned. 'For the first time, yes, I know this is the right thing. I don't know why you're complaining, it was your doubts that gave me the idea.'

'But it never works out, does it?' the blonde knight asked.

'No, but that's why you like me.'

Bowman rolled his head back and stared up into the empty and endless blue sky. He sighed and looked back down. 'Bugger it,' he said, 'let's do it.'

Guy shook his head. 'You two are prize fools. But I think it's time for a little chaos, so I'm going to fight with you.'

Richard frowned. 'You mean to swing a sword at me, or to stand next to me and face the Young King?'

Guy put a hand on his sword. 'I'm no friend of the Angevins,' he said, 'better to stab this one in the back before he stabs me.'

Richard grinned. Then his elation faded as he realised what he was about to face.

The first thing Richard did was to find Roland's sword. Durendal had been driven halfway into a fissure in the white-grey cliffs just outside the holiest building in what he thought could be described best as a pilgrim town. The yellow bricks of the buildings seemed to grow out of the rock face, and the cliffs towered above him when he stood below the sword and looked up at it. It gleamed in the afternoon light, and he could hear a Latin song drift up from a chapel somewhere further down the cliff. Durendal looked out of reach, although a window below it offered a way to get close.

But Richard didn't have time for any more sightseeing, which was a shame because he reckoned the town to be the most beautiful place he had ever seen. Instead, he wanted to find all the entrances to the town so that he could keep the Young King out, and for once do something that could serve as a good example for his children. He knelt in front of the brightly coloured shrine to Saint Amadour as incense wafted about his nose and he whispered a prayer for Sophie's soul. The coolness of the shrine raised the hairs on the back of his neck, and he sensed spirits nearby. Richard wasn't foolish enough to think his wife was among them, he was quite sure she was haunting the tower she had leapt from. He prayed for his children's safety instead, and apologised for leaving them. He admitted that his decision had been a mistake and prayed that the children would forgive him for it. Finally, he said a prayer that Solis would be alive when he returned and Gerold would recover.

Richard found two fortified gatehouses below the castle, each closer to the river than the last. Both gatehouses were of a yellow stone and guarded a doorway big enough for a laden packhorse to enter. They had sturdy doors and battlements. The ground was so rocky that no attacker could ever dig under them, but they were not so tall as to be immune from ladders.

Guy's men worked to stock those gatehouses with boulders to hurl, and cut javelins from saplings they collected on a foraging expedition. Small stones were gathered up and placed next to slings which would be used to shoot them at surprising speed. The castle was easy to defend, but if the Young King could find boats he could sail under it to a small port with no defence at all. At least from their position perched high up the rock face, they would see any boats coming far in advance.

Two days later Guy stood next to Richard on the wall next to the tower as an army arrived. Richard hadn't slept much, he'd feared for his dreams and that fear had kept him awake. When Sophie appeared in his mind, he thought of something else.

'I'm glad we kicked the pilgrims out,' Guy said, 'it's far more peaceful here without them.'

Richard rubbed his fingers on the limestone walls and it came off yellow on his fingers.

The newly arrived army outside the castle was mostly unseen, remaining over the ridge that seemed almost like a natural wall around the castle, but the Young King and his banners were unmistakable when they approached.

The young monarch squinted up at the wall which was illuminated by the sun behind him. 'They told me the gate was shut to all, but I did not believe them,' the Young King said.

'They were right,' Guy replied.

'Why is the gate shut?'

'We can't let you burn it,' Richard said. 'It is a holy place and under God's protection. You can't keep devastating church land. Do you not remember the fate of Sir Rob?'

'I have time,' the Young King said, 'once I am the ruler I will strongly patronise the church. I will love the church more than myself. Their suffering will be repaid.'

'Find another way to fund your campaign,' Richard said, 'Christ might be the forgiver, but God is a punisher.'

The Young King put a hand on his face for a moment. 'I have a war to fight, and you are aware of that. I have no choice but to end it on favourable terms. To do that I need my army at my back, and to keep them, I have to pay them. It is unfortunate but necessary. Open the gates.'

Richard rested his mailed arms on the limestone. He really hoped doing the right thing would work out this time. 'I'm sorry, but I can't let you in. It's for your own good.'

'My own good? What would you know about my good? This is absurd. It is as if I stand before Neufchatel all over again.'

Bowman placed his strung bow on the crenellation so half of it stuck out over the wall. Then he placed an arrow beside it, the iron head in full view of the party below.

'Put that away,' the Young King said, 'you've done enough damage already. I should have you skinned alive for this.'

'I knew it,' Guy said, 'he is as brutal as his father. His words are honeyed and false.'

'You,' the young Angevin snarled. 'We had a deal. A very good deal. I understand Richard has a broken sense of right and wrong and cannot look outside of himself, but you know exactly what is good for you. Explain yourself.'

'We had a deal while you had something to offer me,' the Lusignan said, 'but it is plain to see that your rebellion is nearly over, and you are not going to be the winner.'

'The war will be won.'

'It will,' Guy said, 'but not by you.'

'You dare betray me, all of you?' the Young King shook his head and his words sounded pained. 'You, who I favoured so strongly. Who I honoured so greatly. How can you wound me so deeply?'

'Leave,' Guy said, 'ride north and reconcile with your father. He will apologise, you will apologise, and everyone can go back to what we were doing before you created this mess.'

'Open the gate,' the Young King ordered.

Richard felt anger within, he would hold these walls. 'Open them yourself.'

The Young King simmered for the rest of the day, which gave Guy time to post men at the lower gates and set a lookout watching over the river.

Richard climbed the tower, partly so he could distract himself with the view over the valley to the south, and waited. As a balmy evening fell and bats darted back and forth around the tower, Richard could hear the distinct sound of axes. But ladders, Richard had learned well by now, took a while to build, so he found his pile of blankets and went to sleep. He woke up in a sweat, halfway through a dream about ghosts and haunting flutes, but groggily drifted off again because he was so tired.

The next day brought much of the same, but the axes ceased their chopping as the day cooled and Richard climbed the tower again to watch for movement.

The glow of fires over the ridge lit the night sky while squires lit braziers around the castle walls.

Guy climbed the stairs, looked around the horizon and nodded down towards the two gates far down the cliffs below. 'They're going down there.'

'How can you tell?' Richard asked.

'I can hear them,' he replied, 'but it's also what I would do. No one is scaling these walls. We'll take a gatehouse each and keep them out. They could try both at once.'

Richard flew down the stairs in the tower as fast as he could, but there was no light in them and he was lucky not to tumble all the way down, even though he caught his spurs on a step once and bounced off the curved wall. Richard collected Bowman and went down to the first gatehouse and climbed the short wall next to it. The whole wall was only the length of a spear's throw from sheer cliff to sheer drop, with the gate in the centre. The road that led to it was only a few dozen paces long before it curved back on itself and cut further down the cliff. There it ran towards the second gatehouse halfway down the valley to the river.

'We only have a short wall to defend,' Richard said. Luckily it was the height of two men and made of stone.

Bowman rested his bow on the wall and peered down the road. 'We don't have any ladder hooks, though.'

'We've got slings,' Richard shrugged. The locals who lived in Rocamadour paid for militiamen who had spears and slings, and ten of these men stood next to Bowman and Richard. Two of Guy's squires reinforced the wall.

'It will come down to how many ladders they bring,' Bowman said.

'Less than three and we'll be fine,' Richard said.

When the Young King's army came, they brought four ladders.

It was dark, Richard could smell the river, and the men alongside him moved their weapons around for no reason or went to relieve themselves. Pinpricks of light heralded the attack, although the torches used to light the way were kept far down the road so as not to illuminate the advancing men and give the defenders clear targets.

Bowman nocked an arrow anyway.

'I can't really see them,' Richard squinted. The evening cooled, but he was warm inside his mail. His heart thumped just as much as it had the first time he'd ever sighted the enemy.

The blonde knight loosed his arrow, and the militiamen picked up their slings and selected stones and lead bullets to unleash on their assailants.

Bowman's second arrow found its mark because a man screamed in the darkness, but then the glow cast down from the walls shone upon the bodies of Sancho's mercenaries and their ladders. They'd approached in silence, but now they roared battle-cries and charged.

The defenders whirled their slings around their heads only two or three times before slinging their ammunition down at the Navarrese. The stones flew through the air, and at such a short range, the missiles cracked noses, bruised arms, and dented shields. One mercenary lost an eye and his life to the slingers before the ladders were lifted up.

Richard threw one of the recently made javelins, but without an iron head it served to deeply annoy a mercenary rather than kill him. Richard drew the Little Lord's sword instead.

Crossbow bolts whistled overhead and Richard felt himself duck.

'Don't duck,' Bowman shot an arrow which penetrated the mail of the first man to climb the nearest ladder.

A slinger succumbed to a crossbow bolt in the chest as Richard lined himself up at the top of a ladder. He swung his blue and white shield to his front just in time for a bolt to slam into it and send him back a step.

One of Guy's squires dropped a boulder onto a ladder and its top two rungs splintered with a loud crack.

'Only three left,' Bowman stepped back and readied his arrow for whoever climbed Richard's ladder next.

A head appeared then ducked back down. 'Mercenaries are cowards,' Bowman muttered.

The dog of war found his courage, or perhaps gave in to threats from below, and climbed up onto the wall. His eyes focused on the arrow as it cut through the skin between them and cracked a hole in his skull. He fell backwards off the ladder and Bowman nodded with satisfaction.

'You don't have enough arrows for all of them,' Richard said, 'we have to break the ladders.'

Guy's squires lifted a huge stone between them and staggered towards the third ladder.

A mercenary's shield appeared up their ladder, and Bowman lowered his bow as he was presented with no target. 'Bugger.'

Richard rushed to meet the shield-bearer, rammed his own shield into the green and gold one, and pushed that man straight off the wall. A spear stabbed up from below and glanced off Richard's thigh, but the mail on his shirt just bunched up and muffled it.

The Lusignan squires heaved their stone onto the wall and rolled it down onto their target. As it crashed through the third ladder, a bolt thwacked into one of them and sent the victim to the ground howling in agony.

'Two ladders,' Bowman stepped sideways to shoot whoever dared appear on the wall next.

A bear of a man leapt with surprising deftness onto the rampart and growled at Richard.

Bowman's arrow caught him in his midriff, but whether or not it penetrated his mail, he rushed at Richard, who suddenly felt very small. Richard raised his shield. The bear pushed him backwards and a sword clanged off his helmet. The bear spun around as an arrow sunk into his lower back, but Richard only had time to deal him a glancing blow before the mercenary switched his attention back to him and hammered down on his shield.

Richard fell to a knee beneath the blow and lashed out with the Little Lord's sword. His strike hit the bear but didn't seem to bother him.

Bowman's next arrow buried itself in the bear's shoulder, but the mercenary crashed his sword down and split Richard's shield down to a knot in the wood. Another blow and Richard would be defenceless.

Guy's squire dropped another stone onto the second ladder and Richard heard the crack even as he parried an attack with his sword.

Bowman cried out in frustration as he loosed his last arrow and it sailed into the bear's back. 'How many arrows does it take?' he dropped his bow and drew his sword, but another mercenary ascended the ladder and lunged at him before he could aid Richard.

Richard, still on one knee, raised his shield to take another hit. The bear's sword crashed into the middle of the broken shield and split it clean in two. Held together only by the leather straps on its inside, the two wooden sides flapped down on each side of his left arm. The force jolted him and threw him down onto his chest, which hurt. Richard slashed sideways with the sword with everything he had, into the bear's ankle. The bear lurched away and hopped on his unharmed leg.

Richard followed up with a cut to the good leg and the giant was felled. The bear tumbled and Richard discarded his fractured shield.

But the bear wasn't done. He rolled over, snapping all the arrows sticking out of him, and pulled himself to his feet with an almighty grunt.

Bowman flinched as a bolt whirled past his neck and struck the shield that hung on his back. It hurled him backwards and another Navarrese scaled the ladder and jumped down onto the walkway.

Guy's squire rushed to meet him, but he was out of large enough rocks after destroying the third ladder, and could only slash with his sword.

'There's just one left,' Bowman gathered himself up and killed the mercenary the Lusignan man distracted.

The bear shook himself off and lumbered at Richard. His sword arced down and Richard brought the Little Lord's blade up to block it. The Spanish sword cut through the Norman blade and it snapped.

Richard stared for a split second at the broken sword, and the bear laughed. Richard gritted his teeth and thrust the jagged iron up into the mercenary's face.

The bear swayed backwards out of its range and grinned. He stepped forwards and Richard backed up a step, aware he was dangerously outsized.

Bowman slashed the mercenary across the back of the neck and his mail coif jangled. The bear sensed the danger and tried to move out of harm's way. Richard, still only kneeling on the ground, rammed the broken sword into the bear's thigh.

He roared even as Bowman cut down onto his shoulder. The blonde man's blade only cut a few rings apart, but the force numbed the bear's upper arm.

Richard scrambled to his feet and used the damaged blade with two hands to jam it down into the big man's chest.

Guy's squire killed a dog of war who bounded up the ladder, but then a bolt from outside the wall caught him in the arm and threw him aside.

Bowman hacked at the bear's sword arm and the man dropped his weapon. Richard withdrew his blade, but the Navarrese twisted as he collapsed and the blade snapped a second time as it caught between two ribs. Richard let it go, drew Sir John's dagger and drove it into the bear's skull a moment after the bear hit the stone walkway.

He still didn't die.

Bowman chopped at the bear's wrist again and the hand almost severed from his arm. 'Pick him up,' the blonde man shouted and Richard jumped to help.

An enemy climbed the ladder as Bowman and Richard carried the bear, a load which took all of their hands to carry.

A slinger's stone winged its way to the ladder and cracked the attacker's skull. He clung onto the ladder with one hand and held his face with the other as he yelled out in pain.

'We've got no big stones left,' Bowman grunted with exertion.

'I know what you're doing,' Richard helped Bowman push the still moaning bear up onto the wall. A crossbow bolt hit the floundering mercenary somewhere, and Richard had to brace against the force.

'Now,' Bowman cried and they rolled the huge man onto the ladder, which gave way and shattered into splinters.

The militiamen on the wall ducked behind the wall and grinned with relief.

Bowman threw himself down as a volley of bolts either broke on the wall or flew above it.

Richard joined him behind cover. 'No ladders left.'

Guy's surviving squire checked his fallen comrade, but he was dead. Two of the militiamen had taken fatal bolt strikes, but the survivors said prayers and recovered their strength in silence.

The blonde knight grinned. 'And that still counts as you losing your sword.'

Richard frowned. 'I'm actually going to miss that sword.'

'We'll have to get you another one,' Bowman said as the noise of the defeated enemy retreated back up along the road.

Richard recovered his breathing. 'I've got an idea,' he smiled at Bowman.

'Whatever it is, young lord, don't do it.'

Richard did it. Once he was quite sure the Young King's men had given up their assault, he walked into Rocamadour and through the stone passageways until he reached the shrine of the Black Madonna. He walked through rooms full of huddled attendants who waited for the attack to be declared over, and through store chambers and up stairs. It took him a while to find the window he searched for, but when he stuck his head out of one and looked up, he saw Durendal protruding from the cliff above.

'I thought you might have meant that,' Bowman shouted from the street below. 'You're an idiot. It's probably rusty.'

The old blade twinkled in the moonlight. It reflected silver. 'I think it's sheltered under the cliff,' Richard said, 'the iron is good.' He reached his fingers up towards it but they fell short. He pulled himself back to the room and looked around. In the corner was a wooden pole on three legs that was used to hang clothes on. He tipped the tunics or dresses onto the bare wooden floor and picked it up. Richard brandished it out of the window and waved it in the direction of Roland's sword. The legs of the pole hooked around the crossguard and Richard jerked the sword out of the cliff with a great scraping sound. It sliced through the air and Richard had to duck out of the way when it spiralled into him, cut his hand, and fell to the street below. Bowman dodged it as it clattered onto and down some stone steps.

Richard got rid of the pole and looked back out of the window.

Down below, Bowman retrieved the sword and turned it over in his hands. He flexed it and it bent a long way. 'The sword is fine,' the blonde man said, 'I'd never have believed it was even a real sword.'

Richard returned to Bowman and his new sword. 'You can't tell anyone,' he said, 'they'll either not believe me or curse me.'

'You can't steal a sword like that without being cursed, young lord,' Bowman handed it over.

Richard didn't care, he slid it into the Little Lord's scabbard and the sword rattled around inside.

'We can glue a piece of sheepskin into the throat of the scabbard,' Bowman said, 'it'll be as snug as if they were made for each other.'

Richard nodded, that was a job for the morning.

Bowman glanced up at the empty crack in the cliff. 'Someone is going to miss that.'

Richard grinned. 'I've got another idea.' He left the castle through their defended gatehouse and joined the militiamen who now scavenged everything they could from the bodies scattered on the roadway. Richard pulled the Little Lord's useless sword from the bear and made his way back to the empty scar in the cliff. He wedged the clothes pole between the window ledge and the cliff, and used it as a ladder to jam the Little Lord's sword back where Durendal had been lodged. The pole snapped as he returned to the window, Richard banged his head on its frame, but landed safely inside, his sword swap complete.

When dawn broke it was a warm, still day. Richard couldn't believe that winged insects still flew around at this time of year here, as he swotted one on his neck. His mail coif squashed it against his skin and it mangled up in the rings, never to be fully removed.

Richard settled in, watching from the tower, waiting for something to happen.

Guy did the same on the wall below as some dogs barked out in the Young King's encampment. The day dragged on, but at least a servant of the shrine brought up food for the castle's defenders. The inhabitants of Rocamadour did at least appreciate someone standing up for them, even if those who could had taken the last of the boats and sailed away.

Brian only found Richard as the sun rose the following day. He'd visited all the shrines and spoken to everyone he could find who could converse with him in Latin. 'This is my favourite place so far,' the monk said. 'Did you know this is a stop on the way to Compostela?'

'No,' Richard said, 'but Sarjeant would have. I hope he is well.'

Brian wiped sweat away from his neck with a cloth. 'However much this place gladdens my soul, why couldn't we go to Flanders? Where it is a more sensible temperature.'

'Maynard betrayed us before we got away,' Richard said. 'I was quite ready to go back north, although I don't mind it being so warm.'

'I like it up on the castle because at least there's a breeze here,' the monk said, 'down in the valley I feel as if I might suffocate.'

Richard turned around and gazed along the river, and saw it wasn't empty.

'Will the Young King's army try again?' Brian asked.

Richard sighed. 'They already are. There are boats on the water, do you see?'

Brian strained his eyes but shook his head.

'They are by the shore not far up river. I expect they're loading soldiers,' Richard said. 'We don't have enough men to fight them off. Maybe once, but not if they also attack the gates at the same time.'

'I said something bad was going to happen.'

'You did,' Richard replied, then thought about finding Guy. Instead, just before he left the castle, movement outside it caught his eye.

Brian bumped into the back of him when he stopped and scratched his face on Richard's mail.

'Someone's coming,' Richard said.

'Probably an ultimatum,' the monk rubbed his face.

'If it is,' Richard said, 'they've sent the worst possible person to deliver it.'

Beneath the walls and walking on foot, came Maynard the squire. He scanned the walls and advanced further only when he was certain no one was going to shoot at him.

'What do you want?' Richard asked. 'Have you come to apologise?'

'I did as I was commanded,' the squire answered, 'but that's not really why I'm here.'

'Hurry up,' Richard said.

'The siege is over.'

Richard laughed. 'We've seen the boats, you can't trick us that easily.'

'Oh, those,' Maynard said. 'A company was sent out as soon as we arrived, but we haven't heard from them for over a day.'

'So you're not here to distract us?' Richard asked, although he wasn't sure why he was bothering.

'No,' Maynard replied, 'we didn't even know if they'd find any boats in the first place.'

'Then why are you here?'

'The Young King is sick,' Maynard said.

'How sick?' Richard asked. He turned to Brian and asked him to fetch Guy and tell Bowman about the impending waterborne attack. Whatever happened, everyone needed to know about the boats.

Maynard's eyes moved from arrow slit to arrow slit. 'He's bedridden, the camp is in a depression in the ground you see, and the air is bad. Insects keep biting me and the water tastes odd even after it's boiled or mixed with wine.'

Richard could hear Brian in his head telling him everything was God's vengeance. 'What does he suffer from?' he asked.

Maynard rubbed his ear and looked up after a pause. 'The flux.'

Richard's stomach churned. The flux was dreaded. Victims usually suffered from a fever and threw up, but the worst symptom was chronic diarrhoea. Richard had always suspected Long Tom had suffered from it before he chose death by siege in Brittany, but no one had wanted to talk about it then. But he was going to have to talk about it now.

'How bad?' Richard asked. 'Is blood coming out?'

Maynard glanced around. 'I don't want to say.'

Richard swore. In Brittany almost no one had survived after blood came out. But this was the future King of England and half of France, so maybe it would be different.

'Why are you telling me this?'

'The Young King fears his end,' Maynard said, 'he wanted me to give you a message, but I don't really understand it.'

'What is it?' Richard asked.

'It's very odd,' the squire scratched the back of his neck, 'he said that someone will have to stop the monks removing the incense too early as they did at Lagny. He said you'd understand, and that you are the only one he thinks will perform that service for him.'

Richard understood the message, but didn't think he was the only one who would do it. 'Was there anything else?'

'Obviously our lord wants you to come and see him,' Maynard said. 'Oh, and that the siege is over and his men will not attack.'

'What about the men in the boats?' Richard asked. 'They won't know about the flux.'

Maynard shrugged. 'I'm just delivering the message. Rocamadour is safe from the army on land. The Young King is escaping this place and travelling to Martel as we speak to recover there. He has told no one that yet, though. That's a secret.'

'Hopefully no one is listening to you shout about it, then,' Richard shouted down himself from the battlements. The squire was an idiot.

Guy clambered up the stone steps that took him to the wall. Richard told him the news.

The Lusignan gazed down at the squire. 'We have two problems,' he said.

'The boats?' Richard said.

'That's one,' Guy said, 'but the other is worse.'

Richard looked down at the squire who seemed to be waiting for something.

'The second,' Guy closed his eyes, 'is that anyone who thinks too hard about it will lay the blame for this illness on us.'

An icy shiver ran down Richard's spine. If they hadn't closed the gates, the Young King would probably have spent no time in the bad air at all.

'What can we do about it?' Richard asked.

'Run, I suppose,' Guy said, 'the Old King is going to kill us. Slowly.'

Richard clasped the handle of his new sword. The leather wrapped around it was dry and cracked, but the pommel had a nice weight to it. 'Shouldn't we deal with the boat problem first?' Richard looked down into the valley where three boats drifted towards Rocamadour. They'd reach it soon.

'Why bother?' Guy said. 'I'll have my horse saddled before they reach dry land.'

'The whole point of this was to defend the shrines and the people,' Richard said.

'No, the whole point of this was to stay alive,' the Lusignan said.

'Do what you want,' Richard said, then turned to Maynard. 'I'm going to open the gates for you, you're coming in.'

Maynard backed up a step. 'No, I'm not, you'll kill me.'

'I swear on my wife's soul I won't,' Richard said, 'but I need your help. Also, if you turn your back, we'll shoot you where you stand.'

The squire considered his options, but he wasn't one to risk an arrow. He approached the castle.

Richard let him in and dragged him down the hundreds of steps to the jetty at the foot of the cliffs. Bowman had mustered a dozen militiamen there, and was busy tipping a table over to block the steps that led up into Rocamadour.

The first of the boats drew near, hugging the shoreline, a dozen oars propelling it along.

'We don't have long,' Bowman said. His bow lay on the stones, a sheaf of arrows beside it.

'I'm hoping it won't come to a fight,' Richard said, 'but first you have to promise not to overreact.'

'Overreact about what?'

'Promise me,' Richard said.

Bowman pointed to where he wanted a militiaman to place a second table. 'Whatever makes you happy, young lord, I'm busy saving our lives.'

Richard dragged Maynard by the arm down to the waterfront.

Bowman spotted him and forgot about the tables. 'You,' he shouted, 'I'll gut you and throw you in the river one limb at a time.'

'Calm down,' Richard said, 'he's going to stand here and tell them that the rebellion is over.'

Bowman scrunched up his face but kept his eyes on the squire. 'Why? What happened?'

'The Young King has the flux.'

Bowman's eyes enlarged. 'Is he passing blood?'

Richard nodded.

The blonde man made the sign of the cross, just as the first volley of crossbow bolts peppered the stone platform used to offload cargo from boats.

Maynard dove behind one of Bowman's tables and Richard ducked a bolt which would have otherwise hit him.

'You still shouldn't duck,' Bowman said.

Richard got up and waved both hands at the boats. 'Stop,' he shouted, 'the siege has ended.'

On the ships men were busy reloading their crossbows, sliding new bolts into groves.

Richard looked for Maynard but he was still hidden. 'Come here, squire,' Richard cried, 'this only works if they can see you. You'll get me killed.'

Bowman grasped Richard's plan. He picked the squire up by his mail coif and dragged him out onto the waterfront. 'Shout now, boy, because I'm using you for a shield and even if it doesn't work, I'll still be fine.'

Maynard screamed at the boats to stop, telling them what had happened and that hostilities had ceased.

A bolt whirled through the air and shattered on the stones, but none followed.

Richard let out a breath. 'I've half a mind to let Bowman drown you for your delay,' he said.

Bowman pushed the squire towards the river.

'But you can't do it,' Richard said.

'Why not?' the blonde knight asked. 'Don't tell me you've forgiven him?'

'Far from it,' Richard said, 'but if you kill him in front of that company, they'll just start shooting again. Besides, we'll need him to go and see the Young King in safety.'

'What?' Bowman pushed Maynard away as roughly as he could get away with. 'Why would we do that? We should be fleeing.'

'We're going to the Young King. I have to make sure some incense burns for long enough.'

Bowman sighed.

Contemplating the depression in the ground where the Young King's camp had been pitched, Richard wasn't surprised that disease had spread.

The royal tent, painted red with gold borders, was half down. Servants and squires held the highest guy ropes steady while others knocked out tent pegs with wooden mallets.

The Navarrese wagons had moved off to an area of higher ground a few bowshots away, and lagered up in a circle.

'They'll be deciding their next move,' Guy said. The Lusignan had wavered but decided that an attempted reconciliation with the Young King was worth his time.

'Those dogs of war will scuttle off and look for another war,' Bowman said. 'Or start one.'

The remaining canvas of the royal tent folded in on itself as the guy ropes were let down, but one servant let go of his too early. The tall pole it held upright fell and gouged a great gash in one side of the tent. An argument erupted and a squire smashed the servant around the head with his wooden mallet.

'I'm thinking we shouldn't tarry here, young lord,' Bowman said.

The red shields were all gone, including Maynard, who had disappeared while they prepared their horses for the journey. The thankful residents of Rocamadour had laden them with food and wine, and Richard felt just as deeply proud about that as he felt utterly terrified of what he'd done to the Young King.

'You're right,' Richard squeezed his thighs onto the blue roan. 'We should go.'

A company with colours from the Low Countries began their march north just as a ripping noise sprung from the royal tent. Squires cut up the canvas, folded sections up and tied them to their horses to sell for themselves.

'One word is so powerful,' Richard mumbled, 'mention the flux and the world changes.'

The world had changed. The army broke up and lords took their retinues back to their homelands. Richard retraced the way to Martel, only a short distance, but the air seemed different. A breeze blew, warm but strong, as if heralding a change in the weather.

Brian watched the flight of a heron overhead. 'You remember what I said, don't you?'

'Yes,' Bowman snapped, 'we know you told the royal boy this would happen. He didn't listen, and now he's sick.'

Martel's tower pierced the sky up ahead. A few white clouds puffed up above, but the breeze picked up.

Guy rode right into the camp only recently set up by the red company. He shouted down from his horse asking where the Marshal was.

'Crying at the bedside,' came the reply.

Guy groaned. 'Of course he is. Pathetic.'

The camp grew out of the village of Martel, rows of shelters erected as an extension of the main street, as well as the back street that ran parallel to it.

The tower looked much like the one at Rocamadour, but it didn't have the same size of castle attached. Instead houses sprouted from it, and out of one of those houses two squires in red surcoats dragged a wooden chest.

'It's not any better here, then,' Bowman said.

'The Young King was the person holding the whole thing together,' Richard dismounted. He left the horses in the care of Guy's squires and went to look for the sick monarch.

They walked up the main street and doors were bolted as they approached. A knight guarding the entrance to the tower told them that the Young King wasn't inside, but rather at the house of Stephen the Smith. The knight didn't know where that was, only that a bishop had recommended it as the best location in Martel to treat the flux from.

Smiths were often on the edges or outside of settlements, so they all slogged to the far end of Martel.

The forge had been extinguished and work had ceased when the Young King had first been carried in. Now, all the windows were open and the door had been removed from its hinges and placed on top of a large, square iron fire box. The Young King used the door as a bed. The smith was nowhere to be seen, but the smithy was by no means empty. Two dozen knights crammed into the room along with an equal number of assorted clergy. A breeze wafted across the room and the door-table, and ruffled the linen sheets that lay over the Young King. His golden-red hair waved in the draught, too, but it seemed duller than before.

Bowman inspected a rack of hammers as Richard approached the man he had twice betrayed.

The Marshal stood beside his master, tears streaming down his face. 'You did this,' he said to Richard through clenched teeth.

The Young King lifted an arm and waved the Marshal to silence. 'We are at peace,' he said, his voice muted and his words slow. His face was pale and he wore a rough hair shirt against his skin.

Richard wanted to look away, but the intensity of the Young King's eyes was the only thing that hadn't diminished.

'Thank you for coming,' he said, 'I wish my father would come. I have sent word to him begging for his forgiveness. My last wish is that he will come in person so I can see him one last time, but I fear you are the last visitor I shall receive on this earth.'

'I'm sure he will come,' Richard said, 'but you may still recover.'

The Young King looked up at the beamed ceiling. 'My father will fear a trap. He fears for traps everywhere, and now that I see he is right to do so. I have been a terrible son.'

'You must recover,' the Marshal wiped away only some of the torrent of tears that washed his face.

'Richard,' the Young King held his hand out.

Richard clasped it and the lack of warmth brought tears to his eyes. It was as if the life in the Young King was slipping away before him.

'I need you to ensure things are done correctly after my death,' the Young King said, 'the two of you. Men are fleeing already and once I die the rest will follow. Most of those in this room will go, but the two of you will stay.'

The knights and greater lords who watched and listened either looked away or made a point of speaking to each other and pretending not to be listening at all. Richard knew his lord was right, few of those who surrounded him were planning to be in Martel for long.

'You were right from the start,' the Young King said, 'I was mistaken. My fatal punishment is fair, I can see it now. My selfishness has laid me low. My impatience has killed me. My certainty has led me to the edge of the abyss.'

'You are not certain to die,' Richard said. 'I'm sure that the best healers are already on their way.'

'They are,' the young Angevin said, 'but I have to live long enough for them to arrive. The bishop here already tells me to do things. Taking me here to this room was his idea, as was lifting me off the floor. Yesterday I prostrated myself naked on the floor of the church before his crucifix, and now I wear this.' He ran his dehydrated fingers along the rough hairshirt.

Richard saw Sir Rob the Scot in his mind and tried to prepare himself for what might come. 'If it comes to it,' he said, 'at least you will die with friends around you.'

The Young King could only smile faintly.

'You meant well,' Richard said, 'everything you told me at Lagny, you said with honesty. All your intentions were good, you are to be the light of this world. The Lord knows this and will surely judge you fairly.'

The Young King closed his eyes. 'Bernard of Clairvaux wrote that hell is full of good wishes and desires. And soon I will join my good wishes.'

Richard shook his head. 'You meant well. Recover and see to your soul.'

'I cannot eat,' the Young King said, 'I know my time is drawing to an end. All that remains is to put my affairs in order and die well. All of life is a preparation for death. Mine is simply coming earlier than planned.'

The Marshal wailed and some of the knights frowned at him. 'We cannot lose you, my lord, we cannot. I cannot live without you.'

'You shall be well without me, my Marshal. You have your fame and your prowess. Neither can be matched. The world is yours.'

'You are the light of the world,' the Marshal repeated Richard's phrase as he fought through his tears, 'without you we shall be but deaf men fumbling in the dark.'

Richard coughed to hide his surprise at the Marshal's sudden turn of eloquence.

'Carry my torch, Marshal, serve my family as you have served me. Learn from our time together, the bad times especially. Be the example of loyalty that our world sorely needs. Preserve my family's power and legacy.'

'Not without you,' the Marshal croaked, 'the world will be in shadow in your absence. How can I find joy in the tournament after you are gone? Each sword blow shall be empty, each ransom unsatisfactory.'

Richard walked around the door-bed and put a hand on the green cloak, looking more tattered than ever, that hung from the Marshal's shoulder. 'You need to pull yourself together,' Richard said, 'you can wail for now, but soon you will need to stand strong and set an example to others. Knights will look to you. God only knows why, but they will.'

The Young King laboured a breath. 'Wait for the day of my departure. I know the two of you will be the only ones who will stand by me once life has passed from my body. When I am dead, see the proper rites are performed, then bury me in Rouen.'

Brian raised a hand from where he stood nearby. 'If I may?'

The Young King nodded imperceptibly.

'May I suggest that you are buried in Grandmont Abbey, a gesture which may balance the destruction wrought there on your behalf.'

The Young King closed his eyes and brought his hands up to his chest in prayer. 'Your heart is in the right place, monk. But my rightful resting place is Rouen. That is where my bones belong. Although, I will permit the more perishable parts of me to be laid to rest at Grandmont. You shall see to it.'

'Me?' Brian gulped.

'You will stay with Richard. Even the bishop will run back to my father the moment my final breath leaves me, but you will remain.'

The purple-faced bishop bristled but didn't respond.

'Rouen,' the Young King whispered with closed eyes, 'in the duchy I shall never rule.'

And so they waited for a king to die. Richard and Bowman waited in the hall attached to the tower, drinking Martel wine and distracting themselves with idle thoughts on how to wipe out the Martel family. Brian went to the village's church and prayed that someone else would be given his new responsibility. Guy sat in another corner, deep in conversation with his sister, who Richard did his best to ignore. He made himself look the other way, for every time he looked at her, he heard his wife in his head and his heart broke a little more.

Over the next few days, knights melted away from Martel. Fewer and fewer ate and drank in the hall each night as the red company withered.

The Marshal barely left the bedside of his master and remained with him day and night. Weight fell from his body and darkness clouded his face. Richard was worried about him, but not as worried as he was about himself. Healers arrived with more churchmen, but whatever they did, the Young King kept no food down.

Bowman sat down one day after conversing with some Lusignan knights. 'Even Henry the Northerner has fled,' the blonde man said, 'after all his words and professed loyalty, he's fled the Marshal.'

'Only cowards are as loud as he was,' Richard said.

Bowman nodded and sniffed at the empty table. 'I think we're out of food, too. Martel is dry, the villagers snuck out last night with the last of the food and wine. All we have is the water in the well.'

The next morning, news came from the south, and it was dark.

'The mercenaries are coming back,' a red-surcoated squire said. He wiped the dust from his journey off his face. 'Their wagons roll towards Martel, with the fires of Rocamadour behind them.'

Richard sat up straight. 'Fires?'

The squire shrugged. 'They looted the shrines.'

Richard slumped onto the table and buried his head in his hands. 'What was the point? Why did we bother?'

Bowman didn't know. 'At least it wasn't the Young King who sacked the shrines. His soul can be spared punishment for that, at least.'

'We killed another king, Bowman. We killed him saving Rocamadour, but then we lost Rocamadour anyway. The world would be a better place if I threw everything aside and went into a monastery.'

Bowman thought about it. 'Aye, on balance I think you're probably right about that, young lord.'

Richard lifted his head and glared at his friend. 'That's not what I need to hear.'

In the far corner, in the place that they'd made their own, Alice started crying and Guy tried to console her.

'What's wrong with them?' Bowman asked.

'King Henry is going to set an example to the other rebels with how he deals with a few of them,' Richard said, 'and Guy thinks he'll be the one who is blamed the most.'

'Which is accurate,' Bowman said, 'after you, anyway.'

'You really aren't helping.'

Church bells rang. They clanged together not in any tune, but in a cacophony of violent noise.

Richard and Bowman looked at each other. The chatter in the hall evaporated and Alice's sobbing ceased. The very air seemed to suck out of the chamber.

'Oh, no,' Bowman said.

'To the smithy,' Richard said, 'quickly.'

They rushed to reach the Young King before he died. The bells rang as their feet pounded the street. Knights saddled their horses and vaulted onto their backs as quickly as they could. When the Stephen the Smith's building came into view, a flock of brown-robed churchmen rushed out of it.

A count pushed a squire out of his way behind them, clutching in his hands the Young King's own sword. The squire reached for the sword, but the count swung the scabbard over and clouted him in the forehead before fleeing.

Brian was right behind them. 'The end of the world,' the monk panted, 'the end.'

Richard rushed through the doorless-door and found a handful of advisors and a clerk still there with the Marshal. The Marshal was as pale as his lord, and Richard felt a pang of pity for him.

The Young King waved a flailing finger at a folded cloak on the floor. 'Marshal,' he whispered. 'The cloak.'

The English knight picked up the bright red cloak and held it up to his master.

'This cloak. Has my crusading cross. On it.'

Richard reached to where his own linen cross had been without thought. Although the cross was gone, some of the frayed stitching was still stuck in the worn tunic.

'You Marshal. My most. Intimate friend,' the Young King's voice was a husk of its former self. 'Fulfil my holy vow. Take cloak. Holy Sepulchre. Jerusalem. I took vow. Less seriously. Than ought to have.'

The Marshal nodded, unable to form words. He looked far worse than Richard had felt when he'd lost Sophie, and that stirred up guilt which brought tears to Richard's eyes.

Bertran de Born stood behind the Marshal and attempted to comfort him. The troubadour was one of the most senior knights not to have abandoned their king.

The Marshal sniffed. 'I swear I will lay this cloak at the Sepulchre. I will journey to Jerusalem for you.'

'All has been done properly,' Bertran said, 'our king has prepared himself for death as well as any man ever has. It is time for the last act.'

The Marshal's tears fell on the cloak as Bertran gently moved him out of the way.

'Help me lower the door-bed onto the floor,' Bertran said.

Richard and Bowman did as instructed, the Young King not weighing as much as they'd expected. Then Bertran and Brian scooped up ash from the forge and made a bed of it on the floorboards. Bertran fetched a large yellow stone and placed it and one end of the bed.

'Help me lower him onto it,' the troubadour said, his words failing him and coming on as reverent whispers.

Richard couldn't help but crying as they all lifted the Young King from the door-bed and onto the bed of ash. The Marshal gently rested his master's head on the stone pillow as Bertran draped a noose around the king's neck.

Even Bowman's eyes were not dry.

Bertran nodded. 'Not all kings are lucky enough to leave this world in such a way.'

The Marshal knelt down and clasped the Young King's cold hand.

Bertran knelt down and placed a golden ring in the Young King's other hand. 'Your father did not come, but he sent this ring as a token of peace. Go to your rest knowing that he forgives you.'

The Young King alone did not cry. The clerk who recorded the final act of his master wept and the drops caused his writing to run down his page.

Brian brought in incense and lit it in the smith's forge. He'd almost been too late.

The church bells still rang.

Then, with his army dispersed and his hopes shattered, the Young King, not yet thirty years of age, died.

The lump in Richard's throat made it hard to breathe. The incense caught in his throat and made him want to choke. The Marshal's tears stopped and he glanced down at his lord in a stunned silence, as if he hadn't quite believed the young man could actually die.

Bertran looked at Richard and Richard looked at Bowman. The blonde man dropped his eyes and sniffed.

Brian walked over to the body. He said words in Latin because the bishop was too stunned to do it himself.

Guy stood in the open doorway, Richard didn't know how long he'd been there. He looked worried, a look that Richard hadn't often seen on his confident face. 'I'm going to get smashed by the hammer,' the Lusignan murmured.

'Do not dare to think of yourself,' Bertran hissed at him. 'The light of this world has been extinguished. All who were noble flocked to this man who had no land or wealth. They flocked to him because of his person, not his titles or power. We shall never see this again so long as we live. Knighthood itself, the cornerstone of our world, will fall without the Young King to carry it. He lifted it up to new heights of glory, and without him it shall sink lower than we can imagine. We shall never know the like of the fabled tournament of Lagny again, the world has fallen into black and shall never recover.'

WHAT NOW?

By the following dawn only a handful of knights remained to escort the body of the Young King north.

The space outside Martel, once full of tents, horses, and people, was left a desolate patch of trampled grass dotted with ashen marks where fires had been. The houses in the village hadn't been spared a nighttime spate of looting, and only the tower had avoided being ransacked.

Stray dogs roamed the streets that morning as Richard saddled his spare horse. The Young King's body was laid into a cart by some squires and the Marshal himself, and the remnants of the red company left Martel as his escort.

They rode north back towards Limoges, uncertain of what lay ahead, only that without the Young King, their rebellion had ended. Some knights worried of being executed for treason, but all those who stayed had put duty above personal fear and worried about their fate only privately.

Guy of Lusignan was not one of those. He placed himself at the head of the company with the Marshal, but joined it purely out of self interest.

The inhabitants of the first village they passed through lined their fire-wracked streets and touched the cart as it rolled by, tears falling from their faces and wails on their lips.

Richard watched them with confusion.

'They blame his men, not him,' Bowman said, 'their village lies in ruins, but the Young King was still their saviour.'

'I don't understand,' Richard said, 'he levelled their homes to pay his mercenaries.'

'And these people blame the mercenaries,' Bowman said, 'and mourn their dead king.'

The procession drew the same reverent reaction from a dozen villages over the next couple of days before they reached their first destination.

Guy shook his head as he gazed at the river with its bridge into

Limoges. 'These last few days have been the strangest of my life,' he said. 'How can the farmers love any king so much? Especially one who has recently tormented them so?'

'Maybe you aren't as smart as you think you are,' Richard said. 'Maybe if you treat the common folk well, they will love you. These farmers would work for the Young King twice as hard as that would work for you.'

'From what I've heard,' Guy said, 'you are not one to be giving advice on the running of villages.'

'Suit yourself,' Richard said. The cart carrying the body was filled with wreaths of flowers and anything else of value the mourning villagers had cast into it.

Guy let out a long breath. 'If I return to my lands as the Young King's champion, then some of the love for him may shine through me.'

'You do not have what he had,' the Marshal said. He had spoken but a few words the past few days, and eaten still less. 'He was honest and genuine. You are not.'

'I'm always honest at the time,' Lusignan said, 'but this might be a time for new beginnings. I'm man enough to admit that. Providing the Old King doesn't come seeking revenge, that is.'

Bowman watched voluminous clouds drift over Limoges's red rooftops. 'Maybe the Old King will think of something other than revenge. I wanted to destroy the tower in Martel and everyone in it, but since the Young King died, I'm not feeling the urge anymore.'

'You're not saying you're finished with trying to kill Geoffrey Martel, are you?' Richard asked.

Bowman sniffed. 'If my path and his crossed again I wouldn't slow my sword,' he said, 'but I'm not leaving my path to find him.'

'That's probably for the best,' Richard said. 'And I know what you mean, if the Little Lord was here now I'd kill him, but I'm not going to Castle Tancarville to settle our score. Even though he deserves nothing more than a painful death. If my children are still safe, then that's what I'm going to concentrate on. Nothing is going to bring Sophie back, not even seeing the Little Lord's head roll.'

The company crossed the river, red shields at the front and those with white and blue at the rear. Which was just as well, because while the cart was mobbed by a hundred townspeople, a familiar red and yellow quartered banner appeared on the main street.

'The earl might be very displeased with us,' Bowman said as they watched a baker hurl loaves of bread into the cart.

'Hopefully he never realised we harboured the Marshal and Guy in the first place,' Richard said.

Mandeville had knights at his back, and they outnumbered the merged company they came slowly to investigate. They came slowly because the crowd that had stopped the Young King's body also slowed Mandeville, the townspeople running between his horses and forcing him to push them aside.

Somewhere behind them, the blue roan kicked a monk who strayed too close to his back end. Guy watched expressionless as the monk writhed on the ground.

'What's wrong?' Richard asked.

'The earl will likely still be after the Marshal's blood,' Guy said, 'but if he knows I stood on the walls at Rocamadour, he might be after mine, too.'

Richard cast his eyes up and down their company, which was now spread around the street and square, mingled up with loud mourners. 'You banner isn't flying,' Richard said, 'so just go back and ride with your men. There is no reason for the earl to even know you're here.'

Bowman groaned. 'You really want to help him again?'

'Silence,' the Lusignan snapped, 'Richard has a point. How will I know you won't just give me up for some reward?'

'That's what he would do, young lord,' Bowman said, 'and that's what he will do when our positions are reversed. Don't protect him again.'

'I'm going to,' Richard said, 'he stood by me when I wanted to defend Rocamadour, so I'll stand by him now. We'll say he fled but his men wanted to serve me.'

'You?' Guy sneered. 'This is a ploy to take over my company.'

Richard's lips twitched. 'Do you want to be hidden from the earl's hammer or not?'

Guy grimaced and turned his horse around in the crowd. He pushed his way back towards his knights, kicking out with mailed feet at every townsperson he could reach. Once he moved his horse closer to a cobbler just so he could kick him in the teeth.

'You'll regret that,' Bowman said as Mandeville reached them and frowned at the Marshal. 'It will come back to haunt you.'

'I'm already haunted,' Richard replied, 'I've seen Sophie's face three times in this mass of people already.'

'It'll get easier,' the blonde knight said, 'I've only seen my brother once.'

The Marshal's worn and drained appearance took Mandeville by surprise. 'Are you ill, too?' the earl asked.

The Marshal neither replied nor gestured a response. His eyes lingered only on the road ahead, to where he was going.

'Speak,' Mandeville commanded, 'I am within my rights to kill you for the damage you have spread over our king's lands.'

'Go ahead,' the Marshal said without emotion. 'My lord is dead so I have nothing left to lose.'

Mandeville's eyes found Richard. 'What's wrong with him?'

'The Young King's death has affected him greatly, the Marshal was devoted to him,' Richard said.

Mandeville hadn't bothered to don his helmet so his curly brown hair spilled down his neck. 'He served the wrong king,' the earl said, 'someone should have counselled restraint.'

'It's a bit late for that now,' Richard said.

'King Henry doesn't think it's too late for that,' Mandeville stared at the Marshal, 'and he has studied the list of great knights who signed the letter of rebellion.' The letter of rebellion was signed by knights to remove their allegiance from the Old King, so that their siding with the Young King was technically not treason. It did however give King Henry an exact list of those who had sided with his rebellious son.

Richard studied the Marshal's face for a reaction, because his name must have been near the top of the list.

'He can hang me for all I care,' the Marshal said, 'once I've laid my lord to rest.'

Mandeville snorted. 'Fool. But I will let you bury your lord, for all his faults he was still our prince. However, King Henry will not be lenient on the likes of you, Marshal, nor on the Tancarvilles or Lusignans. He's torn a chunk out of his beard raging at them, so much so that he's had to shave it off. The Brabanter mercenaries are marching to the Lusignan lands as we speak to destroy everything of theirs, it is their misfortune to be closer than Castle Tancarville.'

Richard nodded along, hoping that the earl wouldn't notice the colours of half of the company behind him. 'We are to bury some of him at Grandmont Abbey,' Richard said, 'would you allow us to proceed? We need to get out of this town before things get out of control.'

'Things are already out of control,' Mandeville sighed. 'The king is distraught, he told us that while his son had cost him much, he wished he lived to cost him more.'

Richard felt a lump in his throat, and he heard the Marshal sniff and rub his eyes.

Brian rode up on Richard's left. 'We need to leave, your blue horse thinks the townspeople are enemy infantry and is biting them.' The monk's eyes fell to Richard's new weapon. 'What happened to the Little Lord's sword?'

'Nothing,' Richard shifted his shield to cover it. 'And yes, we need to be moving.'

'Is that?' Brian went to ask.

'No,' Richard replied firmly. He turned to the earl. 'May we proceed?'

'Are you leading here or is the Marshal?'

Richard shrugged. 'Look at him, he isn't leading anyone.'

'And why do you hold Lusignan shields?'

Richard glanced down at his blue and white striped shield. 'Guy's men abandoned him. They answer to me, at least for now.'

Mandeville frowned and searched Richard's face for deception. 'I am not entirely convinced to believe you,' he said, 'but I know you and the Marshal hate Guy with passion, so I'm going to entertain you for now. I would drag the Marshal to the king if he didn't look so pitiful. When I saw your colours ride to Limoges I was looking forward to that, but now I fear it would give me little joy.'

The Marshal turned his head for the first time to look at the earl. 'Before we go to Grandmont, I would like to tell the king how his son died,' he said, 'for he died well.'

Richard wanted to kick the Marshal. They couldn't very well take the company, with Guy in it, into the Old King's camp.

Mandeville nodded. 'That is proper. I will escort you there.'

Richard knew that however stupid it was, he'd have to go with the idea. 'Thank you, we all serve the same king,' he said.

Mandeville raised his eyebrows as he turned his horse. 'A loyal man would feel no need to say so.'

Richard swallowed but shouted back an order to move on. The townspeople cried and some threw themselves in front of the cart and their horses. It was fatal for one woman who was crushed under the cart's wheels, and a child died somewhere from being trampled. Richard wondered if his blue roan had been involved, but decided it was best to concentrate on what they were about to do. For they rode to tell a king how his heir had died.

When Richard set eyes on King Henry, he found an old man with greying hair and a gaunt face. Previously he had been a source of fire and energy, rarely sitting down, but now he languished on his throne with his crown in his lap, his fingers running over the jewels and the cold gold.

Richard followed the Marshal in, preferring to say nothing unless spoken to.

Henry's throne was in the centre of Saint Martial's hall, the place where the Young King had announced he would ride south to Martel and Rocamadour. It was emptier now, the tables pushed to the sides, although the monks and abbot had returned.

The king's eyes pulsed when he saw the Marshal before him, and his body straightened up. 'You,' he growled.

The Marshal knelt down and bowed.

'You have some balls on you,' Henry said, 'I saw whose name was top of the list.'

The Marshal kept his head down.

'But I see that you are at least opening your neck up for the executioner's blade.'

The Marshal remained still.

King Henry growled to himself. 'Have you nothing to say for yourself? You who betrayed me and then failed to counsel my son properly. His death is on your shoulders alongside that ridiculous tattered green cloak.'

The Marshal slowly reached into a pouch tied inside his tunic, rummaged around and produced a golden ring. He held it up to the king.

Henry's eyes misted up and his rage evaporated. 'My ring. And to think I suspected him of trickery. How foolish I was.'

'My lord,' the Marshal said, 'if you would permit me, I would like to tell you of your son's death and the manner in which he conducted himself.'

Henry's lips wavered but he managed a nod.

The Marshal explained how the Young King had managed himself in Martel, all the penances he had undergone and how he had correctly put his affairs in order. He told him everything except for how almost everyone had deserted him at the end, and how Martel had been ransacked.

King Henry wept. He wiped away tears on his red sleeve and nodded. 'I did not expect the bed of ashes and the noose, I thought him too proud to endure death so well.'

The Marshal choked back tears and gave his king the ring.

'You must fulfil his wish to have the cloak taken to Jerusalem,' the king said.

'I intend to,' the Marshal replied.

King Henry sniffed and regarded the knight before him. 'Take my son to Rouen, then journey with what is left of his company to the east. You have leave to travel overseas, providing you leave your two best horses with me as an assurance to your loyalty and your proper return.'

The Marshal frowned. 'I should not need to provide any assurances, my loyalty has always been beyond question.'

King Henry's eyes flamed and his hair almost seemed red and gold again. 'You shed my loyalty as a serpent sheds its skin. You grow back new loyalty now only once you've been defeated and my son is dead. Do not dare to speak to me of loyalty.'

'I only have one warhorse,' the Marshal said, 'and if we are to sail east, I should need him. The Holy Land is a dangerous place.'

'You will be embarked on a pilgrimage. You do not need a warhorse.'

'Take it then,' the Marshal snapped, 'but I do not have another, you would at least leave me with a riding horse? Or would you have your son's cloak escorted by a knight on foot?'

'Watch your tone,' the king said, 'I am but one gust of wind away from changing my mind and removing your head.'

'I will leave my warhorse with you, but I do not have a second animal to give you.'

'Find one.'

The Marshal stood up. 'How? I have no money either, but I could perhaps find some of that. Would I be able to pay you the value of the second horse?'

King Henry nodded. 'The value of a good warhorse, not some nag fed wine to improve it for its valuation.'

The Marshal bowed. 'I will deliver coin.'

The king grimaced and waved them away. Richard retreated from the abbey in relief, for King Henry had ignored him. Guy had remained undetected too, for however unreliable and cruel he was, he wasn't stupid.

Richard wiped his palms together as the pair of them left the abbey to rejoin the company. 'Thank you for not mentioning Rocamadour.'

The Marshal nodded. 'I've been thinking about that. You might have been right,' he said, 'I've never given God or Christ too much thought, not above the normal prayers, but I think desecrating so many holy places was the cause of my lord's death.'

'So you don't blame me?'

'Oh, I blame you,' the Marshal said, 'you broke his rebellion and then you broke his body. But no one could break his spirit, not even at the end.'

'I was trying to warn him,' Richard said.

'I know, but I suppose the warning came too late, and now we shall bury him.'

'Where are you going to get enough coin to pay the king?'

The Marshal stopped and put his hands on his hips. 'You.'

Richard almost tripped on his own feet and had to laugh. 'I'm the poorest knight here, and you're not having the blue roan.'

'Not yet,' the Marshal said. 'But I remember all the talk in Neufchatel about silver the first time we were there. I know the rumours, and I know the Little Lord thinks you had gold. You've got something, and you're going to pay me some of it as compensation for killing my lord and destroying my life.'

Richard scratched the back of his neck. He could hardly argue, and besides, he planned on reclaiming the silver anyway, so maybe the

Marshal could help with that if he had a stake in the enterprise. 'We'll see,' he replied, 'let us bury the Young King, then we can discuss it.'

The Marshal almost grinned in triumph as they rejoined the company, pushed away the locals who had clambered onto the cart, and set off on the short journey to Grandmont.

Richard was glad to leave Limoges and its clamouring masses behind, their devotion unsettled him, even if they had thrown so much food into the cart their company had not gone hungry since leaving Martel.

Richard and Bowman rode at the front with the Marshal, but when Bowman turned back to watch the company climb a small hill, he squinted and frowned.

'What is it?' Richard asked.

'He's been following us since Martel,' Bowman said.

'Who?'

'The damned squire.'

Maynard rode a distance behind the company, but Richard had not noticed him until now. 'What does he want?'

'No idea, young lord, but if he comes too close, I might send an arrow his way. I've still got a sheaf.'

'It's his fault Grandmont burned,' Richard said, 'maybe we should give him to the Corrector and whatever monks survived Guy's carnage.'

Bowman nodded. 'Fair enough,' he lifted his eyes into the distance and squinted again. 'Do you see that?'

Richard shook his head.

'Dust.'

'Who from?'

'If I knew that I wouldn't have said dust, would I?'

'Do you think the earl has changed his mind and come after us?' Richard asked.

'Could just as easily be the king,' Bowman said, 'either way, I think we should do our duty at Grandmont as fast as possible.'

Richard agreed with that and rejoined the Marshal at the head of the company as it ascended Grandmont's hill.

The abbey's courtyard walls still stood, but the broken and charred roof timbers were now piled outside where the monks had dragged them. Shattered tiles lay everywhere, some scorched black, and monks worked to attach new beams to the church building. Their progress was slow.

Brian waited with Richard while the Marshal went to find the Corrector, who presumably would not be pleased to see one of the men who oversaw the destruction of his order's house.

'Who takes the Young King's eyes and bowels out?' Richard asked

Brian as the company disarrayed and went to quarter their horses in the stable building. Guy had left it untouched previously because his horses had still been in it while his men fired the rest of the complex.

Brian groaned. 'I'm hoping the monks here will do it, I don't want to cut out a king's eyes.'

'My brother would have done it,' Bowman appeared next to them and dismounted.

Richard agreed. 'He'd have enjoyed it, too.'

'Probably best he isn't here, then,' the blonde man said mournfully, 'he'd have upset the monks.'

Richard smiled faintly in memory of the fright Nicholas had given Abbot Hughes at Lagny. 'All we seem to do is bury people,' he said softly as a bird flew overhead.

Bowman handed his horse up to Brian, picked up a couple of broken roof tiles, and strode back down the hill. When he'd cleared the company, he hurled a tile as far as he could.

'Is that the squire?' Brian asked.

Richard nodded as Maynard's horse spooked at the tile that crashed into the road in front of it.

'Go away,' Bowman shouted.

Maynard recovered his horse and held it in place.

Bowman threw the second tile, which flew past Maynard's face and exploded into pieces behind him. The horse jumped forwards at the sudden noise and bolted up the hill to the company's horses in order to find safety. He crashed into Bowman's horse which Brian held, and the black stallion lashed out, causing Maynard's horse to rear. The squire's saddle held him in place, but he winded himself on his pommel.

'What are you doing here?' Richard asked. 'You've got some nerve coming back.'

Maynard's face was red from fear, but it was hard to tell if it was to do with his horse bolting, or facing those he'd betrayed. 'I need to apologise to you,' the squire said, 'you didn't deserve what I did.'

'We could have been put to death,' Richard said, 'why? Why did you betray us?'

Bowman marched up behind the squire, grabbed his arm and pulled him from the saddle. The blonde man cast him to the ground with a crunch and placed a mailed foot on his chest. 'Tell me why I shouldn't stamp down on your face?'

Maynard struggled for only a moment. 'The Young King sent me to spy on you from Corbie,' he squealed, 'he feared you would go back to the Old King and tell him about the invasion of Normandy.'

Richard didn't mention that he'd spilled that secret to Brother Geoffrey by accident even before they'd snuck out of Corbie.

'So all this time you've been spying on us?' Bowman asked. 'Why? What threat were we to anyone?'

'You did foil the invasion,' Maynard's eyes were glued to the foot that could easily crush his windpipe.

'That's why you kept telling us to go back to the Young King,' Richard said.

Maynard nodded.

'That doesn't excuse sending the Marshal and Guy here to find us,' Bowman said. 'Had you not done that, the Young King would still be alive.'

The squire sobbed. 'I know, I'm sorry for what I did, but I needed to obey the Young King so he'd grant me a place in his household after Adam died. Without it I'd starve alone on a roadside somewhere.'

Richard sighed. 'Let him get up.'

'Young lord,' Bowman looked up at Richard.

'I know,' Richard said, 'he deserves a punishment, but he's not really done much differently than I did. We both killed the Young King through our actions, and his death won't improve the world.'

'I disagree,' Bowman twisted his foot and Maynard clawed at the mail and coughed.

'Let him go,' Richard said, 'today we bury part of the Young King, let's not spoil it by shedding blood here. We need to be more careful to avoid angering spirits and gods.'

Bowman removed his foot and Maynard coughed as he scrambled to get away.

The Corrector arrived to escort Brian and the body into the roofless church where the removal of the Young King's brain, eyes, and bowels would take place.

Brian went with the Corrector reluctantly, and some time later, as dusk suggested its presence by a cooling in the air, the monks called the knights to the ceremony.

An ornately decorated golden box was to be the resting place for the removed organs. The gold shone in the fading light that poured through the empty roof, even as the stench from the Young King's bowels forced one monk to be sick.

The brain was reverently placed into the box first as the monks sang in Latin, and the Corrector, bloodied hands dripping on the church floor, added the eyes. Richard had smelled the scent of death so much that he wasn't fazed, and seen enough crows eat eyeballs that he remained unaffected by any of it. The long and gory bowels were dragged by three monks and Brian across the church and squeezed into the golden box.

Except that it wasn't really big enough and every time the Corrector pushed down on one length of the guts, another length slipped out of the box and threatened to fall onto the fall.

The Marshal watched it all in stony silence, his face white and his eyes red. His face was impenetrable as Richard stepped forwards and drew Sir John's dagger. The Corrector's arms were red up to his elbows, and although at first he frowned at the dagger, he allowed Richard to shorten the bowels until they would fit inside the golden box. Red blood ran down its decorated sides and pooled on the church floor, and Richard wondered how anyone could have a good death if this could even happen to a king. The Marshal said a prayer, got up from his knees, and left.

The Corrector scooped up the extra bowels and tossed them into a brazier, the smell initially foul, but eventually causing Richard to think of sausages. He banished that thought as soon as he could, and left the church when the Corrector had finished a short service. The monks tended to the Young King's body to prepare it for the rest of his journey to Rouen by packing it with salt and stitching it into a bull's hide. But when Richard went out of the abbey complex and into the open air, he wondered if anyone would reach Rouen at all.

Because the Marshal stood in front of Richard, but he was surrounded by horsemen, men who rode under a banner of green and gold.

Sancho was already off his horse and personally binding the Marshal's hands behind his back.

Richard was still near the abbey's gate and decided not to venture further, for no other men from his company were outside to stop Richard sharing the Marshal's fate.

Sancho looked up, his dark face beamed a smile. 'God favours us today,' he said, 'you owe me a debt almost as large as this man.'

The mercenaries spread out, their column still pouring up the hill from the road. They outnumbered Richard's company at least twice over and some moved to barricade the stables off from the abbey.

The Marshal stared down at the ground, not offering the slightest resistance to his captors.

'Let him go,' Richard said, 'this is not the time for petty kidnapping.'

'Petty?' Sancho left his captive and strode towards Richard. 'The Young King owed us pay for our last three weeks of service. The Marshal is the man who inherited that debt.'

'In whose law?' Richard asked.

'In the law where my company is stronger than any other company in Aquitaine,' Sancho grinned.

'How much do you think he owes you?' Richard asked.

Sancho shrugged. 'Three pouches of gold.'

'The Marshal doesn't have a single gold coin,' Richard said, 'and we just buried part of the man who actually owed you. Turn around and go, your presence is offensive to Christ.'

Sancho laughed. 'Not when I have the greatest knight in Christendom captive. And you, whatever you are.'

'Poor,' Richard spat.

'Your boy killed my man, you owe me silver for that.'

'Your man was useless,' Richard said, 'if a boy could kill him, he had no value.'

Sancho nodded. 'True, but you will still pay me if you want to leave here alive.'

Guy walked out of the abbey and put his hands on his hips. 'I had hoped not to see you again,' he frowned.

Sancho pointed at him. 'And you are here, too. So many captives fall into my lap.'

'You can try,' Guy stood tall, 'but you don't have enough dogs to trouble me.'

Sancho ran his fingers up and down the leather grip of one of his swords. 'I have hundreds of dogs.'

'I've killed hundreds of dogs,' Guy yawned.

'It would be easier if we could pay them off,' Richard said. 'They want a lot of gold or silver.'

Guy rubbed his chin. 'How much?'

Richard coughed. 'What? Are you thinking of paying?'

'The Young King would pay for you both,' the Lusignan said, 'and then you and the Marshal would love him for it. I could buy that love from you by saving you.'

'I wouldn't go that far,' Richard said. 'But more to the point, you don't have pouches of silver on you.'

Guy winked at him. 'Don't I?'

Richard didn't know what that meant as Guy approached the mercenaries. The Navarrese nearest to him lowered lances at him or drew swords. A few started fumbling for crossbows and bolts.

Guy walked past one lance and brushed it aside. 'I told you already, there are not enough of you to trouble me.'

Sancho slid his sword from its scabbard. 'What knight willingly walks into captivity?'

'Not this one,' Guy said, 'you'd be dead before you lifted your blade, so don't try to touch me. I'm here to negotiate payment.'

'You have gold?' Sancho asked.

Guy bargained Sancho down to two pouches of silver for the back pay and the Red Child's victim. Then he reached under his tunic, withdrew two pouches, and threw them on to the floor by his feet.

Sancho regarded them with hungry eyes.

Guy crossed his arms. 'If you want them, there they down are.'

The mercenary captain licked his lips, but didn't bend down.

'Are you afraid I'll remove your head?' Guy asked playfully.

'I'm never afraid,' Sancho said.

'And yet you will not take your money,' the Lusignan sneered. 'Cut the Marshal's bonds and I might walk away from these pouches.'

Sancho waved at the Marshal and his hands were freed.

The Marshal walked towards Richard and Guy stepped backwards.

The captain reached down towards the pouches and Guy jumped at him. Sancho reeled backwards, tripped, and fell onto this rear. Guy laughed at him and his men laughed too. The Lusignan knight turned his back on the green and gold men and went back to the abbey.

'The captain will be killed by his own men within a week,' Guy grinned.

Richard didn't care if that turned out to be the truth. 'Why did you ransom the Marshal? He's sworn to kill you for murdering his uncle.'

'Because now he owes me,' Guy said, 'as do you.'

Richard sighed. 'What happened to being loved like the Young King?'

Guy took a deep breath. 'I've thought about it, and I don't think that approach is truly for me.'

'And yet you've still handed over a lot of silver,' Richard watched the mercenaries lower their weapons and return down the hill.

'It's an investment in my own future,' Guy said, 'now the Marshal owes me. And he counts favours, so he won't forget it. And you, Richard, you still owe me your huge ransom from Lagny.'

'I escaped, so that doesn't count,' Richard said.

'You could take it to the Young King to arbitrate,' Guy said, 'oh wait, you can't, can you?'

'You owe me twice for your life. One of those alone should cancel my ransom.'

Guy chuckled. 'I'm due a fee for saving you from the mercenaries. Your child's murder, too. You very much owe me, Richard.'

The Marshal rubbed his wrists. 'What just happened?'

'You allowed yourself to be taken,' Richard said, 'and now you owe Guy for paying for your freedom. What is wrong with you?'

The Marshal rubbed his eyes. 'Much,' he said. His lips were cracked and there were dark patches under his eyes, but those eyes brightened. 'But I'm back now. My sorrow carried me away, but I can see that I've been selfish, wallowing in my loss and pity instead of thinking of the world around me. That's what knights are for, bettering the world. Without us there is only suffering and fear. I will dedicate myself to improving the realm, that is my purpose, that is what my lord would wish me to do after his passing.'

'Fine words,' Guy said, 'but I'm not really sure what they mean. You'll be back to fawning over the Old King now, still thinking you're the best knight who ever lived.'

'I don't know about *ever lived*,' the Marshal said. 'But I've only been thinking of myself, my lord taught me better. He taught me to consider others. I was a child until I met him, and now that he is gone, I am a man.' The Marshal reached to his shoulders and grabbed the tattered green knighting cloak. He tore it from his back with a great rip and threw it to the ground.

Richard raised his eyebrows. 'He might genuinely be serious.'

'I think he is,' Guy nodded.

'I'll serve my lord's dynasty,' the Marshal said, 'as he asked me on his deathbed. I'll show you all what loyalty is, just watch me.'

Guy sniffed the air and ignored the scent when he realised it was just the smell of the Young King's burning entrails wafting out of the church. 'What about me? What am I supposed to do now? King Henry has sent his own mercenaries off to burn my lands. Most of my knights went to Langy with me, so I expect most of my castles will fall. I'll have no family, no lands, no income. No knights who aren't here with us now. There is nothing for me in Aquitaine any longer, and I'm not going back north, the weather there is foul.'

'I'm going east,' the Marshal said.

'Yes, I know, to throw your stupid cloak at a building somewhere in the land of sand.'

'I'm going there too,' Richard said. 'I've got a mystery to solve.'

'Oh, that,' the Lusignan said, 'Alice told me about that. At least your father could still be alive, ours is dead and gone.'

'I don't think he's alive,' Richard said, 'I think Eustace Martel made sure he wasn't. But I'm going to sail east anyway, I have to know the truth. Besides, like you I have no land to stay for.'

Guy looked up at the sky where clouds stifled what was left of the evening. He shook his head. 'This is a cruel joke, written by some trickster spirit. That I find myself even considering journeying to the Holy Land with the two of you is nothing short of absurd.'

'In the east, your dozen knights and two dozen squires probably constitute an army,' the Marshal said.

Guy's eyes sparkled. 'Really?'

The Marshal nodded. 'That is what we are told. And if you want to cash in your favours with the two of us, you'll have to be in the Holy Land to do so.'

Guy's twinkle faded. 'But I just gave the last of my silver to those dogs, I can't afford passage overseas. I know you can't either, Richard. And you, Marshal, you still need to pay King Henry for his hostage horse.'

The Marshal grimaced. 'It seems bleak,' he said, 'but I have no choice, the cloak must be delivered. Our Lord will show me a way. But I think Richard can solve all our problems and get us on a ship.'

Guy turned to Richard. 'Really? Have you discovered the secret of alchemy?'

Richard dreaded to think what Bowman would make of sharing their silver hoard with the Marshal, let alone Guy. He took a deep breath. 'I'm not happy about this.'

'I knew it,' the Marshal said, 'there is gold.'

'Gold?' Guy jumped on the spot.

'No,' Richard said, 'there's no gold. But there might be silver. We've had it hidden away but now is the time to finally recover it. If I don't do it now, I may never get it back, and if I don't, I'll never reach the Holy Land and find out what happened to my father.'

Guy snorted. 'You might regret it.'

Richard shrugged. 'If something needs doing, do it now before it's too late, that's what the Young King has taught me.'

'Excellent,' the Marshal said, 'then what do we have to do to recover this silver?'

Richard smiled. 'All we need to do is sneak several day's march north into Normandy without angering King Henry, pick up my children, then break three cartloads of silver out of a nunnery.'

'Is that all?' Guy asked.

The Marshal nodded. 'Why not? Pretty much all we've been doing here for weeks is breaking into holy places and looting them, why stop now?'

FUNDRAISING

The company left a trail of miracles in its wake on the journey towards Rouen, although to Richard's disappointment, they always seemed to happen when he wasn't looking. They picked up a wooden coffin in Chateauroux when the body of the Young King began to give off an unsettling odour despite its bull hide wrapping.

Lepers who touched the coffin were cured, frail limbs regained their vitality, and the blind regained their sight. Richard touched the coffin once, but nothing felt any better, and his two stomach wounds had mostly healed anyway. Villagers and townspeople turned out to mourn their lost king in ever increasing numbers as the company finally made its way into the Norman city of Rouen.

The cathedral was a mighty building towering over the city, but Richard by now had seen many and felt himself numb to its grace and majesty. Brian ran off again and was not there as the Young King's bull hide stitching was picked open and the salt packing fell out and covered the floor like snow. Someone found the linen clothes he had worn during his coronation, and solemnly dressed him in them one last time. The stains from the sacred coronation oil still marked the white linen, but the yellows and browns seemed to Richard to signify the sin which the Young King had fallen into during his rebellion.

He was interred near the high altar in front of what looked like a thousand knights, or at least all those in Normandy who were able to travel. To Richard the whole thing was a swirling dance of death performed by others in front of his tired eyes. He wondered where Sophie's body was and if it had been given a Christian burial. He wondered who would bother to bury his own if he and Bowmen got themselves killed at the same time. Not a single person who left the cathedral that day did so with a dry eye, but Richard cried for Sophie and Nicholas, as well as his mother and father. The whole city lamented the passing of the Young King for days, during which it was widely said that the world lying before those who survived the Young King was a joyless and colourless one. Largess and prowess were doomed to wither on the vine, the golden spurs on the heels of knights would shine a little less.

Richard didn't care about that as they stole the cart which had transported the body and drove its tired pony towards Cailly. He had two purposes left in his life: see his children to adulthood and uncover the truth of what happened to his father. If the world now descended into something with less of a sparkle than it had enjoyed before, it wasn't his concern. He needed to sail east, and to do that, he needed the silver. Richard had a burglary to plan.

Maynard followed them to Cailly, and Guy gave him a blue and white shield to add him to his company. That company by now consisted of fewer than forty men and Alice. 'Every man I have will help me carve out a kingdom in the Holy Land,' Guy said.

'He's as bad as the Marshal and his rich heiress,' Bowman said as Cailly drew into view.

'They both believe their own words,' Richard said, 'I wish I had their confidence. Although I don't know what hopes the Marshal has left, his chances of a good marriage have surely been dashed to pieces on the rocks of the Young King's rebellion.'

'Not my problem,' Bowman rubbed the faint scars on his face he'd received at Neufchatel.

Cailly had not exactly been rebuilt in the time Richard had been away, although all the rubble and charred timber had been piled up in heaps outside the village ditch. Crossbowmen watched the company ride up to their bridge, but there were only two of them and they wisely didn't ask too many questions as they stepped aside.

The castle gate was still guarded by the crossbowman who had given them trouble on their previous visit.

'Will you let us in?' Richard asked him. This time he rode up to the gate on the blue roan and craned his neck straight up.

'Why should I?' the crossbowman asked. 'Who are you?'

'You don't remember me? I left my children with you, how could you have already forgotten me?'

'You don't have a memorable face,' the guard said and Richard heard sniggers from the top of the wall.

Bowman rode his black horse next to Richard and shouted up. 'Can you see how many men we have with us?'

The crossbowman pressed his lips together.

'How long do you think it would take us to batter down the gate?' Bowman asked. 'Or build a couple of ladders. How long would it take us to wipe that smile off your face once we've got in?'

The crossbowman sniffed. 'Actually, I think I remember you now. Of course you can come in.' He looked at Richard. 'Your horse won't stop kicking the stable doors in the mornings. Someone shot a crossbow at him last week, it hit the door and he just kicked it harder. He's broken one door, and it isn't as if we don't have enough work for the carpenter to do already. You can come in if you take your cursed horse and leave.'

'I'd like nothing more,' Richard said. He grinned at Bowman as the guard disappeared and shouted for the gate to be opened.

'And you said this castle is one we can't sack?' Guy asked from the head of the column.

'No,' the Marshal said, 'you can't.'

The Lusignan frowned as the gate opened and Richard rode in to find his children.

He didn't have to go far because Judas ran laps around the bailey, barking, with Solis chasing him. Head down and ears back, the yellow stallion playfully tried to catch the black dog's tail while Lora stood in the centre of the yard and giggled at them. Alexander was with her, and he noticed Richard first. The boy pointed, and Lora turned and shouted. She was going to grow up to look like Sophie, Richard thought.

Solis noticed next, and threw himself to the side to change direction. He'd been cantering with a limp on his hind leg, but his change of direction was still swift. The stallion skidded to a halt in front of Richard and whinnied at him. Richard held out a hand and the horse nuzzled it.

Richard's eyes teared up and he grabbed Solis's yellow head to hug it. The horse tolerated the embrace for a moment, then tore his head up in the air and walked off as if offended.

'Fine,' Richard said after him, 'sulk if you want to, but I did come back.'

Judas ran over with Lora, who threw herself at Richard. 'Where have you been?'

'Away,' Richard said, more feebly than he'd hoped.

Alexander stayed in the middle of the bailey, then ran off towards the keep, where Richard presumed he sought Sarjeant.

Richard picked Lora up and held her tightly, her life lifting his worn spirits.

Bowman shouted for Judas, and the black dog leapt at him with his tongue out. 'You look just like my brother,' the blonde man said to him.

Guy remained mounted and shook his head. 'What is wrong with all of you, you're so soft.'

'Have you got children?' Richard asked.

'No,' Guy said, 'I don't have a wife yet.'

Alice dismounted from her palfrey and rolled her eyes at her brother. 'He shall have to grow up at some point.'

'You are the spinster,' Guy said, 'don't tell me what I can or can't do.'

Sarjeant descended the mound's steps as fast as he could with a smile on his face. 'My boy, I even went back to praying to plead for your safe return,' he said.

'You must have been desperate,' Richard said, then he told him everything. Except for the details of Rocamadour and how badly the Young King's body had started to smell.

Sarjeant nodded along, but his eyes were fixed on Richard's new sword. 'I would swear I've seen that handle and pommel before.'

'I doubt it,' Richard said, 'how many swords must there be in all the world?'

'Only one like this one, I'd wager,' Sarjeant said. 'The crossguard is too short and the pommel is more oval than disc-shaped. It isn't that long, either.'

Richard shrugged. 'My old sword broke, this was the closest to hand.'

Sarjeant raised his eyebrows. 'Where exactly were you when the sword broke?'

'In the south.'

'And where was it again that you said the Young King died?'

Richard grimaced. 'Martel.'

Sarjeant sighed. 'Which is near Rocamadour, on the pilgrim trail to Santiago de Compostela.'

Richard shrugged again. 'Maybe someone mentioned that. Perhaps.'

'Did you steal Durendal, the sword of Roland?'

'Quiet,' Richard hissed, 'not near Guy or the Marshal.'

'You thief, what has become of you?' Sarjeant asked. 'Did you rob a shrine?'

'No,' Richard said, 'I merely took a sword that belonged to no one out of a rock that belonged to no one.'

'You have grown insufferable,' the former Templar said, 'you've spent too much time with that blonde man, he's corrupting you little by little. What kind of example will this set for your children?'

Richard exhaled. 'Frankly, the best I think I can. Look, I needed a sword. The Little Lord's finally broke and we were under attack.'

'Yes, you said,' Sarjeant frowned, 'by the Young King himself. I cannot believe that you got him killed. What were you thinking, my boy? His father will cut your limbs off for what you did.'

Richard put Lora down. 'King Henry didn't seem too upset by my actions, although I didn't see the need to tell him every detail.'

'He'll find out.'

'Maybe,' Richard said, 'but for now I'm safe, and it's yet another reason for us to journey east. It is time to reclaim the silver that you and

Bowman hid in that crypt.'

'Ah, good,' Sarjeant said, 'well, good for you. I am not so keen to return to those sandy parts. The heat, my boy, the heat. It makes you drink.'

Richard could see pain in the older man's eyes. 'I'll keep an eye on you,' he said, 'and help you resist the worst of the drink.'

Sarjeant focused on his shoes.

Richard realised Alexander had followed Sarjeant most of the way back to him, but not all the way. Solis sniffed him with an outstretched neck and the boy rubbed the yellow chin.

'Alexander,' Richard said, 'are you not happy to see me?'

His son frowned in the very serious way only children can. 'You killed a monk. That's bad.'

'He was trying to hurt your mother, he didn't leave me with any choice.'

'But she still died,' Alexander balled his fists, 'and now she's gone. Does that mean you killed her?'

Richard felt an ache in his heart. 'Of course not, why would you think such a thing?'

'You left us here,' his son said, 'don't you want us? Maybe you didn't want mother?'

'I had to earn money,' Richard said, 'to pay for everything we need.'

'How much have you got?' the boy frowned as if he knew the answer.

'It didn't work out quite as I'd hoped,' Richard said.

Alexander's face grew red with frustration. 'So you could have stayed?'

Richard sighed. 'Yes, I suppose I could have.' He crouched down to meet his son at eye level. 'I made a mistake, a very big mistake and I wish I could go back and change things so we stayed together. I'm very sorry and I won't leave you behind again.'

'Be careful, my boy,' Sarjeant said, 'take care when making promises you may struggle to keep.'

'He'll understand when he's older,' Richard said, 'I'm not a farmer, I will sometimes leave my village. But we will all go east together.'

Sarjeant shook his head. 'Many grown adults die on pilgrimage, grown adults who were healthy. We'll see very few children on the route, and for good reason. Taking them with you is a terrible risk.'

'Leaving them here is a greater risk,' Richard said, 'but tell me, how has Solie been?'

Sarjeant's face couldn't help lightening. He glanced over to Alexander who pulled up grass and held it to the horse, who to Richard's surprise took it gently.

'He is lame on that leg,' Sarjeant said, 'as you saw when you arrived, but he can still canter. He doesn't appear to care at all. I've not ridden him because if anyone approaches him with a saddle, he bites them and spins around and throws back feet towards their heads. His leg might be damaged, but he can still flick those feet up to head height. I've been letting him run around the bailey during the day, but it takes the entire garrison to herd him back into his stable at night.'

'The guards seemed fed up with him,' Richard grinned a wide grin. Seeing his horse alive and relatively mobile, alongside both of his children, both alive and well, brought Richard as close to happiness as he'd been for weeks, maybe even months. He could ignore Alexander's hesitance, that would improve, but it was more worrying that he'd picked Lora up to hug her so he didn't have to look at her face and her blonde hair. Sophie's hair.

He took his mind off that by watching the guards close in on Solis, who saw them coming and made for the mound on which the keep was raised. The stallion flashed past Richard, giving him a good view of the cross-shaped scar, an indent in his flesh, the skin underneath slightly whiter than his yellow coat.

As the guards tried to use spears to herd the horse off the steep mound, Richard turned to Sarjeant. 'And how is Gerold?'

'His head has stopped aching and his cough has gone,' Sarjeant nodded, 'he isn't helpful, though, he always tells me he's fine and just needs a few more days.'

Maybe he just needed to touch the Young King's body, Richard thought. 'We can put him in the cart for the journey, it worked well enough for me.'

'I will be glad to leave this place,' Sarjeant said, 'its walls may be strong enough, but they are not friendly to us and I have felt uneasy during our stay. We are also far too near Castle Tancarville.'

'We'll leave first thing in the morning and put some distance between us and the Little Lord,' Richard said. 'We might reach the area near the nunnery in the early afternoon, even with the cart, then we can go and see how accessible the crypt is.'

It took longer than Richard had hoped to reach Eawy Forest. Maynard groaned when Richard handed him Solis's rope for the journey, but the squire hadn't dared complain. The pony pulling the cart had done so all the way from Martel and now its steps were tired and slow. He struggled up what passed for hills in the flat Norman terrain, snorting and bracing, and it was almost evening when they pulled into an abbey and the beast could rest. Bowman reckoned the abbey was only a woodland away from the nunnery and the silver.

Richard unharnessed the pony. 'I promise you,' he told it, 'I'll buy a mule to pull this as soon as I can, then you can retire. You've done your life's work carrying the Young King to his final resting place, I think you've done enough. I can't seem to do right by anyone else, maybe I can at least with you.'

The company overfilled the abbey's stable, which was a long room without internal walls where the horses would be tied next to each other. On the way in, the blue roan spooked at a brazier when a log crackled and stood on Brian's foot. The monk swore in Irish and limped off to investigate the abbey.

Alice helped the children to find the guest quarters and make their beds, something Richard wasn't sure he approved of, but as he didn't have time to do it himself he ignored it.

Gerold sat up in the cart as the company milled about, and when no one bothered to lend him any assistance, he gingerly climbed out of the cart himself.

Bowman pointed it out to Richard. 'I suppose the Young King's body was as holy as everyone says it was.'

'He never even touched it,' Richard said.

'No, young lord, but he did lie where the coffin did.'

'Don't tell Brian,' Richard said, 'he'll start declaring the Young King a saint.'

The Irish monk returned to the darkening stable courtyard before the company had fully organised itself for the night. Travelling with forty men and sixty horses was not a simple matter.

Brian wore a frown. 'What was the name of the abbot whose crypt your silver is hidden in?'

'Quiet now,' Bowman said, 'not everyone in Normandy needs to know what we're planning.'

'Why?' Richard asked. 'Is he here?'

'What was his name?' Brian repeated.

'Anfroy,' Richard shuddered.

Bowman swore. 'An unholy man.'

'On, no,' Brian said.

'What?'

'Abbot Anfroy is indeed here,' the monk bit his lip for a moment, 'but that is not the problem.'

'Who cares if he's here?' Bowman asked. 'So long as he isn't in his tomb.'

'That is going to be the problem,' Brian said. 'Abbot Anfroy is dead.'

Richard froze.

Bowman went to make a joke before he realised the implication of the abbot's death. He swore again.

'When do they plan to inter him?' Richard asked.

'Tomorrow.'

'What?' Bowman cried.

'But we were going to spend tomorrow making a plan,' Richard said.

'It looks like we'll have to enact it tomorrow now, too,' Bowman said, 'I always hated that abbot. I hate all abbots.'

'I'm sorry,' Brian said.

'It isn't your fault,' Richard said, 'you didn't kill him.'

Brian's gaze fell to the ground. 'I think it's a punishment for the monk I did kill.'

'So we need to get into the crypt before his body reaches it,' Bowman said, 'or at least before anyone opens it up to prepare it for him.'

Brian made the sign of the cross. 'Your hiding place was sacrilegious, this is your punishment for that.'

'Not every misfortune is God's punishment,' Bowman said.

The monk shrugged. 'So what now?'

Bowman grinned. 'It seems obvious to me, young lord. We have over thirty armed men, and the nunnery has nothing but nuns. We'll just go in there and take it. We'll need three carts, too, so we'll have to borrow two from here. Or hope the nunnery has some of its own. We could repay the loan of the carts with silver once the job is done, if you're feeling righteous, that is.'

'If I'm feeling righteous?' Richard coughed. 'We're claiming the silver in order to go on crusade, what is more righteous than that?'

Bowman blinked in disbelief. 'You're agreeing with me?'

Richard rubbed his eyes. 'Before we retrieved the children, I might have agreed with you, but now, no. Fathers are supposed to set a good example, so I have to at least try to do that. Besides, have we not desecrated enough holy places?'

Bowman looked at Richard as if that didn't need an answer.

'Do you not remember what happened to the Young King?' Brian asked. 'What his fate was and what caused it?'

'*He* caused it,' Bowman folded his arms and looked at Richard.

'The monk has a point,' Richard said, 'I've lost my wife, and you, your brother. Do you want to lose anyone else?'

'You are both taking things too seriously. It's for a good cause, I'm sure Christ will look the other way,' Bowman said.

'That's not how forgiveness works,' Brian said.

'Isn't it?'

Richard watched the Red Child walk up to Guy and ask him about his mail. 'I know Christ preaches forgiveness, but I'm more worried about his father in heaven. And my soul. You've seen how Alexander looks at me, my own son fears me, thinks me evil, and worries I don't want him. If we take the silver by force, some nun will only get hurt, and then I've lost my son forever.'

'He'll grow out of it,' Bowman said.

'Like you've grown out of your hatred of the Martels?'

Bowman's eyes widened. 'I have, thank you very much.'

'Yes,' Richard said, 'but how long has it taken you? Ten years? Fifteen?'

'Fine,' the blonde man said, 'but you had better come up with a plan quickly then. But it will have to be a good one, not like all the others where something goes horribly wrong and something nearly kills me.'

'I don't think even a horde of nuns are going to kill you.'

Bowman's face darkened. 'No, young lord, but we didn't think a tournament would kill my brother, did we? Or that a trip to Castle Tancarville would…'

'Don't,' Richard hissed.

Bowman held his hands up. 'You're right. We can't lose anyone else, not when we're this close to getting the silver. Just tell me what to do and I'll do it.'

'We'll need two more carts to start with,' Richard said, 'I don't want to risk leaving that task until we reach the nunnery, in case they don't have any carts.'

Bowman cast his eyes around the stable courtyard, where no extra carts happened to be standing around. 'It'll take time to do that,' he said, 'and we don't have enough of that if the funeral is tomorrow.'

Richard scratched his chin where hair was growing unusually long. 'You're right,' he said, 'but what if we could move the date of the funeral?'

'How?' Brian asked. 'The proceedings are already underway.'

Richard grinned at Bowman. 'What would Nicholas do?'

Richard followed Brian into the abbey to find Abbot Anfroy. The sun had long set and most of the monks had retired to bed. In the church however, praying underneath the raised platform that supported Anfroy's wrapped corpse, were four kneeling monks who were very much awake.

Their prayers were spoken, and loud enough to almost chime together, although they didn't pray in time with each other. Four candles burned near the corners of the platform, but the rest of the church lay in cold darkness.

Brian crept into the blackness and Richard followed. He disturbed a mouse which squeaked and scurried along the floor until it vanished into the shadows.

The monks continued to pray, their words disguised any sounds

Richard or the local vermin made.

Richard caught up with Brian by walking into him.

The monk grunted, but Richard apologised with a nod and they both turned their attention to the platform. Cloaked in gloom, Richard and Brian were now invisible in the church.

'What now?' Richard whispered in Brian's ear.

'I don't know, you just asked me to show you where he was.'

'Well, how long will they stay here?' Richard asked.

'I don't know,' Brian replied, 'probably all night.'

'Do you think they'll fall asleep?'

Brian shook his head.

Richard remembered when he'd needed to stay awake all night to save the Queen from the ambush at Niort, a task he'd failed. 'They will fall asleep eventually.'

'And so will we.'

Footsteps on cold stone interrupted the prayers and two of the monks ceased their chanting. Two fresh monks entered side-by-side with their hoods up over their heads. Richard wished he'd brought his own cloak, for the church had no fire and the evening chill seeped through the stone walls.

The newcomers bowed to two of the monks, who stood up, rolled their hoods over their tonsured heads, and left the church. The new arrivals replaced them and started to pray themselves. Richard groaned inside. The monks wouldn't fall asleep if they were rotating their duty.

'Where would we find three more robes?' he asked.

Brian thought about it. 'The dormitory, probably. Hanging on some clothes poles, or maybe drying in the warming room after being washed.'

Richard nodded. 'That will have to do, come on, let's go.'

They slipped out of the church. 'Can you fetch three robes?' Richard asked. 'No one will look twice at you, you already look the part.'

'You want me to steal from an abbey?'

'It's either that or let Guy start killing people,' Richard snapped.

The Irish monk shook his head but plodded off to where he thought the dormitory might be.

Richard returned to the guest wing where the company had been allowed to set out their beds. The space was littered with saddles, swords, and heaps of mail.

When Brian returned with three robes in his arms, Richard found Maynard, who winced as he approached. 'Right squire,' Richard said, 'it is time to start earning your forgiveness. It will be a very long road, but it starts here. Put this on.'

Maynard squinted at the robes. 'But I'm not a monk?'

Richard groaned. 'Obviously,' he took a robe from Brian and threw it at the squire. Then he found Bowman and grinned. 'I can't wait to see you in this.'

The blonde knight snatched the robe and slipped it over his shoulders without saying a word.

Guy gave them a questioning look, but Richard told him that their plan didn't need his help, and the Lusignan didn't care enough to challenge him. The Marshal ignored them too, for he had put some of the squires to work in the monk's empty kitchen to make something worthwhile to eat. The late hour did not deter him.

Richard led his three new monks along the dark corridors to the church.

Richard looked at Brian and Maynard. 'You two go in now, Brian knows which pair of monks have been in for the longest. Replace them. We'll change for the other two in a while.'

'So I have to kneel there and pray?' Maynard asked.

'That would be the point,' Bowman said.

'I don't know Latin, though.'

'Brian does,' Richard said, 'just repeat what he's saying in a mumble. You might learn something.'

The squire grumbled but followed Brian off into the church.

'Are you sure letting the squire do something so important is a good idea?' Bowman watched the two brown robes move towards the light.

'I think Maynard just needs somewhere to belong,' Richard looked Bowman in the eyes. 'Like you did.'

'I'm not stopping you,' Bowman said, 'just don't come crying to me to fix things when the squire betrays us again.'

They hid around a corner as the two relieved monks left the church and Brian started to pray in their place.

'That abbot deserves curses rather than prayers,' Bowman said.

'I don't think he's in purgatory waiting to be allowed into heaven,' Richard said, 'I think he's deep in hell and these prayers are wasted.'

Bowman grunted in approval as the two of them waited until they both started to fall asleep, then entered the church.

Richard bowed solemnly to a monk when he reached the platform, and the young man looked thankful to be done for the night.

The light from the tall candles flickered on Brian's face and the linen shroud around Abbot Anfroy's body as the fourth monk let Bowman take his place.

Retreating footsteps echoed from the stones and up into the high roof. Brian kept up his prayers until he was very sure the monks were out of earshot.

'You can stop that now,' Bowman said.

Maynard had continued to echo Brian's prayers until he also stopped. The church fell into deathly silence, the candles burning away without sound. One flickered despite the still air and went out.

'I can't believe that worked,' Bowman said.

Richard stood up. 'Don't think too much about it,' he said, 'but we need to be gone before the next pair of monks arrive. They will raise the alarm and all hell will break loose.'

Richard was the first to reach the body. The linen had been wrapped around it twice and sewn shut, the abbot's corpse long and thin and nothing like the Young King's body had looked.

'Help me pick it up,' Richard said when Brian and Maynard both hesitated.

Brian flexed his hands.

'Come on,' Richard said, 'you can't be squeamish about this, it wasn't that long ago that you were handling the eyeballs of a king.'

The monk pursed his lips and went to help the squire with the abbot's legs. The four of them easily managed to lift the body from the platform, but the difficulty was actually to see where they were going as they moved deeper into the church.

'Are you sure there was a window?' Bowman asked.

'I swear it,' Brian said, 'at the end here somewhere.'

They had to drop the body to search for the window, fingers feeling the cold stone walls hunting for the recess of the window.

Bowman stilled. 'Here,' he said, 'I can feel the flow of air.'

Richard went to him, and sure enough, he'd found the window.

'I'm not sure he's going to fit,' the blonde man said, 'this is almost an arrow slit.'

'We have to try,' Richard and the others picked the body up and pushed it towards the window.

Where it got stuck. The head passed through, but only one of the abbot's shoulders could fit at a time. They strained for a moment trying to force the matter, but gave up.

'Told you,' Bowman sighed.

'We have to get him out of here,' Richard said, 'we can't rightly just carry him through the abbey and hope no monks are around to see us.'

Bowman stood for a moment in thought. He looked up at Richard. 'You know what my brother would do?'

Richard saw the blonde man grin. 'I haven't brought an axe.'

'No,' Bowman replied, 'but have you ever seen a man dislocate his shoulder?'

'You can't,' Brian whispered, 'he's an abbot.'

'He was a sinner,' Richard said. 'Bowman, do it.'

The blonde man felt around the linen wrapping until he located the shoulder, then put a heavy foot down on it. He jerked the arm and something snapped.

Richard winced as much as Brian did.

Bowman sniffed. 'He deserved that.'

They hauled the body up to the window again and fed it through the opening. With an almighty push they dumped it down outside, where it landed with a bump on the grass.

'Good,' Richard said, 'now we fetch the cart.'

They crept like stalking cats out of the abbey and led the long suffering pony and its cart around to the back of the church. The creaking of the wooden cart seemed loud enough to wake the dead, and Richard searched the abbey for light and strained his ears for shouts.

Neither came as they found the body and hoisted it into the cart.

Bowman did most of the lifting and dropped the abbot onto the wooden boards with a grunt. He wiped his brown. 'The Young king's spirit better not bring him back from the dead,' he murmured.

'Don't even joke,' Richard settled back into the cart's driving seat and clicked his tongue at the pony.

'Where are we going with it?' Bowman asked.

The pony strained with the weight of five men, but grunted to get moving and then settled into a walk.

'I haven't thought that far ahead,' Richard said.

Bowman stretched his arms out and yawned. 'He was an evil man, we'd be within our rights to dump the body in a forest and let the wolves have him. They won't be opening up the tomb for a while if we do that.'

Richard turned back to look at Brian. 'Aren't you going to argue against that?'

The monk went to speak, but Bowman told the monk about Abbot Anfory when they'd originally met him.

The monk shook his head in disapproval. 'If what you just told me about him is true, he does not deserve to be buried on consecrated ground. I'm for the wolves.'

Richard would have laughed had they not still been on the abbey grounds. 'Really? You're not going to preach forgiveness?'

'I threw a priest from a tower,' Brian said, 'and stood by as you Normans killed hundreds of monks in Meath, what do I know of right and wrong?'

Bowman laughed. 'That's good enough for me.'

Richard drove the cart along the first road he found, a road flanked in the dark shadows of trees and with precious little moonlight to guide them. The pony knew well enough where the road was though, and Richard kept going until they found a small track branching off from it.

'This should do,' Richard followed it for a little while until Bowman pointed to a ditch containing a stream that joined the road and ran alongside it.

'There,' the blonde man said and Richard whistled the pony to a halt.

Bowman and Maynard took an end of the corpse each and rolled it from the cart. It thudded into the earth, flattened a bush, and rolled into the stream. It barely made a splash and Bowman rubbed his hands together. 'There we go,' he said, 'the funeral is off.'

They returned to the abbey much relieved, although stayed as quiet as possible in order to not alert the monks to their return. It was as Richard shut the stable door on the pony and threw him a handful of pieces of horsebread that the alarm was raised. The bells inside the church rang out, piercing the still night, and the fearful cries of monks echoed from the abbey complex.

Guy wandered over, the only member of the company not to be eating the feast the Marshal had rustled up. 'Does all that fuss have something to do with you?'

Richard shrugged, but his grin gave him away. 'Let's just say we don't need to worry about them burying the abbot tomorrow. We just need to get to the nunnery and break the silver out.'

'Good,' Guy said, 'how much of it did you say there was?'

'Three cartloads.'

The Lusignan glanced at their solitary cart. 'We'll be needing two more, then.'

Richard nodded. 'I was going to worry about that tomorrow, I'm exhausted.'

Guy thought about it and shot a grin at Richard which was mildly unsettling. 'You get your sleep and leave the carts to me.'

Richard agreed, although not without hesitation, and then went swiftly to bed. The bells stopped ringing soon enough, and Richard slept through whatever the monks did to investigate the theft of their abbot.

By mid morning, the new abbot had questioned the Marshal, who was the self professed leader of the company, but found him genuinely clueless about the incident. The abbot was outraged at the Marshal's banquet however, but was suitably convinced that the company had nothing to do with Anfroy's disappearance.

The abbot forbade the company from receiving any breakfast as a result of the Marshal's late night feast, and it was with a gurgling stomach that Richard watched Guy return from a foray into the countryside.

He returned with two carts and a handful of his squires who yawned and blinked with tiredness.

'Where did you get those?' Richard inspected the carts. They were sturdy enough and the ponies attached looked in decent enough health, but he couldn't help noticing what looked like smears of blood in the bottom of one.

Guy noticed what Richard had spotted. 'I wouldn't ask questions you don't want to hear the answers to,' he said with a sly grin.

Bowman walked out of the guest wing and joined them. 'I'm impressed with the speed you got the job done,' he turned to Richard after looking at the bottom of the cart, 'but are you really sure we are on the side of good?'

'Not really,' Richard said, 'but we'll pay the owners of the carts once we've got the silver.'

Guy looked away.

Richard's shoulders slumped. 'Surely you didn't have to kill anyone? Who would have resisted so many armed men?'

Guy's face hardened. 'What did I tell you about asking questions?'

Richard felt unease, but there was no going back. 'What's done is done,' he said. 'We just need to decide how we get into the nunnery.'

'We snuck into the castle at St Malo pretending to be stonemasons,' Bowman said, 'can't we do the same thing here?'

'Do you see any stonemasons tools lying around?' Richard said. 'And how would we even know if the nunnery needs any repairs? At St Malo it was obvious because half the wall had fallen down, but that nunnery is almost newly built.'

Guy sighed. 'Nuns don't have swords, even in Normandy,' he said, 'we can simply walk in the front door and take what we please.'

Bowman's face lit up. 'That's exactly what Alan with the big red balls did, remember?'

'I do remember,' Richard said, 'but we've just desecrated the remains of an abbot, and Guy's done God only knows what to get those carts. After everything I said about needing to be righteous and set an example for my children, we are not going in with swords drawn. We will get into the crypt without threats or violence.'

'You're making this far harder than it needs to be,' Bowman said, 'and for once Guy is right. We can be in and out quickly without hurting anyone.'

The Marshal entered the courtyard, his eyes bleary from sleep.

'Have you only just woken up?' Richard asked him.

The English knight yawned and asked what they were discussing.

Once informed, he nodded. 'I agree with Richard, we are on a holy mission and have already deviated far from the path of good. As the leader of this company, we will act with decency.'

'You're not the leader,' Guy said.

'I am,' the Marshal stood his ground, 'and we shall treat the nunnery with the proper respect.'

'What in God's name is wrong with you?' Guy asked. 'You are the strangest man I have ever met.'

'I'm a new man,' the Marshal said, 'a good man.'

'Tell that to the abbot after you stole all his food last night,' Bowman said.

The Marshal frowned. 'Knights must eat. And now we can ride to the nunnery and complete our task peacefully.'

'You're making me feel sick,' Guy said.

The Marshal almost snarled. 'And I still remember how you murdered my uncle.'

'Enough,' Richard said, 'we'll enter the abbey with no weapons or armour, just a few of us. Brian can lead us in and present us as penitential knights on our way to join a holy order. Guy, you can wait outside with the company, far enough away that the nuns can't see you.'

'If you're planning on cutting me out of the silver,' Guy said.

'Calm down,' Richard said, 'we just need our story to be believable. We couldn't run off with the silver even if we wanted to, we'd be far too slow.'

Guy crossed his arms.

'Although,' Richard said, 'it's mostly because I can't trust you not to kill the nuns.'

The nunnery had added a small statue of Empress Matilda to its entrance as Brian led Richard, Bowman, and the Marshal through it. The plan was for Sarjeant and the rejuvenated Gerold to lead the three carts up the hillside to the stables where they had quartered their horses during the last unsuccessful visit. They would wait to be summoned down to the nunnery once Richard had accessed the crypt. His plan was to pass the silver out of the same window they had used to get into the nunnery last time.

Bowman scuffed the floor as Brian spoke to a nun who stood in the entrance doorway. 'If Eva was here, we could just repeat what we did that night,' he said.

'What, run away empty-handed?' Richard asked.

The blonde man scowled. 'Everything went wrong only after we left her.'

'We can argue about that later,' Richard said, 'but she's not here, so forget about her.'

'I can't forget about her,' Bowman hissed, 'or my daughter.'

'Alright, I'm sorry,' Richard replied, 'let's just do this, can we?'

The sister speaking to Brian scrutinised the orange and black stains on their tunics, and wrinkled her nose at their pungent smell.

'They mean you no harm and have no weapons,' Brian told her, 'they are humble knights seeking to serve the Lord in the Holy Land.'

That was good, Richard thought, Brian wasn't even really lying.

'Prove it to me,' the nun said, 'whilst I carry your request to the abbess, have them prostrate themselves where they stand.'

The Marshal straightened up and his eyes blazed with resentment.

'You have to lie down,' Brian said nervously, 'on the ground.'

'I know what it means,' the Marshal said through clenched teeth.

'Then why aren't you doing it,' Richard got down on his knees. 'Holy knights have no pride to protect.'

Bowman dropped down heavily. 'My knees aren't getting any younger, young lord.'

The Marshal grunted but followed, all three of them lying face down on the earthy ground as the sister nodded with satisfaction and disappeared.

'See,' Brian said, 'it's not so bad.'

The Marshal instantly went to get back up.

'You can't,' Brian said, 'she might be watching. And the Lord is always watching.'

'That's what I'm afraid of,' Bowman said to himself.

Richard studied the compacted earth and short grass around his face until the sister returned, checked the men were still down, and waved Brian in. 'You have been granted refuge for one day,' she said.

Richard hauled himself up as the Marshal sprang to his feet and brushed down his tunic with disdain.

They followed the sister down a cloister and into a chamber with a small window set near the ceiling. It was small, dark, and claustrophobic. They walked in and their eyes took a moment to adjust to the lack of light. The air had a musty smell.

The sister stood in the doorway. 'Here,' she said, 'you may spend the day here, you may come out to eat in the afternoon.'

'Wait,' Richard said, 'you want to shut us in here?'

The nun stepped backwards. 'We have been robbed before,' she slammed the door and turned a key.

'If Alan wasn't already dead, I'd kill him,' Bowman said.

Richard groaned and went to the door to rattle it. It was truly locked.

'Great plan,' the Marshal said, 'now we'll be stuck in here while Guy gets bored and sacks the nunnery. He'll find the silver and leave us here to rot.'

'I'm sure he won't,' Richard gave up and slumped down against the cold wall. 'Or would he?'

Bowman shrugged. 'He's done worse.'

'He has,' the Marshal said, 'he killed my uncle and his men stabbed me through the thigh.'

'We know,' Richard said, 'and we don't need to hear about it again.'

'This is your fault,' the Marshal said, 'all your false talk of righteousness put us in here.'

'You agreed with me,' Richard said.

The Marshal gritted his teeth and sat down on the stone floor. The light from the window was dim and each other's faces were only smudges in the gloom.

Brian sat down, too. 'It gives us time to pray.'

'We don't want to pray,' Bowman said, 'we need to get out of here.'

'How?' Richard asked. 'The door is secure and the window is too small. You're not breaking my shoulder just so I can fit out.'

'Why would he break your shoulder?' the Marshal asked.

'Don't worry about it,' Bowman replied. 'Can't we pretend to be sick?'

Brian shook his head. 'I think they are suspicious enough as it is, we shall have to wait until mealtime.'

The Marshal dropped his head into his hands. 'This is just like being locked up at Castle Lusignan again.'

'No, it isn't,' Richard said, 'you know this is only for one day, not even the night.'

The Marshal snapped his head back up. 'I'd have been out of there quicker had you not dallied so long with my ransom.'

'I have had enough of you,' Bowman snapped, 'he lost a finger and nearly an eye for that ransom.'

'Everyone stop,' Richard said, 'we've only been in here a moment and we're nearly fighting each other already. We need to just calm down until they release us.'

The Marshal and Bowman glared at each other but held their tongues. Richard let out a deep breath and tried to relax. He thought everything had been going too well. The time dragged by visibly as the beam of light shining through the high window moved agonisingly slowly around the chamber. No miracles occurred and no cunning plans presented themselves. Instead, each man suffered alone with his own thoughts until the key turned in the door and the sister opened it with a slow creak.

'You may eat,' she turned and stepped away.

Brian eased himself up and rubbed his lower back.

Richard got up quicker. 'I'm hungry, we should eat and then see what options we have.'

The Marshal pushed him out of the way and followed the nun towards the refectory.

A table had been set out apart from the others, and the sister stood beside it with her arms folded.

Richard sat down on the table and felt exposed as the two dozen other nuns peered over their food at the scruffily dressed men.

'I don't feel very welcome,' Bowman sat down with a thud and reached for a pewter jug.

'Can you blame them?' Richard thanked the sister, who left them alone.

Bowls of thick pottage greeted them, cool already and mostly beige in colour. Richard lost his appetite.

Bowman groaned at the contents and pushed it away, the discarded bowl quickly scooped up by the Marshal and placed next to his own.

Richard drank some water, which he direly needed. 'What's the plan?' he asked.

'Don't look at me,' Bowman said, 'this was your plan.'

Brian ate his pottage happily enough. 'They will not leave us alone,' he said, 'either we leave and say we are going on our way, or we stay the night locked in that chamber again.'

'I have no wish to be locked in there again,' Bowman said.

'And we can't just leave,' Richard sighed.

'We can always resort to force,' the Marshal said through a stuffed mouthful. Some yellow vegetable fell from his mouth.

'What happened to you being a good man?' Richard asked.

'No man's patience is limitless,' the Marshal shrugged.

Bowman pursed his lips.

'What then?' Brian asked.

Richard considered the nuns. Who were not intimidating. 'They are just nuns, even without weapons we are a lot stronger than they are. They are not going to physically get in our way.'

'Ha,' the blonde knight said, 'your righteousness act didn't last long, did it?'

'Fine,' Richard replied, 'then I need a distraction to go into the crypt and check if the silver is still there.'

'A distraction?' Bowman licked his lips. 'So what you're saying is, we need to create some noise and fuss, and then you can then run off and start work at the crypt.'

Richard nodded. 'Yes, then we don't have to hurt any nuns.'

'Well, why didn't you say so,' the blonde man poured cold water slowly into his cup until it overflowed.

Richard watched as Bowman gently put the jug down and grinned at him. Then the blonde man looked up at the Marshal, who sat opposite him spooning pottage into his mouth. Bowman picked up the cup, turned to wink at Richard, then hurled the contents into the Marshal's face.

The cold water swamped him, chilled the knight's shocked face and made him gasp. His pottage bowl flew over and fell into his lap. The Marshal half tried to catch it, but while he looked down, Bowman stepped up onto the bench, then the table, and launched himself at the Marshal. The blonde man pushed the Marshal right back off his bench and the two of them clattered onto the floor.

'I'll kill you,' the Marshal shouted.

Richard couldn't tear his eyes away as they struggled.

Brian gently tugged at his sleeve. 'I think this is his diversion,' he whispered.

'Oh,' Richard said as Bowman punched the Marshal in the cheek.

The nuns jumped up and the abbess screamed for the fighting to stop. The Marshal rolled Bowman over and clubbed him in the stomach.

Bowman jumped to his feet and picked up the Marshal, flinging him into the nearest table and sending food and drink into the air along with the shrieks of the sisters.

'Now,' Brian stood up.

Richard got to his feet as someone's nose crunched behind him. 'Shame really, I was enjoying that.'

No one noticed them leave. As Richard ran down the cloister, he heard a table snap in two back in the refectory. Brian scurried behind him with a slight limp from where the blue roan had trodden on his foot. They passed the chamber with the window they'd used before, and Richard paused. 'Go out the window and bring the carts down,' he said. 'Sarjeant should be up the hill at the stables. Tell them to come and we'll start loading the silver.'

'Shouldn't we wait until we know it's still there?' Brian asked.

Richard shook his head. 'If it's not there, we'll escape on the carts, just go.'

The monk nodded and clambered up and out of the window. Richard continued on down the corridor until he found the dark entrance that dropped down into the crypt. Except the door was shut. He looked down for a lock near the handle. If they needed a key, he was going to have to let someone torture the abbess.

Fortunately, there was no lock. Richard breathed a sigh of relief and turned the handle and barged his shoulder into the wooden door with all his might. The oak door squeaked. He pushed it again and it jerked open a small way. Richard was about to put in one last shove to open it when a finger tapped him on the shoulder. He turned around, ready to congratulate Bowman on a perfect distraction, but instead his eyes had to shift down to find the pointed face of Brother Geoffrey.

'What in God's name are you doing here?' Richard asked.

The monk's eyebrows were raised in triumph. 'I would ask you the same question,' he said, 'except that I tracked you here so I know precisely what you are doing.'

'You followed us?'

'No,' Brother Geoffrey said, 'you see, I have deciphered your scheme. I observed you at Rouen when the Young King was buried, and your company has men with loose lips.'

'You didn't decipher anything,' Richard said, 'you just got some bored men drunk.'

'That is half of my job,' Brother Geoffrey said, 'and it revealed your dark plan. All these years you've been waiting to come back and recover the hidden gold. And now that your greed has finally got the better of you, I am here to return the gold to its rightful owner.'

'I don't know how many times I need to say it, there is no gold.'

'Keep lying to me if you wish,' the monk said, 'but your plot has been uncovered. Your deceit will be the final nail in your coffin, if the king even grants you a coffin.'

'This isn't the king's silver,' Richard said.

'Silver? Who said anything about silver?'

'You are a terrible spy,' Richard said, 'now leave me alone before you get hurt, and don't tempt me, hurting you is an extremely appealing thought.'

'If you surrender quietly, I will put in a good word for you,' Brother Geoffrey said.

Richard sighed and turned fully to face the monk. 'A good word? Like you did when you reminded the king about Yvetot? Like you did when you made sure he remembered to deny me Keynes as well? I am only here because of that, this is all your doing. You are a filthy serpent wrapped around my neck.'

'Boy,' Brother Geoffry spat, 'you have no guile at the game in which I am a master. You are trapped, cornered, and beaten.'

'I might be lacking guile,' Richard said, 'but do you know why your plans always fail? It's because they are obvious even to someone as oblivious as the Marshal, who is as good at reading people as a stone is at reading scripture. You're an idiot. Now get out of my way, your influence over me is very much gone. You threw it away when you tried to have the king execute me. What more can you do to me?'

'I'll have you hung,' the monk raged, 'you should fear what I can do, what I have done to those who dared cross me.'

Richard couldn't believe what he was hearing. 'Fear you? I don't fear you, you're nothing but a silver tongued lackey. You should fear what I have done. Leave now or I will kill you.'

Brother Geoffrey pushed his chest out. 'I am sure you have done a great many terrible things, you even managed to have the son of the king killed, but you would never dare harm a holy man. Your threats will not quake my soul.'

Richard tensed his hands into a fist. 'Do you remember back at Castle Tancarville, when the monk flew from the tower?'

'Of course,' Brother Geoffrey said, 'he was my companion.'

'You suspected me, did you not?'

Brother Geoffrey nodded. 'I did, but the iron bar proved your innocence in the trial by fire. I confess it was a surprise to me, but the Lord spoke and cleared you of wrongdoing.'

'No,' Richard said, 'he didn't.'

'He didn't what?'

'Clear me of anything,' Richard felt the scars on his palms even as his fists urged him to pound the monk's face into a pulp.

Brother Geoffrey frowned then took a step back. His chest sank and his eyes lost their shine. 'What are you telling me?'

Richard stepped forwards and grabbed the monk's robe under his neck. He thrust his face down to Brother Geoffrey's. 'I threw the monk from the tower, right in God's view. The Lord saw it and judged that it was no crime to murder him. What do you make of that?'

Brother Geoffrey shuddered and Richard lifted his body up onto its tiptoes.

'And now I'm reclaiming the silver that's mine,' Richard said, 'it will be used for a righteous cause, and there is nothing you can do to stop it. This is your very last chance, and for all you've done to me, you do not deserve to have even that. Stand aside now, without uttering a single word, I will not give you a third chance.'

'Or what?' Brother Geoffrey spat in Richard's face.

Richard's right fist took revenge for the burning iron bar it had endured and punched the monk right in the nose. Richard threw him to the ground and blood spattered across Brother Geoffrey's face. The back of the monk's head hit the stone floor with a bang, he groaned for a moment, then his body relaxed.

Richard watched him, but the monk's chest still moved. That had been a very long time coming, he thought.

He nodded to himself, then pushed the crypt door open and descended the steps into the murk. The air tasted of mould and damp, and there was a watermark running around the crypt from when it had flooded during the nunnery's construction. A few steps in and the light from the doorway dissipated and Richard had to feel his way to Anfroy's tomb. His fingers dragged over rough stones, some of which were damp and uncomfortable to touch, until they found a wooden board. Richard smiled, he hadn't sealed the tomb himself but he'd heard the nails being driven in, and just then his fingers found their small iron heads. Not every nail was all the way in, for Bowman and Sarjeant had finished their work in a rush. Richard however, had nothing to prise the wood off or pull the nails out with, so he walked back out of the crypt to where Brother Geoffrey lay.

Richard crouched down and fumbled for a dagger but didn't find one. There was only a pouch so Richard opened its leather flap. Inside was an iron eating knife, which Richard grabbed and took down to the tomb. He used the blade to lever out the nails which were protruding, and then ran the knife under the plaque and pulled. Half of the wood split and came away. A splinter dug into Richard's thumb but he didn't have time to worry about that. He used the eating knife to pull off the remnant of the wooden board, although its iron blade snapped as he did so. Richard didn't care, because as long last, he was inside the tomb.

He reached into the black recess and his hands touched cold wood. The chests, the chests were still there. Richard's heart surged, and he had to use both hands to drag the first one out. He almost ran back to the chamber with the window, the wooden chest clenched tightly in his hands, where his eyes stung from the light of the late afternoon.

A cart jerked to a halt with Sarjeant pulling on the reins. 'I don't really know how to drive this thing,' he said.

'Who cares,' Richard held up the chest, 'look.'

'My boy,' Sarjeant's blue eyes glimmered.

The second cart was right behind him, Gerold with the reins, his face pale and gaunt, but he looked steady enough. 'I honestly thought you'd been spinning tales the whole time,' the old knight said, 'but you really have silver?'

'We really have silver,' Richard tossed the box through the air to Sarjeant.

The third cart with the tired pony joined the queue, along with Brian who was out of breath. 'Is that it?' he watched Sarjeant place the silver into the cart.

'Not all of it,' Richard said, 'come on, Brian, you and Sarjeant can help me ferry the chests up here to load.'

They raced down into the crypt, Sarjeant stepping over Brother Geoffrey but asking no questions.

Brian got lost for a moment in the crypt when he went the wrong way, but soon found the tomb and hauled a chest out to carry.

They loaded the first cart before their enthusiasm waned and they slowed down with the weight of the wooden boxes. When Richard went back to bring the first chests for the second cart, Bowman and the Marshal staggered along the corridor. One of Bowman's eyes was swollen and black, and blood poured from both of their noses and stained their tunics even more than they already had been. Sweat matted their hair and the Marshal had a wide cut across his cheek. Blood dripped from his mouth and he spat a globule of red onto the stones. The two of them walked together, holding each other up.

Sarjeant stopped dead when he saw them. 'Holy Mother of God,' he said, 'what in sweet hell happened to the two of you?'

Bowman grinned a crimson grin. 'I think we have made up,' he said.

The Marshal nodded. 'I think I needed that, there's nothing like the taste of iron in your mouth to set your mind straight.'

Richard smiled at them. 'But even better, the silver is still here and we've loaded a third of it.'

The Marshal spat some more blood out and his smile faded. 'That's a shame,' he said.

Richard stilled. 'Why? What's wrong?'

'The nuns lost interest in us when someone was sighted at the foot of the hill,' Bowman said, 'and they are in a frenzy now because it's a mounted column.'

'Has Guy lost his patience?' Richard asked. 'That wouldn't be the end of the world, we can talk him down. We could do with a hand loading the silver, anyway.'

The Marshal shook his head. 'We looked,' he said, 'it was some sort of red banner.'

'A banner?' Richard asked. 'We haven't been flying one.'

'That's my point,' Bowman said, 'but I couldn't tell you if it was a plain red banner, or one with a silver shield and spur rowels.'

Richard's blood froze. 'We need to know which it is. Neither is good, but one would be the end of us. If Lord Tancarville himself is here, we are all dead men.'

'I don't know,' Bowman said, 'this nunnery isn't on the main road to anywhere, we only blundered into it originally because of that lightning strike. Why would Lord Tancarville ever come here?'

Richard's breath stuck in his throat. 'No, he wouldn't,' he said, 'and there's only one person who knows what might be here.' He looked down at Brother Geoffrey. 'And this one could have easily let slip what we're doing after he found out.'

'He found out?' the Marshal asked.

'Yes,' Richard said, 'so it is either Sir Roger or the Little Lord who is outside, and Sir Roger wouldn't be flying any sort of red banner.'

'Oh, no,' Bowman moaned. 'Not that little turd.'

'He's not so little now,' Richard said, 'we should leave with the one cart we have. If we drive hard and get lucky, we could escape while they fight over the rest of the silver between themselves.'

The Marshal shook his head. 'I didn't get this beaten to let even one coin of the silver go.'

'I thought you weren't greedy?' Richard asked. 'I think it's better to escape with some than die here with all of it.'

Bowman let go of the Marshal. 'I can't believe I'm agreeing with the peacock, but he's right. The carts will never outrun horses, we might as well stand and fight. They'll track the carts up the paddocks, so we can't sneak off either.'

Richard groaned in frustration. 'We could lose it all,' he said, 'or more of us.'

'Give us a better plan then,' the blonde man said.

Richard turned to Brian. 'Tell Gerold and Sarjeant to drive that cart as far away as they can. Pick up the children and make for the coast, we'll find them. Then run as fast as you can to where Guy is hiding and tell him to charge whoever is outside the front gate. If he wants to see a return on his investment, he'll have to fight for it.'

Brian nodded. 'I doubt he'll mind,' and climbed out of the window.

'We'll need weapons,' the Marshal said.

The corners of the chamber were empty and it was devoid of even a chair or table. 'Find anything you can,' Richard said. 'Smash a chair up if you have to, find something stout and long.'

'What happened to not desecrating and looting more holy sites?' Bowman asked.

'Not now,' Richard rushed out of the chamber and towards the refectory. Richard picked up a wooden stool and smashed it against the table to break a leg off. He held the stool with one of its remaining legs as a shield, and took the broken leg as a club. The Marshal found a broom while Bowman ran to the corner of the room and took a long iron candlestick in both hands, the candles still burning and their flames trailing through the air as he moved.

Richard gripped his new weapon tightly. 'All we need to do is hold them off long enough for Guy to get around and charge their rear.'

Bowman brandished his candlestick, rubbed at his puffy eye and went off towards the entrance. 'What if we can't hold them?' he asked.

'Of course we will,' the Marshal said, 'it'll be just like Newstead Abbey all over again. Or was that a nunnery?'

'If we can't hold them,' Richard said, 'we'll fall back to the chamber with the window. If we can't hold the doorway there, we'll slip out of the window and run for it. But it would be better if we could hold this door.'

The Marshal followed Bowman. 'I'll hold it.'

Richard reached the entranceway last, just as Bowman stalled his advance. He stalled because the door already swung open, revealing the mailed figures of the Little Lord and Sir John.

The Little Lord stepped through the doorway and Bowman lowered his candlestick at him. The Marshal took a stance next to him and held his broom like a two-handed spear.

'Your plan lasted even less time than usual,' Bowman said.

Richard took his place next to the blonde knight and held the stool out in front of him.

Sir John laughed. 'What are you doing? Two of you already look like you've fought a battle.'

'Yes,' the young Tancarville sneered, 'and lost it.'

'This one hasn't started yet,' Richard said.

'Look at you,' the Little Lord's red hair framed his face, a face wrought with satisfaction. 'I knew you'd be here, Richard. I knew it all along that you'd hidden the gold here. You came back, I told my father you would, but he didn't care. It will be his loss to miss out on the gold.'

'Good for you,' Richard wanted to keep the Little Lord talking. 'But how did you know we were here?'

'The monk with a rat-like face.'

'So this was his idea, not yours,' Richard said.

'I am here by my own doing,' the Little Lord said, 'and I'm going to finish what I started at the castle. You will be put to death as a traitor.'

'I've betrayed no one,' Richard said.

'My father was your lord, and you sided with Sir Roger against him.'

'That's nonsense, you're the one who's wronged me.'

'I'm not here to talk to you,' the Little Lord said, 'I'm here to kill you and become rich. Richer than my father, and far richer than my brother.'

'They aren't here with you, then?'

The Little Lord shook his head and his mail coif reflected in the candles which still burned on Bowman's candlestick. 'They are not part of this.'

'That's good,' Richard said, 'very good. We can settle this now just between the two of us. Let everyone else stand back, and we can finish this man to man.'

The young Tancarville laughed. 'A heroic duel, is that what you want?'

'Why not? Why should anyone else here die on our behalf? This quarrel is between the two of us alone.'

'You're only saying that because I have an army behind me and you're armed with a broken chair.'

'So you're too much of a coward to fight me on your own? Even when I don't have a sword?'

'Where's the gold?' the Little Lord snarled. 'I know you put it in the crypt, I just couldn't find it before. Tell me where you hid it.'

'There is no gold,' Richard said, 'I swear it on my soul and the souls of my children, I have no gold hidden here.'

The Tancarville groaned. 'Have it your way, we're going to kill you all and then destroy this place looking for it.'

'You can try,' Bowman waved the candlestick in their faces and half the candles fell off and went out on the floor.

'Are you sure you want to fight the great Marshal?' Richard nodded to his right.

Sir John laughed. 'We know who he is, he's in disgrace after the Young King's revolt failed. No one will care if he's killed here.'

'You will regret saying that,' the Marshal stepped forwards, 'I'll have you on your knees begging to be taken captive before I break a sweat.'

Sir John studied their bruised and torn faces. 'You already have. You look like you lost a fight with a bear.'

'They did that to each other,' Richard said, 'so just imagine what they're going to do to you.'

'Fine words,' the Little Lord said, 'and very amusing, but we have swords and mail, and you are unarmoured. You'll be dead in moments.'

Richard's temper bubbled, the sight of the Little Lord looking smug grated him. 'Then why are you still out there?' he asked. 'Are you too scared to face us? If you're so confident of victory, cross the threshold and come and test yourselves.'

'I thought you were speaking for time,' Bowman said, 'why are you antagonising them?'

Richard clenched his jaw tight in the way he often did before combat.

The Little Lord raised his sword carefully, for they hadn't brought their shields into the nunnery. 'Push through the door and flank them, our numbers will crush them,' he said.

Sir John drew his sword with a sigh.

'Come on,' the Little Lord said to the two squires behind him, 'attack them if you want to earn your golden spurs.'

Richard raised his club and rotated his wrist in anticipation.

The two squires, not armoured with mail, but wielding real swords, edged forward then charged.

Bowman poked forwards with the candlestick and a squire halted to avoid running onto it. The other ran at the Marshal, who thrust up with the long end of his broom and clouted him straight between the eyes. The squire fell to the floor.

Richard stepped forward and struck at Bowman's opponent. The squire saw him coming, but it meant he missed Bowman, who jammed a candle into his cheek.

The Tancarville squire howled and Sir John groaned. 'They've got sticks and candles,' he roared, 'what are you doing?'

The next knight and squire through the door both hesitated.

'There's four of us,' the Little Lord said, 'what are you waiting for?'

'We're waiting for you,' Sir John sneered.

'I'm out of candles,' Bowman said in full seriousness.

Richard would have found it funny had four men not been facing them.

'There's only three of them,' the Tancarville said, 'attack them.'

'We'll kill you two or four at a time,' Richard said, 'it makes no difference to us.'

Sir John shook his head and stepped forwards. 'I have had enough of everyone, we're in mail so we'll swat them like stray dogs. Follow me.'

'You'll lose more teeth,' Richard said, 'and we have no quarrel with you. Just go Sir John, don't suffer more for this arrogant upstart. He treats you too badly to suffer for him more than you already have.'

Sir John frowned even as he stepped over the unconscious squire and batted Bowman's candlestick aside. The knight and squire charged.

'I can treat him how I like,' the Little Lord shouted as another squire flew past him from the entrance.

Richard caught that squire's sword with the stool and the blade bit into the wood. He clubbed the squire on his upper arm but his padded woollen jacket absorbed the blow.

Bowman tangled his assailant's sword in his candlestick and twisted it, sending the weapon flying through the air.

The Marshal parried Sir John's attack and deftly brought his broom across to push back the knight who advanced on him. Sir John tried to swing his sword again, but the Marshal was so quick that he could bring the broom back across to push the older knight backwards.

Sir John tripped on a bench and landed awkwardly on a table.

Some nuns appeared in a doorway but screamed and ran off.

Richard's club lost some splinters when he blocked a sword thrust with it, but he rammed the stool into the squire's face and the young man reeled back with a yelp. He slipped on one of the dropped candles and fell backwards onto the stone floor.

The Little Lord shuffled towards Bowman as his men poured through the doorway. Two knights approached Richard, their nasal helms glinting in the candlelight. He glanced to his side and saw a third knight join Sir John as the Marshal poked and prodded them to keep them at bay.

Bowman stepped back as the Little Lord was joined by two squires, his eyes darting from one to the other and his feet shifting backwards.

They couldn't hold on any longer. 'Back down the corridor,' Richard shouted and retreated.

Bowman didn't need to be told twice, but the Marshal held firm and broke the nose of one knight.

'It's a damned broom,' Sir John shouted, but the Marshal was so fast the broom cracked him in the face and two teeth broke and fell from his mouth.

'You can't hold them all back,' Richard said, 'you can't always be the hero.'

'I'm doing the right thing,' the Marshal parried a sword cut to his head and kicked the opposing knight in the stomach.

The Little Lord pushed towards Richard, and the Marshal was almost cut off from the corridor.

'If you die here,' Richard shouted, 'I won't tell anyone what happened.'

The Marshal paused for a split second, stabbed a squire in the foot with his broom, and then leapt towards the corridor. He swung the broom around as he bounded past the Little Lord and smacked him around the back of his red-haired head as he entered the corridor.

The Little Lord grabbed the back of his head where he'd been hit and winced as the Marshal joined Richard and Bowman in the walkway.

The three of them filled the cloister and brandished their assorted weapons at Sir John and the dozen men who packed in behind him.

Two crossbowmen streamed in and the Little Lord screeched at them to shoot at Richard.

One of the crossbowmen had a beard. He nudged his companion and they both took aim and squeezed their trigger levers. Both bolts clattered into the stone above the cloister and rebounded back at the Tancarville soldiers. One bolt snapped in half and the half with the iron top slashed a squire on the hand and he dropped his sword.

'How can you shoot so badly?' the Little Lord cried.

Bowman grinned, but it was hardly visible beneath his swollen and bruised face.

'We should go back to the chamber,' Richard said.

'Do you think so?' the blonde man started creeping backwards.

The two crossbowmen reloaded about as slowly as it was possible to while Sir John led his men into the corridor. They moved slowly, aware of the longer reach of the candlestick and broom.

The Marshal lunged forwards and two knights jumped backwards out of his way. 'Fight me,' the English knight shouted.

'Cowards,' Sir John muttered.

The knights came back and charged with Sir John. One was stunned by the broom, but the other pushed Richard's club aside and hit him around the side of his face with the flat of the blade.

Richard staggered backwards as Bowman fended off Sir John.

'You two fight like children,' the Marshal cried as he brought the broom down on Sir John's shoulder and knocked the Tancarville knight down onto a knee.

'Only because you never taught me,' Richard backed up and almost fell through the doorway into the chamber with the window.

Bowman joined him inside while the Marshal's broom took out a squire's eye then broke the fingers of another. The English knight hopped into the chamber and the three of them faced the door and waited for Sir John or his men to attack.

'Shoot them,' the Little Lord pointed through the doorway.

Rob and Jean were at the back of the throng of knights and squires who dared not cross the threshold. 'We can't see them, my lord,' Rob shouted. 'So we can't shoot them.'

'Let the crossbowmen through,' the Little Lord ordered and the squires parted to allow them to get to the doorway.

'What now?' Bowman asked. 'We don't exactly have anywhere to hide.'

Richard held his battered stool up but didn't think he'd have much luck blocking crossbow bolts.

The bearded crossbowman lowered his crossbow. Richard was sure that when he squeezed the trigger he saw him wink. The bolt sailed a whisker from Bowman's chin and flew straight out of the window. The other crossbowman pointed his weapon at Bowman, too, and that bolt whistled over his head and chipped some masonry from the window frame as it disappeared outside into the paddock.

The Little Lord howled and cracked the pommel of his sword into the side of the bearded crossbowman's head. He fell backwards and Bowman grimaced.

Richard's chest pounded and he felt dizzy. His arms were drained, and judging by Bowman's heavy breathing, he wasn't doing any better.

The Marshal alone balanced on the balls of his feet and brandished his broom with enthusiasm. He was enjoying himself, Richard thought.

The Marshal sallied towards the door, struck a squire on the nasal guard, but Sir John slashed down on the broom and severed the furthest foot of its length.

Shouts came from down the corridor. Those shouts and loud voices rippled up the Tancarville men. 'A company is coming,' one shouted.

The Little Lord exchanged a glance with Sir John.

'We don't have another company,' Sir John said.

'Surely my father can't be here?' the Little Lord said.

Bowman chuckled, but it turned into a cough.

Richard wanted to grin, but the chamber was almost spinning, and he badly wanted to sit down. 'I told you,' he said, 'you shouldn't have tried to fight us.'

The Little Lord's confidence melted away. 'What do you mean?'

The Marshal waved the broken broom in Sir John's face. 'Come on Sir John, you are a name known to many, let me defeat you before Guy spoils everything.'

'Guy?' the Little Lord snatched a look behind him. 'Which Guy?'

Richard lowered his stool. 'The one you're hoping it isn't. Surrender now or flee, it's all the same to me.'

'You're trapped,' Bowman flourished the candlestick and one of the Tancarville squires backed through the throng and fled.

'We should leave,' Sir John said, 'no sense in being stuck inside the abbey without our horses. We don't have so many men outside holding our mounts, we should return to them.'

'But the gold,' the young Tancarville cried.

'Do not let greed blind you, my lord, there is nothing to be gained by staying, we may already be trapped.'

'No, no, no,' the Little Lord stamped a foot, 'the gold is mine, it's destined to be mine.'

Rob and Jean had been edging towards the back of the armed men in the corridor, and now they simply turned and ran.

A knight followed them and Richard allowed his arms to relax.

'Come back,' the Little Lord shouted, 'you serve me, obey me.'

'They have no wish to die for your feud,' Sir John said, 'and none of them believe there is any gold here. Leave now before all the men abandon you, for once that happens, you'll never be able to lead them again.'

'I don't think he's really leading them now,' Bowman twirled the iron candlestick.

'I know there's gold here,' the Little Lord said, 'I saw them hide it.'

'How sure are you?' Sir John asked as two more squires melted away from the company. 'Sure enough to die for it? We will kill these three, but if Guy of Lusignan is outside, you could die a very uncomfortable death.'

The young Tancarville swallowed. 'What about Richard? He has destroyed my life. He made me a joke at Castle Tancarville, and his wife made that even worse. He unhorsed me outside his worthless village and stole my sword, I need to hurt him.'

Richard bristled. 'You did all of those things to yourself. You tried to bully me, you tried to steal my wife, and you tried to burn my village. And twice you and your father did burn my village. Anything bad that's happened to you has been a fair punishment. And you killed Sophie, nothing I did to you could come close to that.'

'Your wife killed herself,' the Little Lord snapped. 'Because you were not strong enough to save her.'

Richard's limbs no longer ached or felt empty, instead they felt as if powered from a fire inside. He raised the stool and charged.

The Little Lord, just as angry, stood his ground and swung his sword.

Richard caught it with the stool, but his club only connected with his enemy's mailed forearm and did no real damage.

The Marshal charged and pushed Sir John out into the corridor.

Bowman howled and rammed the candlestick into a squire, who blocked with his sword to no effect whatsoever and found himself stabbed by the ends of the iron candlestick.

The Marshal tripped a knight up with the broom and suddenly Richard was alone in the chamber with the Little Lord, his two friends pushing the Tancarvilles back down the cloister.

The Little Lord slashed the sword and shaved a corner off the stool. Richard didn't see the follow up quick enough to parry it, and the sword gashed a tear in his sleeve and a burning sensation flared across his upper arm.

'You've got your duel,' the Little Lord struck again, but this time Richard brought the stool up to contain it.

Bowman tripped backwards into the chamber and the candlestick sprawled from his grasp across the stone floor.

Sir John strode in after him. 'It is time to go, my lord,' he said.

'Stay and fight,' the Little Lord replied, 'obey me or I'll knock the rest of your teeth out myself.'

Bowman scrambled back for his weapon as Sir John turned to his lord. 'I have not forgotten the mockery you made of me that night at the castle, in front of all the men. Stay here if you will, but I will not lose my life in your defence. You have cost me enough.'

Bowman clasped the iron shaft of the candlestick and used it to haul himself back up to his feet.

The Little Lord ignored his knight and lunged at Richard. His blade knocked the stool from Richard's hand and the red-haired man grinned. 'I've dreamt of this moment.'

Bowman swung the candlestick around at him and the Tancarville had to jump it.

Richard brought his club down, but the Little Lord somehow batted it away with so much strength it flew from Richard's grip and crashed into the wall.

Bowman held the candlestick at the Little Lord. 'Last chance,' the blonde man mumbled through a split lip.

Richard lowered his body in case he needed to dodge an attack, he held his empty hands out but felt more vulnerable than he'd ever been in a fight.

The Little Lord had to pick which man to go for.

'Give up,' Richard said, 'whoever you tackle, the other of us will have you.'

The Little Lord glanced at the doorway, but then turned back and clenched his teeth.

'You're choosing this to stay and fight over some imaginary gold and an imaginary grievance?' Richard asked. 'This is what you want to die for? You know what, I thought I didn't need to kill you, but this is going to make me feel far better than I thought it would.'

'Are you sure?' Bowman asked. 'You've been awfully righteous lately, killing him like this might haunt you forever.'

Richard readied his feet to spring into action. 'I told you before, I'm already haunted. I may as well rid the world of this creature before he can harm anyone else. He's killed too many women already. This will be for Sophie and Matilda.'

'Sir Roger's girl?' the Little Lord smirked. 'I barely even remember what she looked like.'

Richard went to lunge, but his empty hands checked his aggression.

A scraping noise came from outside the window, and Maynard appeared with a bundle of three swords in their scabbards. He dropped the bundle through the window and started to climb in. 'Guy is attacking,' he said.

'We know,' Bowman replied.

'Don't let him leave,' Richard ran over to the swords and drew Durendal from its loose-fitting scabbard.

The Little Lord went for Richard but the candlestick caught him in the abdomen and stopped him. The Tancarville pushed the iron shaft out of the way and Bowman recoiled backwards.

Richard slashed with his new sword and caught the Little Lord on the arm, but his blade wasn't truly sharp and no rings were severed.

The Tancarville struck Richard, their swords tangled and both twisted out of their hands with a chime of iron scraping iron.

Bowman put all his strength into a thrust and threw the Little Lord back and onto the ground, where he pinned him to the stones with the candlestick as if it were a pitchfork.

The Little Lord clawed at it to push it away, but the spikes to hold the candles were sharp and dug into his skin through the mail.

Richard retrieved Durendal. 'A fitting use for Roland's sword,' he said.

'Are you sure?' Bowman asked. 'He's without a weapon now.'

Richard contemplated kicking his foe's sword over just so he didn't have to kill an unarmed man.

'Roland's sword?' the Little Lord struggled to breathe, but his right hand stopped clawing and shot to his waist.

'Watch out,' Richard cried as Bowman realised the danger, and the Tancarville drew a dagger and swished it at the blonde man's ankle.

Richard cut down, but the Little Lord moved too swiftly and they both missed everything.

Bowman drove the candlestick forwards again at the dagger-hand and Richard took his chance.

Except that his sword cut bounced off the candlestick, glanced off the Little Lord's helmet, and Richard overbalanced when it didn't dig into anything.

The Little Lord flung the dagger out and cut Richard's shoulder and he dropped Durendal.

'Seriously,' Bowman said, 'we really need to work on that.' This time the candlestick rammed into the Tancarville's helmet and brought him crashing down in a clatter of metal and iron rings.

Bowman brought his heel down on the dagger-hand and the Little Lord cried out in pain.

Richard checked his shoulder, but even though it hurt, he could still use it. 'I'll use his own dagger,' he said.

'Are you sure, young lord?' Bowman asked. 'What happened to being a good example?'

Richard picked up the dagger. 'I want to do the right thing,' he said, 'but now he's here, all I can see is Sophie leaping from the tower. He needs to die, Bowman, he needs to die.'

'Aye, I'm not arguing about that,' Bowman twisted his heel and the Little Lord screamed, 'but can't it be someone besides you who does the deed? It doesn't have to be you that swings the blade.'

Richard's breathing caught up and he felt lightheaded again.

Guy burst into the chamber from the corridor, a red sword in his hand and a grin on his face. The grin only widened when he saw Bowman.

'What happened to you? This whelp here can hardly have beaten you so badly, can he?'

'It was the Marshal,' Richard said, 'they've made up their differences. Maybe you should fight the Marshal next.'

Guy kicked the Little Lord's head and his helmet flew off and clanged along the stones.

'Let me go,' the Little Lord whined.

Bowman laughed, then had to spit out more blood.

'Are you going to kill him, then?' Guy asked. 'His company was streaming out of the nunnery when we charged, but we caught a few of them.'

Richard went to belt on his scabbard and put Durendal back into it. 'Bowman is insisting I don't kill him, apparently I have to be righteous about it.'

'Stop saying righteous,' Bowman said, 'the word is grating on me now.'

'I find the men who use that word are usually those who are furthest from it,' the Lusignan crouched down over the fallen Tancarville. 'Do you think your father will save you?'

The Little Lord tried to respond but the candlestick on his chest restricted his breathing.

'No one is coming to help him,' Richard said.

Maynard stared at Bowman's face and Richard shook his head at him so he didn't ask. 'We need to load the rest of the silver,' Richard said to the squire, 'find someone to ride after Sarjeant and Gerold and tell them they can come back. Then find some of Guy's squires and have them finish loading the other two carts.'

Maynard nodded hurriedly and stuck his leg back out the window. In his rush he fell out and landed awkwardly on the paddock.

Richard looked down at the Little Lord. His urge to slit his throat had been a passing one, and now the wish never to kill anyone again took over. Richard remembered that he'd wanted to find a quiet life and hang up his sword on the wall, leaving it there as he watched his children grow up.

Bowman looked up. 'What are we doing with him? I'll kill him for you, or I'm sure Guy will happily help you if you want him to.'

Richard shook his head. 'I don't want anyone else to have to do my work for me. When Maynard gets back, we'll get some torches and go down into the crypt.'

Maynard and a dozen of Guy's squires arrived quickly, and it wasn't long before two of them dragged the Little Lord kicking and screaming down into the dark depths.

'I don't know what he's complaining about,' Bowman said, 'he wanted to go and see the silver.'

'He'll be disappointed when he finds no gold,' Richard grinned. 'Are you alright? Your face looks like a horse has kicked it. Twice.'

Bowman tentatively touched his face and flinched. 'If you told me to gain all that silver I needed to get kicked by a horse in the face,' he said, 'I'd have crouched down and poked the animal myself.'

Richard descended the stone steps into the crypt ahead of the Little Lord.

The Marshal came down with his broom in hand, shorter now than before and snapped into a sharp point, its tip soaked in blood. 'I've heard so much about this,' he said, 'I can't wait to see what we've got.'

Guy sneered at him. 'You are just a greedy little man, aren't you?'

'Bring the torches over here,' Richard said. He had to lean on the wall as his head spun.

Two squires brought light with them as two others hauled the Little Lord over on his knees. They dumped him on the cool floor and he looked around like a cornered deer. 'You can ransom me back,' he said.

Guy laughed. 'We have three cartloads of silver, I'm told, why would we need your paltry ransom?'

'But I'm a Tancarville, you can't just kill me.'

'Like you slaughtered my villagers?' Richard asked. 'Today is the day you face justice for all that you've done. You can't talk your way out of it. Even your company left you, and from what I hear, your father will not even mourn your passing.'

'My passing?' the Little Lord rubbed his chest. 'You can't kill me. My blood on your hands will stain your soul.'

'There will be no blood on my hands,' Richard said.

'Can I kill him, then?' Guy asked. 'If only to silence his moaning.'

Richard shook his head. 'You wanted gold,' he said, 'and I told you many times that there wasn't any. There still isn't, I was telling the truth all along.'

'But?' the Little Lord stammered. 'What are we doing here?'

'Bowman, can you supervise the squires moving the rest of the chests out?' Richard asked.

Bowman nodded and barked commands at Guy's men. The first chest came out and Guy snatched it. The Marshal walked over and peered into it as the Lusignan tore it open. They both smiled at the contents before Guy slammed it shut. 'This one is mine,' he said.

'What is it?' the Little Lord asked, his eyes pleading.

'You still care about that?' Richard asked.

The Tancarville nodded. 'I need to know.'

'You will know,' Richard glanced over to Guy and the Marshal as the squires stacked up the chests on the crypt's floor. 'Pick him up and put him in the tomb,' Richard said.

Guy raised his eyebrows. 'Oh, that's very clever.'

'That's a job for a squire,' the Marshal waved Richard away and went to pick up a chest for himself.

The Little Lord's mouth flapped open and he shook his head. 'You can't do that, I'm a Tancarville.'

Guy picked up one arm and Richard grabbed the other. 'When you're locked in there,' he said, 'I want you to picture Sophie leaping from your tower. I want you to think about what you did and why it was wrong.'

The Little Lord struggled, but Guy alone was far stronger and they took him to the now empty tomb. Guy did most of the lifting to cram his legs in first, and the Marshal appeared with his broom to push his body in. The Little Lord clawed and cut Richard's face with his fingernails, but he couldn't resist the three of them. He wailed and cried.

'I never liked him,' the Marshal said, 'he never behaved like a knight should.'

Guy chuckled. 'So this is behaving like a knight, is it? Shutting a man in a tomb to suffocate or die of thirst?'

The Marshal shrugged.

'Nail it shut,' Richard stood back as the flames of the torches flickered on the Little Lord's pitifully desperate face. Richard opened a chest and took out a pouch of coins. He threw it at the Tancarville and it bounced off his face. 'Here,' Richard said, 'here are the coins you were so willing to die for. You'll never know what sort they are either, because you'll never see them in the darkness. I just wish I had a bowl of pottage to throw in there with you.'

Bowman picked up half of the broken wooden board and held it up over the tomb. The Little Lord stuck a hand out of the gap and cried out, but Guy slammed his sword hilt into his fingers with a crunch. The hand withdrew.

'What do we do about Brother Geoffrey?' Bowman asked while the squires scrambled around on the floor looking for all the nails.

Guy grinned. 'We can't let him go, can we? He knows we're here and I suppose he knows why. If he lives he'll run straight to the king.'

'I can't kill him,' Richard said, 'he is a monk.'

'Is he?' Bowman asked.

'I can remove his tongue and fingers,' Guy said, 'then he cannot speak or write of us. I will take his eyes as well, just to be sure.'

'You can't mutilate anyone that badly,' Richard said, 'not in a nunnery.'

Guy frowned. 'I think it's a bit late for that sort of thinking. You can't let him go, so I'm giving you another option.'

Richard knew the Lusignan was right. Brother Geoffrey couldn't be allowed to live. 'But what of all the Tancarville men who escaped? We can't kill all of them.'

'We got enough of them,' Guy said, 'and I think Sir John may not tell his lord the truth of what happened, for he won't want to be sent after us.'

'That's a leap of faith,' Richard said.

'You might as well believe it,' Guy said, 'we can't go chasing after them, we need to catch a ship instead.'

Richard sighed. 'Nothing is easy, is it?' he whispered to himself. 'Fine, wall the monk up too, what's another corpse on our list? At least we aren't shedding any more blood doing that.'

Richard watched as the Little Lord sobbed. Two squires dragged the unconscious Brother Geoffrey in and shoved him into the tomb, which at least served to drown out the Little Lord. The two bodies didn't really fit in the space, but Guy pushed the monk in and the Little Lord's protests became very muffled. Richard was having second thoughts about the whole thing as Bowman held the wooden boards in place and a squire used a knife pommel to hammer the nails back in. It was slow going.

The Marshal sniffed at the damp air. 'This is a darker end to the affair than I had expected,' he said.

'I'm quite impressed,' Guy said, 'I really didn't think you had this in you, I underestimated you. I would not even mind if my sister chose you, she is rather fond of your children.'

Richard had done his best to ignore Alice. 'We should load the chests and be gone,' he said, 'we don't want the nuns to even think of coming down here.'

The Marshal picked up three chests and staggered away up the steps with them loaded in his arms.

'Let's get this done,' Bowman said, 'if the nuns open the tomb up then all your good intentions will be for nothing.'

'I hardly think walling up two men counts as good intentions,' Richard picked up a chest to carry himself. 'But we're leaving the matter in God's hands. If they deserve to die, no one will hear their screams. Which means we are free from guilt.'

Bowman snorted and grabbed some chests as the squires hauled off the rest one by one. 'So long as you believe yourself,' he said, 'if I said that, you'd never let me get away with it.'

Richard climbed up the steps and into the corridor. 'I can truthfully say I killed neither the Little Lord nor the monk, and that they got the justice they deserved. If God sees fit to punish them with death, then my children will be safe from both of them.'

'It will help if we're across the ocean and in the Holy Land,' Bowman walked behind him.

Richard agreed and dropped his chest on the windowsill where Maynard picked it up and stacked it on the third cart. 'Your men in the cart didn't get far,' the squire said, 'and your family are preparing to leave.'

'Good,' Richard nodded.

Bowman threw his chest at Maynard who caught it only after it had crashed into him. 'I can't really believe it,' the blonde man said, 'after all those years and after trying so much,' he reached into a coin and produced a silver coin, 'I think we're finally rich.'

EXODUS

The sun peaked behind Richard as the company crested a hill and the fishing port of Dieppe came into view. The clear blue sky stretched out far to sea, where distant waves sparkled in the sunlight. Dieppe was small, not big enough to be guarded even by a castle, but it was to its fishing fleet that they marched. A ship would take them to Harfleur, they had enough silver to buy a ship outright if they needed to, and then they would find passage east.

'I don't think I'll ever return to Normandy,' Richard told Bowman who rode next to him, 'I can feel it. This feels like a goodbye.'

'That's probably wise,' the blonde man said, his face a mass of yellow and black bruising. 'At least until the Old King dies, oh, and Lord Tancarville. And Geoffrey Martel while we're at it.'

Richard shook his head. 'There is nothing for me here. I'd write to Adela in Ireland, but I don't know where to send the letter, so I can't even do that. All my family is with me here and now.'

Solis limped along behind Maynard, pulling the squire's horse to a stop whenever he decided a bush or tree needed trimming. Alexander had taken a liking to the palomino and walked along with him, the horse happy to occasionally nudge him, which both of them seemed to enjoy. Lora rode in Sarjeant's cart atop boxes of silver, sometimes accompanied by Judas when the dog decided he needed a rest. Alice seemed drawn to the children, but hopefully that was because they were more preferable travelling companions compared to the knights and squires. The Red Child was learning to ride a spare Lusignan horse, and he sat tall on the wooden warsaddle and insisted on wearing his full sized sword while he did so. Richard was more worried about him than the other two children, Guy was certainly not the sort of role model the child needed.

'I can't believe we're riding with Guy,' Richard said, 'and with the Marshal in the same company.'

'I think it's a loose definition of the word company,' Bowman tried to chuckle, but his top lip had swollen up so much he couldn't. The blonde knight watched Guy tell the Red Child to loosen the reins. 'Although, if Guy wants to add him to his little army, I'd say good riddance.'

Richard was inclined to agree, but he felt responsible for the child, even if he already had one murder to his name. He was also officially a bastard of King Henry, so Richard didn't want to discard him and risk angering the monarch. The official parentage of the Red Child also might explain the time Guy seemed to be willing to give him. Maybe it was another one of his investments.

'I think we should be rid of Guy as soon as possible,' Bowman said. 'Nothing good will come of that man, or any Lusignan.'

Richard knew which other Lusignan he meant. 'You're right,' Richard watched a flock of seagulls fly overhead towards the coast. 'And that's the first thing we'll do in Harfleur if we can. We'll try to find a different ship to him.'

'I won't be able to sleep until our silver is away from his greedy eyes,' Bowman said, 'not that I'll be sleeping well for a while with this face.'

Richard didn't think he'd be sleeping well for a while, either. Guy told them the sea crossing could take months depending on the weather, which meant months of him not sleeping while on ships, or waiting out storms in strange harbours. It also meant loading Solis on and off ships again and again, and Richard did not look forward to that. He hadn't kept his promise to his horse about never sailing with him again, but at least he had kept his promise to the cart pony. At a village on the edge of Eawy Forest, Richard had found a kind-looking farmer with a great brood of children. The farmer had agreed to take the pony and give it no work in exchange for a pouch of silver coins. Bowman had protested. 'You can't give everyone we meet a pouch, young lord,' he'd said, 'we'll have none left before we know it.' But Richard had given over the pouch anyway and the pony had gone into retirement. The grumpy mule he'd swapped it for pulled the Young King's old cart along well enough, but it looked so old it was unlikely to survive the impending sea crossing.

Richard nodded with satisfaction on the pony's score. But everything else was still dangerous. 'Did we do the right thing?' he asked.

Bowman coughed. 'You mean with the Tancarville and the monk?'

Richard sighed.

'I suppose so,' Bowman replied, 'as long as the sisters don't go ripping the wooden board off too early. If the Little Lord survives, then Normandy will never be safe for you to set foot in again.'

'I told you,' Richard said, 'I don't think I'm coming back.'

'You can think about that later,' Bowman said, 'we have to get there first, and from what Sarjeant says, the heat might change your mind.'

Richard tightened up his reins. 'We'll have to watch him if it gets bad. While he has thrown himself into protecting my children, I don't think he's faced his demons yet.'

'We'll have to keep him away from the Templars,' the blonde man said.

'That could be difficult,' Richard said, 'the Marshal is heading for Jerusalem to lay down the Young King's cloak, and I need to speak to the Templars there to ask them about my father. That's the only clue I have to go on, so like it or not, we'll be spending plenty of time with Templars.'

'I was talking about in Harfleur,' Bowman said, 'where we're going to have to deal with them there. We can't ship three cartloads of silver to the Holy Land. Someone somewhere is going to rob us if we do that. That much silver should clearly not be in our hands, having it will draw too much attention.'

Richard sank down into his saddle. 'Their clerks are always so irritating,' he said, 'but you're right, we'll have to give most of the silver to the Templars and take letters of credit with us to the east.'

'I don't trust them.'

'Neither do I, but it was your idea,' Richard said, 'and I don't think we have much choice. We can keep one cartload of silver to split between the three carts and then it won't be too obvious what we're carrying. If the two of us, Sarjeant, Guy, and the Marshal each take out our own letters of credit for the rest, we can avoid arguments.'

'I guarantee there's going to be arguments.'

'Of course, but there's enough silver to go around. We can give a pouch to each knight and squire, except for Maynard, and make that division at Harfleur. I remember Nicola's warning, she said we'd all be murdered over it.'

Bowman grunted. 'I'll be sleeping with my knife beside me,' he said, 'and I think we should take turns watching over each other.'

'I was hoping the paranoia would take a little longer to set in,' Richard said.

'It would if Guy wasn't here.'

Richard knew they'd have to put up with the Lusignan's company for a while longer, but he also thought Guy wouldn't last long in the east. He'd throw his weight around and make a mistake. All Richard had to do was keep his family away from Guy, and hope someone in Jerusalem remembered his father. The roll of parchment in Solis's mane was gone, Richard assumed it had disintegrated by now, but the question he'd written on it was as alive as ever. For the first time, the answer seemed almost within reach, and the thought energised Richard. He would do better for his own children, for he was not leaving them behind, and the truth he sought would be uncovered.

Richard remembered back to when they had been riding towards Neufchatel in the fading light of the evening, mourning the loss of Nicholas, but feeling hope for the future. Now, riding towards the sparkling sea, but mourning the loss of Sophie, he dared to hope again. He headed east, into a world of unending sand, baking heat, and a multitude of dangerous enemies who believed in another god. At long last, Richard's crusade had begun.

HISTORICAL NOTE

The Young King's two rebellions and death are lesser known episodes in English and European history. As he never became king, and his two younger brothers who did are so much more famous, he has been relegated to somewhat of a historical footnote in mainstream culture. Everyone knows of Richard the Lionheart or Bad King John, but what of their older brother? While there are fantastic books written by historians about him, it is only recently that his reputation seems to have been given a closer look. Often dismissed as feckless, petulant, and down right useless, I personally think he needs to be given a second chance. How was he supposed to react to the life he was given? A boy educated to be a king, lifted above everyone else, and treated as almost divine, then was given no lands with which to hone his skills or learn his trade? The way in which his brother Richard was made Count of Aquitaine, and a third brother given Brittany, could only have antagonised the Young King. He must have felt that his father never intended for him to rule anything, and egged on by both the King of France and his own mother, and supported by every nobleman King Henry had pushed away, what else was he to do but run out of patience? This was an age where disgruntled noblemen rebelled against their overlords and their kings. William Mandeville's father had been one such man, and William's overt loyalty to King Henry was surely part of an effort to make up for it. That the Young King rebelled is not surprising, nor necessarily blameful, for his brother Richard had rebelled by his side in the first of his two revolts, and history remembers Richard as one of England's great warrior kings.

The conduct of the Young King's rebellions is another matter. Even with French troops alongside him, and the King of Scotland invading England, Henry II was still able to crush everyone who raised their banners against him. The Young King was young, and although his tournament prowess is not up for question, his real life campaigning skills were perhaps not yet sharpened. Whether by accident or design, the Young King's approach to the tournament circuit ensured that his father's greatest threat - disloyalty - would not be an issue for himself. The likes of William Marshal and Robert of Meulan, and literally hundreds of others, would probably have never rebelled against the Young King. Edward III was a successful king because he had a super-loyal group of knights he could rely on, and perhaps had the Young King lived longer, he may have left the same stamp on history that Edward did. However, with no lands to use as a power base, he relied on his allies and mercenaries, and to pay for the latter, he ravaged the countryside and pillaged a succession of shrines and holy sites. Rocamadour, with its saints and stunning cliff-based location, was ransacked, and Roland's sword apparently taken. There is still a sword to be seen up in the cliffs today, but it is clearly of a newer design than Roland's would have been. The monastery at Grandmont was also a victim, and the Young King's brain, eyes, and bowels were interred there as a form of compensation for the destruction he'd caused. The manner of his death has been reproduced in this book in that he died painfully of dysentery that he caught while pillaging another holy site, and then did everything he could to die well. His final bed of ashes, the stone pillow, and noose around his neck seem very odd to modern sensibilities, but that is how the Young King died. He clutched the ring his untrusting father had sent to him, a father that, despite everything, genuinely mourned his loss. King Henry is supposed to have uttered the words Mandeville speaks in this book, that his son had cost him much, but he wished he lived to cost him more - but in truth they were said in relation to paying off Sancho of Savannac. Sancho and his mercenaries were very real, and after the Young King's death, Sancho kidnapped the Marshal in lieu of his unpaid wages. In reality, the King had to pay him off to settle the matter.

Bertran de Born is one of the most famous names of the twelfth century. A landholding knight in the area of the rebellion, he was also a troubadour, and many of his works are still available to us. If you want to get into the mind of a medieval knight, you can do little better than to track down his writings. I have paraphrased some of it for him to speak in this book, and his lament over the demise of the Young King has echoed vividly down the ages. He comes across as bloodthirsty to modern readers, but then to us war is bad and to be avoided. Indeed, only a hundred years after him, Dante Alighieri included him in one of his circles of hell for his warmongering. But in his time, war was not just necessary, but the fabric of life onto which all else was stitched. Knights came into being to create parcels of land which were safe enough to farm without being constantly raised to the ground, and that meant they had to gain and maintain the skills of war. War was good. War made men better. If we can get our heads around that viewpoint, it can help to understand the men of the time and their seeming propensity towards violence.

Lord Tancarville joined the second rebellion, King Henry's distrust of him either finally being confirmed, or finally driving him to revolt in a self-fulfilling prophecy. The Chamberlain's name would forever after be tarnished with his disloyalty, although his son Raoul was free of it when he inherited his father's lands. The conflict between the Tancarvilles and de Cailly represents the terrible chaos and disorder created by the rebellions, which were essentially civil wars. Normandy was fractured by the uprisings and knights had to take sides, in no less a traumatic way than any other civil war. There is no evidence de Cailly himself ever fought against Lord Tancarville, but the skirmish outside Yquebeuf represents the infighting that characterises these times. The death squad de Cailly formed to hunt for the Little Lord was, however, a favourite Norman tactic. It was used at the Battle of Hastings, and small groups of handpicked knights, special forces if you will, were used to headhunt important enemies from then right up to the Wars of the Roses in the fifteenth century.

The rebellions must have seemed like momentous and historic events for those who took part in them, but as soon as the Young King died, they faded and became a rather awkward memory everyone wished to forget. William Marshal's biography mentions the death in huge detail, but strategically doesn't even mention it happened during a rebellion, or while the Young King was ransacking monasteries. The Marshal was at his master's bedside and was deeply affected by what he saw. He was passed the Young King's crusading cloak and asked to take it to Jerusalem. Henry II did take two horses as insurance against the Marshal's leaving, and the knight escorted the body to Rouen to be buried. That journey deserves more attention than I gave it, because apart from the miracles and outpouring of sadness, he actually was buried twice. The people of Le Mans buried him first, purely so people would visit their city to venerate him, and it took a lawsuit and King Henry's intervention to get him dug up and taken to Rouen. The staggering reaction of the people of Aquitaine, Anjou, and Normandy certainly flies in the face of the feckless reputation sometimes attached to the Young King. His father was a king who many people were waiting for to die, and his son represented hope for a slightly less harsh regime. In Aquitaine, his brother Richard ruled so harshly that the inhabitants wanted him gone too, and in the Young King they saw their champion. So when he died, hope died with him. Not just the hope that knighthood would continue to shine brightly, but hope that the future could be better. There was a genuine hysteria around his death, a mass mourning that reveals that there had to be something more to the Young King than a spoiled boy. William Marshal served four kings, but when he later founded an Augustine priory, it was the long dead Young King out of all of them he called his lord, 'dominus meus', not Henry II, Richard, or John. William found something alluring in the Young King, something he could never let go in all his life, and it therefore not surprising that he ventured all the way to the Holy Land for him, an adventure which we will see unfold in the next book, Crusader.

Next up - Book Six in The Legend
of Richard Keynes series:

Crusader

Sign up to the mailing list on the author's website below
to be the first to hear when new books are released.

But if you can't wait, investigate the author's non-fiction work:

The Rise and Fall of the Mounted Knight

www.clivehart.net

Printed in Dunstable, United Kingdom